Language,
Brain and Hearing

J.G.Wolff

Language,
Brain and Hearing

An introduction to the psychology
of language with a section on deaf
children's learning of language

Methuen & Co Ltd
London

First published 1973
by Methuen & Co Ltd
11 New Fetter Lane London EC4P 4EE
© 1973 J. G. Wolff
Printed in Britain by
Richard Clay (The Chaucer Press) Ltd
Bungay, Suffolk

SBN 416 77360 5

Distributed in the USA by
HARPER & ROW PUBLISHERS INC.
BARNES & NOBLE IMPORT DIVISION

*To Jennifer
and Daniel*

Contents

Plates *Between pages* 146 *and* 147

Acknowledgements

Figures

Grateful acknowledgement for permission to reproduce figures is made to the following:

BRITISH MEDICAL BULLETIN and the author for Figs. 2 and 3, which are based on Figs. 3 and 5 of E. R. F. W. Crossman, 'Information processes in human skill', *Brit. Med. Bull.* **20**, no. 1 (1964), pp. 33 and 36.

HARVARD UNIVERSITY PRESS and THE COMMONWEALTH FUND for Fig. 3a, which is adapted from H. L. Teuber, W. S. Battersby and M. B. Bender, *Visual field defects after penetrating missile wounds of the brain* (1960), pp. 20 and 28.

TEACHERS COLLEGE, COLUMBIA UNIVERSITY, and the author for Fig. 4, which is from R. F. Street, *A Gestalt Completion Test* (1931), p. 41.

THE AMERICAN PSYCHOLOGICAL ASSOCIATION and the authors for Fig. 5 from L. Carmichael, H. P. Hogan and A. A. Walter, 'An experimental study of the effect of language on the reproduction of visually perceived form', *Journal of Experimental Psychology*, **15** (1932), p. 80; and for Fig. 36, which is Fig. 7 from H. Martin, 'Toward an analysis of subjective phrase structure', *The Psychological Bulletin*, **74** (1970), p. 163.

CAMBRIDGE UNIVERSITY PRESS for Fig. 19, which is based on Fig. 8 from John Lyons, *Introduction to Theoretical Linguistics* (1968), p. 211.

PENGUIN BOOKS Ltd for Fig. 20, which is Fig. 10 in John Lyons (ed.), *New Horizons in Linguistics* (1970), p. 117.

UNIVERSITETSFORLAGET, OSLO, and THE ACADEMIC PRESS INC, New York, for Figs. 26–29, which are based on Fig. 11 in R. Rommetveit, *Words, Meanings and Messages* (1968), p. 259.

JOHN WILEY AND SONS INC. for Fig. 30 from D. McCarthy, 'Language development in children', in L. Carmichael (ed.), *Manual of Child Psychology* (1946).

MCGRAW-HILL BOOK COMPANY for Fig. 32, which is Table 5.1 from R. Brown and C. Fraser, 'The acquisition of syntax', in C. N. Cofer and S. Musgrave (eds.), *Verbal Behavior and Learning: Problems and Processes* (1963), p. 170.

LINGUISTIC SOCIETY OF AMERICA for Fig. 31, from M. D. S. Braine, 'The ontogeny of English phrase structure', *Language* **39** (1963), pp. 1–13.

JAMES NISBET AND COMPANY LTD and HARPER & ROW PUBLISHERS INC. for Fig. 33, which is taken from p. 6 of (hænj about (1951/1964).

ACADEMIC PRESS INC. and the author for Fig. 35, from N. F. Johnson, 'The psychological reality of phrase structure rules', *Journal of Verbal Learning and Verbal Behaviour*, **4** (1965), pp. 469–75.

HOLT, RINEHART AND WINSTON INC. for Fig. 37, which is based on Fig. 6.1 in S. Richard Silverman and H. Davis (eds.), *Hearing and Deafness* (1947, 3rd edn. 1970), p. 170.

THE ACOUSTICAL SOCIETY OF AMERICA for Fig. 38, from S. S. Stevens and H. Davis, 'Psychophysiological acoustics: pitch and loudness', *Journal of the Acoustical Society of America*, **8** (1936), pp. 1–13.

THE ROYAL NATIONAL INSTITUTE FOR THE DEAF, London, for Figs. 41 and 42, which are from *Conversation with the Deaf* (9th edn. 1971), pp. 43 and 44.

DR R. ORIN CORNETT, Vice President of Gallaudet College, Washington D.C. for Fig. 43.

Plates

Grateful acknowledgement for permission to reproduce plates is made to the following:

DOVER PUBLICATIONS INC. and BELL TELEPHONE LABORATORIES, for Plate 1, which is from Ralph K. Potter, George A. Kopp and Harriet C. Green, *Visible Speech* (1966), pp. 55 and 200.

THE ROYAL NATIONAL INSTITUTE FOR THE DEAF, London, for Plate 3, which is from *Conversation with the Deaf* (9th edn. 1971), p. 20.

Preface

I should like to thank all those who have given me help in the preparation of this book. In particular, I am grateful to Miss Mary Plackett, Librarian at the Royal National Institute for the Deaf, who has sent me numerous books and articles and has, when necessary, taken a lot of trouble to get them. Mr Hector Thomas, F.R.C.S., formerly Senior Consultant Otolaryngologist for the Children's E.N.T. Hospital, Cardiff, has made the writing of this book possible through his longstanding concern for the welfare of deaf children. The work was supported, in part, by the Jane Hodge Foundation. I am grateful to Sir James Pitman for discussing the uses of i.t.a. in deaf education. Dr Esther Simpson of the Department of Education and Science has kindly supplied information on her surveys of children in schools for the deaf. Miss Cherrill Peake of the illustrations department in the University Hospital of Wales has prepared some of the illustrations, and given valuable help with others. Mrs Linda Williams kindly posed for the speech phoneme pictures in Appendix I. Last but not least I should like to thank my colleagues, Mr Alun B. Thomas, F.R.C.S., Senior Consultant Otolaryngologist, Mr F. G. Hart, Audiologist, and Miss Mair Lewis, Teacher of the Deaf, for their advice and encouragement. Miss Lewis has read the entire manuscript and has made many useful comments. The responsibility for all defects is, however, my own.

Introduction

This book is intended to give an insight into most of the major ideas and issues in the young science of psycholinguistics and to be, at the same time, intelligible to non-specialist readers. It should serve as an introduction to the subject for psychology or language students, clinical and educational psychologists, speech therapists and practising or student teachers. These readers are invited to view Part Two as a 'case study' in which some of the theoretical ideas of Part One are applied to the practical problem of facilitating deaf children's learning of language.

But this second part will obviously be of special interest to teachers of deaf children and to educational psychologists. A child born deaf or becoming deaf early in life has the utmost difficulty in learning language and his teacher needs as good an understanding of language processes as is possible in order to tackle the handicap effectively. This book should at least partly meet the need.

The first four chapters introduce those ideas from psychology and linguistics which are required later in the book. Chapter 5 sketches the normal sequence of language development and Chapters 6 and 7 attempt to put these observations into an explanatory scheme.

In Part One I have given emphasis to those topics which strike me as particularly important or interesting, and in a similar way I have not attempted to be impartial in describing controversial issues. A recurring idea is the importance of economy and efficiency in the brain's handling of information and the role of 'schemata' in this. Related to this is the parallel between the linguist's problem in developing a formal grammar, the child's problem in developing an intuitive grammar and the philosophical problem of induction. Although the bright star of Chomsky's transformational grammar seems to outshine earlier linguistic theories I have chosen to describe Fries's ideas fairly fully, both because they form a firm foundation to later developments in linguistics and because they seem to be more directly relevant to the psychology of language: in nasty jargon, the notion of distributional equivalence (or paradigmatic relations amongst words) together with the idea of syntagmatic relations amongst words is the basis of the explanatory frame outlined in Chapter 7. This is the opportunity to say that such jargon has been used only when necessary, and then it is fully explained.

Part Two includes some background material on deafness, audiometry and history of deaf education. I have proposed some general principles for solving the deaf child's language problem and have discussed present methods in the light of these principles. Chapters 10 and 11 cover in more detail two kinds of possible solution.

The continuing debate about teaching methods for deaf children tends always to settle into the 'manual versus oral' groove. I hope readers acquainted with this debate will read the book without prejudice because, although I have criticised oral methods as presently conceived, I have tried to avoid the usual tramlines and to put a fresh psycholinguistic angle on the problem.

J. G. W.

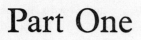

Part One

1 Some background ideas

Before we start looking at language itself, there are three ideas which we should examine which have become very important in psychological thinking and which seem to be proving very useful in thinking about language.

The first idea is that some parts at least of our behaviour and mental processes only make sense if we suppose that the brain can and does build up inside itself some kind of map or model of the outside world.

The second idea is really a set of ideas which has grown up as psychologists have looked at skilled behaviour like driving a car or drawing. The 'skill' of using language has certain similarities with these other skills.

Last is a body of theory borrowed by psychologists from telephone engineers which treats information as something which can be measured. This 'information theory' is obviously relevant to language as a medium for conveying information. It is also relevant to our models in the brain as we shall see.

1. Models in the brain

It has not been and perhaps is not still fully accepted that 'models in the brain' or 'maps in the head' really exist. A contrasted view typified by the theories of psychologist C. L. Hull and his followers is that all behaviour consists of a series of responses which are triggered at some time earlier by stimuli impinging on the animal (or person). The process of learning is seen as attaching new responses to old stimuli or new stimuli to old responses. This is commonly known as S-R (stimulus-response) theory while the alternative is S-S (stimulus-stimulus) because learning is then seen as relating one stimulus to another, which is equivalent to remembering the pattern of stimuli or building up a map or model of the outside world.

There has been a lengthy controversy over which view is right but the conclusion must be, I think, that while S-R theory applies to much of behaviour certain features make much better sense in terms of 'models'.

To forestall any possible misunderstanding it should be said that the idea does not necessarily mean that one could find a three-dimensional or two-dimensional pattern amongst the brain cells. All that is meant is that there is some kind of record of external objects and events in a form which allows the brain to relate one set of stimuli to another set directly without always relating them to actions or responses at the same time. A computer programmer can easily arrange for architects' plans or an engineering model to be recorded in a computer memory store as, say, a series of numbers which would have no physical resemblance to the originals but could still be described as models of them.

The notion of models in the brain has been introduced into psychological discussion repeatedly and usually independently by various people at various times. The terms used have not always been the same and there are differences in the ideas but the underlying similarity is clear.

Thus Henry Head (discussed by Oldfield and Zangwill (1942)) used the term 'schema' to mean a kind of mental model people seem to have of the position of their own body and limbs. His evidence came mainly from patients who had lost limbs or suffered paralysis or loss of sensation in parts of their bodies. One possible theory, which Head rejected, is that each part of our body sends information continuously to the brain about its position. Instead Head supposed that the brain simply remembers the bodily position at some short time earlier (the schema) and only records the *changes* in position by different parts. This is obviously a much more elegant and economical way of doing the job and is rather like the use of a peg board to record the score in a card game like cribbage. It is simpler and requires less effort than recording all the individual scores and adding them up afterwards.

The same term 'schema' was used by Sir Frederick Bartlett (1932) in discussing memory of a more familiar kind. He suggested that a lot of remembering takes the form of adapting a pre-established model. He asked people to listen to a story, the 'War of the Ghosts' and to remember it. When he tested them at various intervals afterwards he found that in addition to the usual forgetting there were systematic distortions apparently because his subjects were applying their Western schemata to a story which came from a different culture; Piaget uses the same term with recognisable similarities in meaning.

Although he did not use the term, Kohler's field theory and the general approach of his fellow Gestalt psychologists obviously embraces the idea. In studying how apes solve simple problems Kohler (1924) was impressed by how the animals' 'insights' could appear quite suddenly and apparently from nowhere. The 'trial and error' behaviour which other psychologists had suggested was necessary for problem solving was occurring, if at all, inside the animals' head by some kind of manipulation of an internal mental model of the situation.

We have now seen how our model idea has been applied to the learning and remembering of past events and problem solving in the present. It should not be surprising therefore to find it applied to the future. Miller, Gallanter and Pribram (1960) have now made respectable the notion that we can build models of future situations and events, i.e. we can make plans.

Non-psychologists will probably wonder why so much trouble should be taken in stating the obvious. The reason is that the whole idea has hitherto been regarded as 'mentalistic' or non-scientific. That psychology should confine itself to things which could be seen objectively was a necessary phase in the development of a young science but this is now past. The notion of stored 'models', 'schemata' or 'patterns' proves very relevant when we study learning and memory, problem solving, plans and, as we shall see in the next section, it is very significant in perception and recognition processes. The relevance of the idea to our study of language will be seen in Chapter 2 where we discuss concepts and meanings, in Chapter 4 where we relate these to the patterns of sounds or written characters which made the language medium and in subsequent chapters.

2. Language as a skill

The study of skilled behaviour is a field which, like our third topic, owes much to ideas borrowed from engineers. The techniques developed during the last war in trying to improve the accuracy of anti-aircraft guns and the more recent work on guided missiles is part of the relatively new science of cybernetics. The similarity between the military and the behaviour problem may be seen if we consider how a tennis player runs and hits a ball.

First of all if he runs directly at where the ball is he will miss it just as surely as the gunner who shoots directly at the aeroplane. In both cases the target will have moved by the time the missile gets there. The motion of the target must be assessed and the 'missile' aimed at where the target will be when the 'missile' has traversed its route. Skills thus often involve *anticipation* or *prediction*.

However, if our player is not quite accurate in his prediction of where the ball will be all is not lost. As he runs he notices his own movement and the position of the ball and can adjust his route and speed to keep himself on target. Thus he has *feedback* of his own movement and can use this information to adjust the direction and speed at which he runs. The guided missile works on this principle as does the humble thermostat which switches an electric fire off when the room is too hot and switches it on again when it gets too cool. The diagram illustrates this.

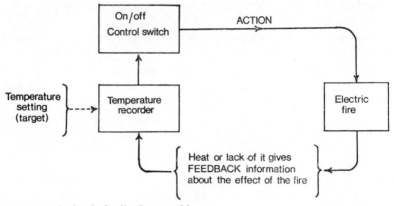

FIGURE I A simple feedback control loop

A third feature of the tennis player's skill is the fact that it can be analysed on a series of levels or a *hierarchy*. On the highest level are the broad facts of running and then hitting the ball with the tennis racket. At a lower or finer level the running may be controlled step by step so that one step is not begun until the previous one is nearly finished. At an even finer level individual muscles are controlled so that they work together and not against each other. Similarly there are constant adjustments of posture so that the player does not lose his balance and such things as the grip on the racket is adjusted by feedback processes so that it is not too strong or too weak.

At most levels in the hierarchy, feedback loops are very common. However, there are probably some areas where this kind of control is abandoned and series of movements are fired off as complete sequences which we can say are *automated*. In fact there is probably a large element of this in running which is highly practised; we sometimes experience this when we follow a familiar route, perhaps that which we take every-day to work. On a holiday or weekend when we intend to turn off our normal route to go somewhere else we may still find that we have missed our turn and gone the familiar way because it is so practised, habitual and automatic.

The ideas of feedback and hierarchy are illustrated in the following diagram. To explain the diagram let us take another example: what happens when we want to fry an egg!

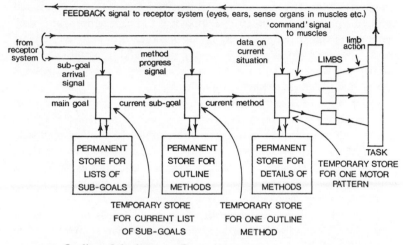

FIGURE 2 Outline of the human effector system

Based on E.R.F.W. Crossman 1964

The main goal, obviously, is to obtain a fried egg. The sub-goals are to obtain a frying pan, egg, fat, spatula, to light the gas, put the pan on the gas, the fat in the pan and crack the egg into the pan, etc. For each of these sub-goals there is an outline of methods. Thus to obtain the frying pan one walks to where it is stored, grasps it by the handle, lifts it off the hook, walks to the stove and puts it down on the stove. Again at a finer level still there are details of methods (walking, grasping, etc.) and at the finest level there is the control of individual muscles. The whole process is controlled by feedback which provides information through the sensory system about the progress of each sub-goal and method at every level. This is important for controlling the sequence so that, for example, you do not start cracking the egg until the pan is there ready to receive it.

All this may seem too easy and obvious to require discussion but its simplicity is deceptive and derives perhaps from our marvellously sophisticated nervous system which allows us to do all this so unthinkingly. In certain patients suffering from wounds to the brain this kind of activity may be upset.

One famous aphasic chef was just such a case, and would indeed crack the egg on to the stove instead of into the pan. His language was also disordered, which underlines the parallel I wish to draw between the organisation of language and these other activities.

The importance of feedback to the control of speech is illustrated by Yate's (1963) well known experiments in which people's speech is fed through a microphone and special apparatus to headphones which they are wearing but it is delayed by about one fifth of a second. In most cases people in these conditions find it very difficult to continue talking and what speech they do produce is very distorted, somewhat resembling the speech of a stammerer.

So far we have talked mainly about the active, 'motor', or 'effector' side of the nervous system. However, the part of the nervous system which gathers information about the outside world and, by feedback, about the person's own activities is also very important. This 'sensory', 'perceptual' or *'receptor'* system (vision, hearing, etc.) is at least as complicated as the effector system. What follows is the barest outline of its general organisation to guide our thinking later.

The diagram shows schematically the various stages of analysis for visual information but similar analysis in successive stages has been

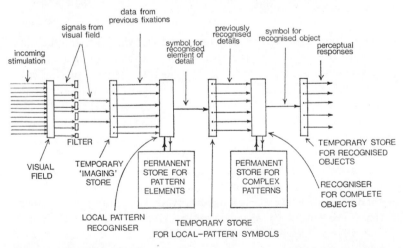

FIGURE 3 Outline of the human effector system

Based on E.R.F.W. Crossman 1964

recognised in the other sensory systems including hearing. Modern neurophysiological studies have shown that a considerable amount of reorganisation and analysis occurs in our eyes and ears themselves. We shall ignore this in our simplified scheme and consider that the first stage after the sense organ is a kind of filter, namely selective attention. The processes which allow us to attend to or select out only certain parts of our sensory input are undoubtedly very complicated but we can think of them as a kind of sieve or funnel.

Next there is some evidence that comparatively raw, unanalysed, input may be stored for a second or two in a temporary 'imaging' store. Occasionally we may be aware of this when we see or hear something but do not recognise it immediately and have to scan a rapidly fading mental picture to decide what it is.

A very important feature of perception is the process of *recognition*. What this means is that the incoming patterns of stimulations are compared with stored patterns and the system 'decides' which of the stored patterns fits the data best.

There is some evidence that the stored patterns for small commonly occurring features (lines at various angles, curves, dots, etc.) are present at birth. Most of the more complicated patterns have to be learned. Very little is known about babies' vision and hearing but it seems very likely that in their first few months and later they are busy storing new patterns which can be then used for future recognition. From time to time throughout life we are likely to meet new patterns which do not fit any of those that we have in store. When this happens we have to set about storing these new patterns for future reference. Anyone who has some experience of looking at microscope slides will remember that it took some time before they could see what was present on the slides. At first many slides look like a confusing jumble of fuzzy shapes but after a time we learn to recognise the various features.

As the incoming stimulation passes from the eyes or ears through the various stages of the receptor system it seems that the small details are the first elements to be processed. At later stages collections of these details seem to be handled as larger patterns and these in turn are put together in the identification of large-scale patterns or whole objects, events, situations, etc.

This recognition may be used as feedback to the effector system, it may be stored in memory or it may cause us to take some new action, like raising our hands in mock horror because our beloved tiny tot has just appeared under a sheet pretending to be a ghost!

There is one important respect in which this account is an over-simplification. Most of the time we ignore the majority of details in what we perceive and attend only to the few needed to identify an object. It is only when there is some doubt about the identity of an object that we need to look more closely at all the details. The stored patterns for small details are, as it were, kept in reserve for special occasions. Most of the time our perceptions are geared to the larger stored pattern, i.e. our general schemata or models of the world. What this means in effect is that our schemata are constantly in use enabling us to guess or predict what is coming next. Providing there is a reasonable match with our expectations we do not bother to check every tiny detail. Here are some examples to illustrate the powerful organising effect of these schemata on what we perceive.

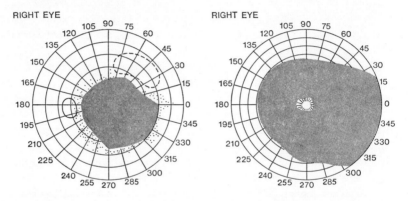

FIGURE 3a Two cases of visual scotomata incurred by damage to the visual cortex   *Adapted from Teubner, Battersby and Bender* 1960

One line of evidence comes from studies of people with damage to their visual systems. Such people may, through accident or disease, have areas of their fields of view in which they cannot see anything. Using special techniques it is possible to map out these blind areas which can be quite large as shown in the diagram. The curious thing is that in mild cases the patient may be unaware of the defect. He fills in the blank space apparently from his general schema of what ought to be there. In fact we all have a blind spot in our visual fields of which we are unaware. The reader can demonstrate this by closing his right eye and looking at the + from a distance of about one foot.

●   +

At a certain distance from the page the ● will disappear as its image falls on the blind spot.

The effect of our overall schema of expectations is also illustrated in our ability to read the following incomplete text:

M–N– H–NDS M–K– L–GHT W–RK.

Similarly we have no difficulty in identifying the incomplete picture. Anyone who has tried proof reading, looking for errors rather than content, will know how difficult it is to detect every defect.

FIGURE 4
From R. F. Street 1931

Our schemata not only help us to fill in gaps, they also force interpretations on ambiguous patterns and may thus produce distortions. The middle series of drawings shown overleaf were presented to people singly and were named. Some people were given the names on the left and some the names on the right. The people were then asked to produce drawings from memory. The drawings on the left and right illustrate the way the original drawings were distorted to fit the names given.

The phenomenon of automatisation, mentioned earlier, is an analogous process on the motor side of the nervous system. Again, the large scale, well-established patterns may take control and may sometimes produce inappropriate behaviour if the situation does not fit the pattern.

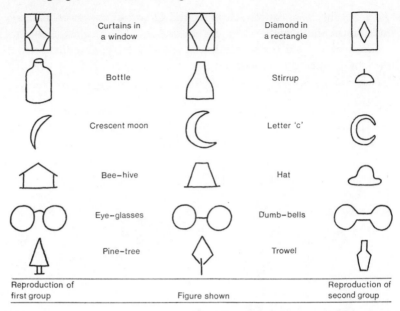

Reproduction of first group		Figure shown	Reproduction of second group
	Curtains in a window		Diamond in a rectangle
	Bottle		Stirrup
	Crescent moon		Letter 'c'
	Bee–hive		Hat
	Eye–glasses		Dumb–bells
	Pine–tree		Trowel

FIGURE 5   *From Carmichael, Hogan and Walter* 1932

As we shall see in the next section both effects are probably the by-product of a nervous system which is organised in such a way as to handle large amounts of information as economically as possible.

3. Information theory

If someone tells us that the Houses of Parliament are standing up and have not fallen down we consider this a trivial and uninteresting thing to say. If, however, they tell us that they *have* fallen down this surprises us and it is real news. In the one case we are told something which was entirely expected and did not convey much information and in the other case the reverse is true. The effort to create surprise value or news is behind the old 'man bites dog' principle of journalism.

Telephone engineers have pinned this down into a mathematical theory which allows them to measure how much information a telephone line or other medium has to carry.

Imagine that you have heard that one of the houses in your street has been struck by lightning. You have no reason to think that some houses are more likely to be struck than others so there is some uncertainty about which house it is and whether it might be yours. If, say, there are thirty-two houses in the street this gives a yardstick of the uncertainty, the more houses there are in the street the greater the uncertainty about which one has been struck. If you are told that the house is amongst the first sixteen this reduces the uncertainty by half and, in information theory terms, conveys one *bit* of information. If you are then told that it is between numbers nine and sixteen inclusive this reduces the uncertainty by half again and gives another *bit* of information. By repeating the process we may see that identifying the actual house which has been struck conveys five bits of information (let us hope that you have been lucky). The more houses there are in the street the more 'bits' of information are conveyed by saying which one has been struck.

Any message may be thought of as a series of 'events' of this kind. Thus speech may be seen as a series of speech sounds or *phonemes* and about forty-four are generally recognised. (See Appendix I) If they were all equally likely to occur at a given moment then each one would convey a little over five bits of information. However, they are not by any means equally likely and this makes things interesting. Our knowledge of the English language tells us that some sounds are commoner than others and that if we hear the sound 'm' for example at the beginning of a word it is very much more likely to be followed by 'a' or 'u' or another vowel than by 'p', 's', 't', etc. As a general rule a series of 'events' (such as phonemes) conveys a maximum of information when they are all equally likely to occur at a given moment. When some are more likely than others then less information is conveyed.

Look at the pattern of black and white squares here. It has been made

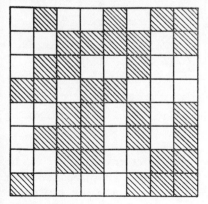

FIGURE 6

in such a way that each square is equally likely to be black or white regardless of its position or what squares precede or follow it. Look at it for say, ten seconds and then try to draw it from memory.

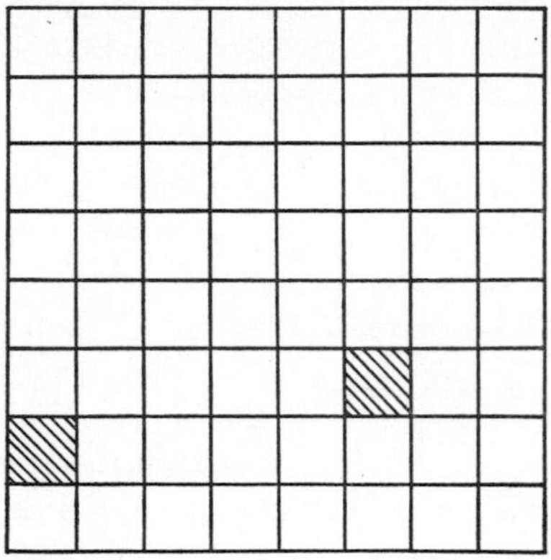

FIGURE 7

Now look at this pattern for the same period and try to produce it from memory. Clearly, the second pattern is much easier than the first. The same applies to the other patterns shown here. Looking at the difference from an information theory point of view we can see that in

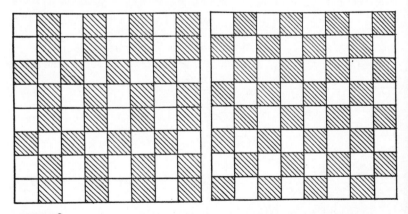

FIGURE 8

the first case there is no way of predicting whether each square will be black or white and we have to make a separate memory record of each square individually. Here the information content is at a maximum. In the second example we only have to remember the position of two black squares and the fact that all the rest are white. In the third and fourth examples black and white squares are equally frequent but we can see from a short sequence regularities and rules which allow us to predict the rest of the sequence. In these three cases the information content is less than the maximum and we say that the patterns are *redundant*. In general, the more redundant a pattern is (the smaller its information content), the easier it is to remember.[1]

The importance of information theory in psychology is that it gives us a way of studying the nervous system as an information handling system. It can be shown, for instance, that when one is looking at a typical scene the visual information impinging on our eyes is far, far greater than can possibly be transmitted along the optic nerves connecting the eyes to the brain. This means that the eyes must make maximum use of any redundancy in this information to find regularities and 'rules' which can be transmitted more economically. This is called *recoding* and a picture is emerging from research of how this is done in the eyes. Similar findings apply to hearing.

Let us consider some possible ways in which a redundant visual pattern or auditory sequence might be recoded so that it can be assimilated and memorised economically in terms of information. Some of these possible methods have been described by Attneave (1954).

A simple idea is to assume that the pattern is uniform unless we have evidence to the contrary. There is very clear evidence that our eyes tend to regard an area of colour as more uniform than it really is and to accentuate the boundaries. This obviously saves a lot of effort compared with recording whether each tiny area is, for example, blue or not blue. A very similar effect has been found in the way our ears record the pitch of a sound.

The two pictures of a yacht shown overleaf are offered as a means of picturing this idea. In the first one we imagine that each point on the sail is recorded as blue. In this case fifty entries have to be made in the memory store. In the second case all that is recorded is that one point is blue, all the rest are the same and they form a triangle: three entries in the memory store.

[1] Actually 'redundant' has two meanings (see Corcoran (1971)) depending on whether one is concerned with regularities within a pattern (Corcoran's Redundancy 1) or whether one is viewing a given pattern as an element in a set of patterns. (Corcoran's Redundancy 2) Clearly the two meanings are closely related, because in the second case the set of patterns can be viewed as one pattern with internal regularities. In this book we shall be using the term in the first sense.

Another device for dealing with very large information inputs like a speckled surface is not to attempt to record each 'speckle' individually but simply to notice the average density of the speckling and its randomness.

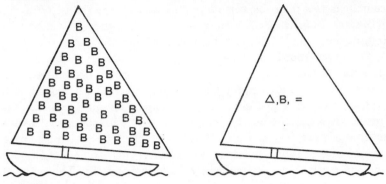

FIGURE 9

Induction

An extremely important strategy, allied to the first one described above, is to make use of patterns already in store. If we already have in store a fairly complex pattern, like that of a chair, there is a tremendous saving in information storage space if when we see another chair we can say, as it were, 'there is another one like the one I saw before' rather than set about recording all the details of this new chair. The amount of storage space required would become impossibly large if we had to record the details of each of 1,000 chairs in a hall instead of recording '1 chair × 1,000'. If the new chair is slightly different from the original one we simply record 'a chair like the old one but with longer legs and decorative carving'.

In fact we simply could not cope with all the information impinging on us as effectively as we do unless we use these strategies. Amongst other things our models or schemata enable us to make a permanent assumption that 'things are as they were unless we have evidence to the contrary'. We have seen the enormous benefits that this brings but the penalties are that we will make mistakes when something changes without our noticing it. The practical joker who moves someone's seat when he has stood up to speak capitalises on the speaker's assumption that it will still be there when he sits down again.

There is a very close parallel between these processes and the ancient philosophical problem of induction. When we say 'all swans are white' after seeing a limited number of white swans we are making an assumption which cannot be justified logically. We are constantly making assumptions about the future on the basis of past experience which, if we stopped to think, are outrageously daring. Just because the sun has always risen regularly each morning there is no logical reason why it should rise again tomorrow. Just because every paving stone on a path has held our weight so far we are really most unwise to trust the next one not to drop us into a deep hole. It is really an act of faith when we crack an egg into a frying pan that it will not be filled with confetti (although we are aware of the possibility that it might be bad). For some reason we seem to get away with all these things most of the time and, as we have said, this fact is a tremendous convenience to us. Induction and prediction discussed in the last section are both variants of our very general tendency to go beyond the information given.

Chunking

Before we leave this subject there is a further parallel to be made between this use of stored patterns and an interesting demonstration by the psychologist George Miller (1956).

He was concerned with the fact that most people seem to have a certain fixed capacity to hear or see a string of digits, letters or words and repeat them back. Whatever the items used this memory span always seems to be about seven or eight. What Miller did was to train some volunteers to convert decimal numbers (0, 1, 2, 3, etc.) into their equivalent binary numbers (which use only 0 and 1) and vice versa. Most binary numbers are longer than their equivalent decimal numbers (9 is equivalent to 1001). When the volunteers were fully trained he presented them with a string of binary digits for them to remember and repeat back. What the volunteers did was to convert the binary numbers into decimal numbers as they went along. In this way they could keep going up to their limit of about seven decimal digits. When they repeated them back they converted the decimal digits into binary digits and in this way they could hear and repeat back up to forty binary digits – much longer than their original memory span. Miller called this 'chunking' because the binary digits seemed to be grouped into 'chunks' corresponding to the decimal numbers. He suggested that we have a fixed short term memory capacity for about seven 'chunks' regardless of what is contained in the chunks.

The same effect is illustrated by these examples. The reader should look at each of the following strings of letters and after each one close his eyes and try to repeat them.

> XMAHQ,
>
> TDLIBCJ,
>
> ONQZUFMRIIGDVTY

He will probably find he can manage the first two but not the last one. Now try these:

> THECHICKENSCRATCHESINTHEFARMYARD
>
> IMMACULATEMOTORCARSFORSALE

Suddenly one's memory span for letters is much larger and it is obviously because we can recognise words already known and remember the letter sequence in terms of the words. This then is a further illustration of how what we have already got stored in memory makes a great difference to what new things we can remember. We are able constantly to make use of the fact that certain patterns are already in store so that they do not need to be recorded again. Many mnemomic devices capitalise on this.

It was remarked earlier that the memory span for words themselves is about seven. The following sequence of words is probably near the limit of most people's span:

> show each names familiar of shapes with

But it is at least as easy to remember the following sequence although it is much longer:

> Several fat men were walking over a bridge when it collapsed under their weight and they all fell into the river.

Somehow a sequence of words modelled on familiar sentence patterns, especially if it is meaningful, is much easier to repeat than a random sequence of words. We shall see the relevance of this to language learning in Chapter 7.

2 Concepts and meanings

Whatever uncertainty we may have about the meaning of the word 'meaning' it will be agreed that language is primarily a means of conveying meanings from one person to another. It is for this reason that I wish to devote some attention to this idea as well as to the related one of concepts.

We shall side-step all debate and review of how the word 'meaning' is and has been used by simply choosing our own way of using it. We shall say that the meaning of speech or other forms of language embraces any work which the speech is used to do, or function which it has, including the transfer of information or concepts of any kind from speaker to listener. As philosopher John Hospers (1967) says, it is in many ways better to think of words as tools to do a job than as having meanings. Our definition is perhaps a little rough and ready, but it is not important to be very precise here. The point I wish to make is that 'concepts', which we shall examine in a moment, are not the whole of meaning. To take a familiar example, the expressions 'How do you do?' or 'Hello!' can hardly be said to deal with concepts, but their meaning is that of greeting or making social contact. We shall extend the discussion of meaning in Chapter 4 and we shall see that while language uses quite a range of devices to help communication many of them are not directly concerned with concepts.

Concepts

None the less concepts are a very important part of meaning and the rest of the chapter will be devoted to them.

By a concept I shall simply mean any collection of objects, events or situations which we group together for certain purposes and treat as being the same. Thus if we see something which is composed of a horizontal platform with a 'back' supported on four legs, which is suitable for sitting on we are likely to group it mentally with other similar objects and call it a 'chair'. Similarly, if we see someone using a sharp piece of metal to try to divide a piece of string into two parts we are likely to group this situation mentally with others where sharp objects are used to divide other objects; the appropriate verbal label is of course 'cut' or 'cutting'. Before we proceed we should perhaps distinguish between a concept and an image. It is quite possible to form a concept of something without having a mental picture or image of it. A man born blind can have a concept of redness through studying the physics of light, but he will not have an image of it. In the same way seeing people can have a concept of ultra-violet or infra-red light without being able to picture it.

A digression

At this point let us pause briefly and consider how widespread in psychology is this phenomenon of recognising sameness or similarity or constancy. Imagine that we could somehow get outside our own skins and examine ourselves like the proverbial Martian would. Our Martian might look at our eyes and recognise them as organs for perceiving the surroundings. Looking more closely he would notice the similarity between an eye and a camera and he would notice how the lens in the eye casts an image on the retina or 'screen' at the back. The image is a flat (slightly curved) pattern of light and dark, variously coloured patches of light. The Martian would probably conclude that this is how we see the world. In fact we see the world as composed of objects not flat patterns of light.

The matter is by no means settled but there is quite a lot of evidence to suggest that babies and other young animals have to learn to see the world as objects. The baby is unlikely to see his rattle or toy car from exactly the same viewpoint on any two occasions and yet every different viewpoint will produce a different pattern of light on his retina. However before long it is clear that he treats it as the same object whatever view he sees it from.

The Swiss psychologist Piaget has recognised this very clearly. (His ideas are well summarised in Flavell (1963).) He also realised that young children take a little while to learn that when an object disappears behind another object it is 'really' still there and may reappear before long. Piaget's famous discovery of 'conservation' is but an extension of the same idea. He found that young children do not realise until comparatively late that when, for example, water is poured from a tall thin glass into a short wide one the amount of water remains the same. Recent work has cast doubt on the validity of some of Piaget's results and few have imagined that his theoretical edifice is correct in every detail, but many of his ideas, including 'conservation', seem to be basically sound.

The reader will probably recognise these phenomena as further examples of one of Attneave's principles for handling information economically:

1. We organise the raw, unanalysed 'sense data' into a model of the world composed of objects and other entities which we recognise as being the same regardless of viewpoint. This 'real world' model seems to be populated also with events (actions), qualities and, perhaps, situations.
2. These entities are themselves grouped into concepts on the basis of similarities.

Both these processes and others, like Piaget's conservation, are instances of the very prevalent tendency of our nervous systems to sift out 'sameness' or 'constancy' in the incoming information. This tendency is itself an example of one of a number of possible strategies for recoding the incoming information to make the most economical use of any redundancy or pattern.

We can recognise these processes without, at this stage, being able to say exactly how they work. The Post Office has commissioned research to try to discover how it is that the human eye can recognise alphabetic letters and words although a given letter or word may come in many different shapes and sizes and may perhaps be seen on its side or upside-down. Their hope is to make a machine do the same job so that addresses on envelopes can be read automatically. It has proved a baffling problem; we have at present to be content with noticing this ability as a very general property of our nervous system.

Distinctive features and dimensions of concepts

It is obvious that all the instances which make up a concept are very rarely identical in every respect. Under the heading 'cats' we are quite happy to include black cats, white cats, toms, queens, tabby cats, Persians, etc. and within each of these sub-groups owners will fondly note their own pet's special foibles and individuality. What is it then that enables us to lump them together? What, so to speak, is the cattiness of cats? The plain truth is that no-one knows but the most popular approach to this problem has been to think in terms of *distinctive features*.

It will be agreed that most cats have fur, four legs, eyes, ears, mouth and that these somehow contribute to their cattiness. While it is true that the vast majority of cats have these things they are not enough in themselves to distinguish cats because they are shared by dogs, horses, cows, etc. These then may be called *inclusive features*. We might be getting warmer if we suggested that cats purr. This seems promising because very few, if any, other animals purr so that we can be fairly sure that an animal that purrs is a cat. However, numerous cat lovers will testify that certain cats do not purr. This may be called an *exclusive feature*.

What about the possession of a tail? There is difficulty with this on two counts; not all cats have tails and other animals have them. The possession of a tail contributes rather weakly to 'cattiness' and this type of feature has been called *probabalistic*.

The ideal feature, which we would say was *definitive*, would be one which only cats had and no other animal had. Retractile claws are apparently such a feature and there are details of the teeth which distinguish cats from all other animals with certainty.

We seem to recognise cats and other concepts, then, on the basis of a collection of distinctive features of varying 'strengths', very few of which are sufficient in themselves to mark off cats from other animals.

This idea may be extended by allowing that each distinctive feature can vary in degree. We would then call it a *dimension* and think of it rather like a co-ordinate on a graph or map. If we look at concepts in this way they will appear as 'envelopes' or 'balloons' whose boundaries are marked off by the dimensions. However, they will not be 'flat' two-dimensional enclosures as could be drawn on a piece of paper, nor will they be three-dimensional balloons but rather they will be multi-dimensional. This idea of space marked out in more than three dimensions is, of course, very difficult to picture but it is an idea familiar to mathematicians. For our purposes we shall be content to represent concepts as flat enclosures drawn on paper. Figure 10 overleaf illustrates crudely the kind of way we might picture the related concepts of 'van' and 'bus'. For the sake of the diagram we shall assume that only two dimensions distinguish them; the amount of window space and the amount of seat space. Buses generally have more of both but one can imagine examples falling near the borderline which have too few seats or windows for a typical bus but more than one would expect in a van. Of course we have been talking about colloquial usages; in law there are sharply defined features especially chosen to distinguish the two types of vehicle clearly.

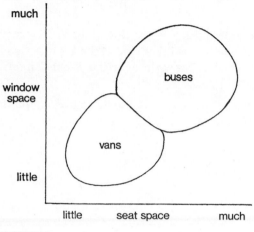

FIGURE 10

Relationships between concepts

We can illustrate the use of our 'balloons' by looking at how concepts may relate to each other.

1. *Distinct concepts* Two concepts may not be related in any recognisable way and we can represent them like this:

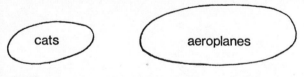

FIGURE 11

The space between them shows that there is never likely to be any uncertainty about whether something is a cat or an aeroplane. The bigger the space, the surer we can be.

2. *Adjacent concepts* Colours are familiar examples of concepts in which one of their important dimensions is shared between them (in

physicist's terms this is the wavelength of the light) and we can arrange them in a row like this:

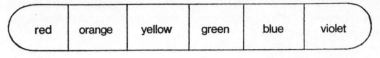

FIGURE 12

By doing this we have recognised that a colour close to a boundary may be very similar to another one on the other side of the boundary and there may be some difficulty in deciding what colour it is. We shall return to this shortly.

3. *Overlapping concepts* Not all cats are pets. Some animals are both cats and pets. Not all pets are cats.

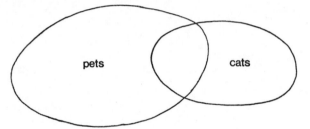

FIGURE 13

4. *Embracing and included concepts* All cats are animals. Not all animals are cats.

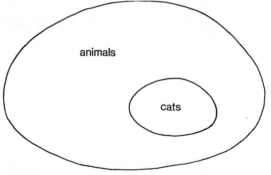

FIGURE 14

An important point is that a given entity has a large range of features which can in theory allow it to be grouped in a large number of different concepts. Thus our tabby cat may of course be grouped with other cats but it may also be grouped under the headings 'pets', 'animals', 'mammals', 'quadrupeds', 'solid objects', 'objects which move themselves', 'striped objects', etc. etc.

The similarity between our balloons and those of logic and set theory is not coincidental. They are basically the same. There are certain logical problems in defining distinct and adjacent concepts as we have described them here but these need not concern us.

Some other properties of concepts

These illustrations show concepts at various 'distances' from each other and we are thus thinking of them as having positions or *locations* in their special kind of 'space'. We can locate any concept by pointing to one example but this does not tell us the other important thing about it: where does its boundary go or what is its *range*? A little girl in our street used to ask my wife from time to time: 'Where's your father?'. She meant me, not because I look old enough to be my wife's father (I hope) but presumably because Maria's concept of 'father' was something like 'grown up man', probably because she had only heard the word applied to the grown-up man in her house and she had assumed the range was bigger than it really is.

We have assumed so far that the boundaries of concepts are sharp and clear. In fact this is very rarely the case. If we saw an animal with fur, four legs, etc. which had whiskers and purred but which also barked and chased rabbits we would find it difficult to decide whether it was a dog or a cat. The boundary of both concepts is to some extent *vague*. It is only because we rarely see cases which come so close to the boundary that this is not often a problem in practice.

Another assumption we have made is that concepts exist somehow independently of the people who have them. However, it frequently happens that two people use the same verbal label but the concepts which each of them attaches to the same label are different. A radio engineer is likely to have a much narrower and more precise concept of a 'transistor' than other people. Providing there is some overlap between the layman's concept and the engineer's they may use the term successfully in talking to each other providing the layman does not have to use it accurately.

Can we have concepts without words?

This last example brings us to the question of whether deaf people without language or young hearing children before they have acquired language can have concepts. The answer to this question is almost certainly 'yes' but with reservations which will appear later.

The evidence we must look for is whether the child or other person treats two or more objects or situations as if they were the same. Thus a baby who sees a new rattle and knows immediately what to do with it on the basis of his experience with other rattles may be said to have a concept of a rattle. He may, of course, shake every new object given to him and it would be rather trivial then to say he has the concept. Part of what we mean is that he can distinguish rattles from other things which are not rattles.

It is clear that in as much as most animals can distinguish items of food from things which are not edible they may be said to have a concept of food. More than this is not so clear. David Premack of the University of California (1970) has made some tests on chimpanzees as part of a surprising and interesting project to try to teach them language. He found that chimps, when presented with two objects and a third sample object, could choose correctly which of the two objects matched the sample. Later he taught them to put one plastic 'chip' on a board when two objects were 'identical' and use another one to show when two objects were 'different'. The chimps' groupings were very similar to those of humans. There are certain problems in interpreting these results but they do suggest strongly that chimpanzees have concepts of common objects which agree very closely with our own!

A related question is whether and in what way people without language can think and the effect of language on thought. This interesting but problematic field has been tackled effectively by H. G. Furth (1966 and 1971) and the Russian psychologist A. R. Luria (e.g. 1961) has a reputation for work on this subject. Justice cannot be done to these studies in the space available. Suffice it to say that the common assumption that thought is impossible or nearly impossible without language is almost certainly wrong.

Natural and conventional concepts

As pointed out earlier the possible ways of grouping objects, situations, events, etc. are legion. However it seems as if certain ways stand out more prominently than others, are more *salient*, and, as it were, invite them-selves to be recognised as concepts. It seems likely that humans (and chimps) are more ready to put fruits into the conventional apple, orange, banana categories than into such other possible groupings as 'fruits that have been pecked by birds' or 'fruits weighing more than three ounces'.

As a working hypothesis we may guess that *'natural'* concepts of this kind are those distinguished by fairly large numbers of distinctive features which regularly occur together. In information theory terms they will be the ones with most redundancy.

The alternative we may call *conventional* or *artificial* concepts. An extreme example of this latter might be 'pieces of wood which have been partly burned and then used as doorstops and then painted with red and green stripes'; since this odd combination of characteristics very rarely occurs there is little usefulness in recognising it as a category much less giving a name to it. However certain concepts which do have names in regular use seem to be more artificial than our 'cat', 'apple', 'orange' examples. The greengrocer's distinction between fruit and vegetables is less immediate and obvious than the distinction between oranges and bananas; young children seem to confuse them. Matters are complicated by the fact that the botanist's idea of a fruit is rather different from the greengrocer's.

A further illustration of the arbitrariness or artificiality of some conceptual groupings is in the use of colour terms in various languages. The English word 'brown' may be translated into French as 'brun', 'marron' or 'jaune' according to the shade and the kind of noun it qualified. The term 'jaune' in particular overlaps with the English word 'brown' so that some colours might be described by both words while other colours could only be described by one or the other. No-one is suggesting that English people cannot distinguish the three groups of colours corresponding the three French terms. It is merely that the conventions of English divide up the 'conceptual space' of colours differently.

Rather than make a rigid distinction between natural and conventional concepts it is perhaps better to think of concepts as varying in *salience*. Although information theory offers a possible lead into measuring salience it is not yet a working proposition. Returning to our question of whether people without language can have concepts we can now suggest that the answer is 'yes' with two qualifications:

1. We cannot guarantee that the pre-lingual person's concepts have the same locations and ranges as those of people with language.

It does seem likely however that very regular or salient combinations of characters will be grouped in similar ways by people with and without language.

2. By the same token it is probable that the more artificial groupings employed by people with language will not be shared by those without.

Sam X

At this point we shall introduce the case of a man, pseudonym Sam, who has a rather unusual history. He was born deaf in 1928 and at the present time, and presumably throughout his life, has a severe to profound deafness (80–90 dB in the speech frequencies). He spent a short period in a school for the deaf but apparently there were one or two incidents of erratic behaviour which, coupled with the difficult circumstances of his older sister who was caring for him, led him to be taken into a hospital for the mentally subnormal at the age of twelve. It has not been possible to get a full picture of how he came to be placed in the hospital but he has lived there for 31 years and for most of that time has been treated as a 'high grade' subnormal patient who is allowed to visit his relatives outside the hospital, work in the kitchens, etc. Recently it was recognised, following non-verbal intelligence tests, that he is in fact of about normal intelligence and some efforts have been made to give him tuition appropriate to a deaf person. It was at this stage that my colleague, Miss Mair Lewis and I took him for 'lessons' to see what language he might be able to acquire. A discussion of our attempts to teach him some language will be reserved until Chapter 10. In this chapter our interest is in Sam's conceptual groupings.

We found that he was able to say his own name indistinctly and also 'shut the door' very indistinctly. He had no other expressive speech and no comprehension of speech either through hearing or lip-reading. He knew the written alphabet almost completely in capital letters although he confused I and L. He could form lower-case letters in the old fashioned copper-plate style appropriate to his school days; he was obviously less happy with these. He also knew about three-quarters of the manual alphabet. (See Appendix II) His sister had taught him to write a few single words but, in effect, his vocabulary was minimal and his knowledge of sentence structure was non-existent.

As a subsidiary to the main task of discovering what language he might be able to acquire we were interested to see something of his conceptual groupings if any. We could be fairly sure that these groupings would have been arrived at quite independently of language. We were interested to see what similarities and differences there might be between his groupings and those recognised in English.

It was fairly obvious that Sam's concepts of most common objects were at least approximately equivalent to ours. At the outset he had no difficulty in matching objects with pictures of them (knife, fork, spoon, mug). We started a vocabulary notebook for him in which words were illustrated by pictures. At the outset we drew pictures and supplied words but later he would come to lessons with his own pictures, easily recognisable in most cases, and ask us to give him the appropriate names. His own pictures were always of distinct objects detached from their surroundings showing that he was isolating these entities in the way described earlier. Having learned the word for the picture he had little difficulty in applying the word appropriately to objects resembling the picture. There were occasional revealing errors where he did not appear to distinguish 'saucer' and 'plate' conceptually or 'bag' and 'purse'.

It was clear that Sam located many concepts in the same way as the common 'nouns' of English. The next question was whether he drew the boundaries between concepts in the same way. To test this we laid out a random array of pictures cut from a catalogue showing various kinds of flowers, fruits, plants without flowers and a range of other objects. We taught him the word 'flower' as applied to one sample picture of a red dahlia bloom, gave him a bunch of labels with the word written on them and indicated that he should label the other pictures. At first he misunderstood the task and labelled all the pictures. It was interesting that the first two to be labelled were red dahlias very similar to the sample and all other flowers were labelled first. We then gestured that one of the pictures (of a guitar) was *not* a flower and indicated that he should try again. This time he labelled all the pictures which English speakers would call flowers and excluded all the rest. This suggests quite strongly that, at least for the range of pictures given, the conceptual grouping 'flower' was more prominent or salient than, say, the grouping of all plants together or all pictures showing a red colour or all dahlias or any of the manifold other possible groupings. As far as we could tell he had never at any time had an opportunity to see the range of application of the word 'flower' and yet he chose the appropriate grouping to match the sample red dahlia quite precisely. The fact that we used 'flower' rather than 'dahlia' or 'X' is irrelevant.

In a second test we used various kinds of footwear plus a range of other objects. The sample picture was of a man's brown lace-up shoe and the labels were marked 'shoe'. In the first trial he labelled all but one of the objects (a mirror, probably an oversight) but he started by picking out all the footwear (men's and ladies' shoes, boots and slippers) and only after a pause went on to label the other objects. This shows quite clearly that he is using 'footwear' as a conceptual grouping.

On the second trial we indicated that the mirror was not a shoe and on this occasion he successfully excluded all objects which were not footwear. Curiously, he omitted to label one article of footwear, a red and black checked slipper, which we interpreted again as a mere oversight.

On the third trial we indicated that the mirror and a boot were not shoes. This time he excluded all boots, non-footwear and slippers but he also excluded ladies' stilletto heeled shoes, a lady's lace-up shoe and a man's casual shoe. The pictures which were labelled were all shoes, some lace-up and some casual, mostly men's but including a lady's – there seemed no obvious reasons for the two shoe exclusions. In general it seemed fairly clear that Sam was not observing the conceptual distinctions made by most English speakers between boots, shoes and slippers.

Other tests suggested that he observed the distinction between bags and suitcases or other objects except for labelling a picture of a cushion as a bag – this is perhaps understandable as it did rather resemble some casual handbags!

In conclusion these results suggest that someone without language may share the conceptual groupings of people with language, but by no means always. We cannot be sure in advance which groupings will be observed and which will not. These results are clearly pertinent to the problem of language acquisition as we shall see.

Some other types of concept

We have discussed how concepts may be thought of as varying in salience and have tentatively suggested that this reflects variations in redundancy. So far we have been assuming that the mental 'model' on which our concepts are based is one which shows the world as populated by objects, events, situations and qualities. We have been concerned with putting these different entities into groups. As discussed earlier it seems that both these processes of grouping and of seeing the world in terms of objects, etc. can be regarded as ways of recognising constancy or sameness in the welter of stimulations impinging on the senses: an object is the same object whatever the viewpoint, a colour is the same colour whatever object it appears on, apples are basically the same in spite of variations in colour and markings, etc.

But there are other ways in which we can isolate sameness. We come to understand that objects can be thought of as having length, breadth and height and we can apply this three-dimensional frame to a great variety of objects. We also come to understand that there is a quality of sameness when we see, for example, a marble, a penny and a rubber or a marble, a marble and a marble, etc. (i.e. there are three objects in each case). This is perhaps the origin of the number scale and other mathematical concepts in geometry, algebra, etc. may have a similar origin in the 'real world'.

Other concepts of a mathematical or quasi-mathematical type include the notion of time as a kind of stream flowing from the past through the present to the future. Another example is the abstract frame of human relationships: father, son, mother, sister, aunt, uncle, cousin, etc.

Most of these concepts are conventionally recognised as *abstract* and this term will serve our purpose. We shall contrast them with concepts based on our 'real world' model which can be called *concrete* although the boundary between them is not sharp. They are based on mental models which are in some sense detached from the world of objects, events, etc. It is as if we had ceased to be content to use our modelling 'clay' merely to reproduce the real world but were using it to invent new forms and structures. It is not by any means clear how children acquire abstract concepts but language probably plays an even bigger role here than with concrete concepts. Most hearing children have to be taught arithmetic and it seems unlikely that many would discover these mathematical ideas without formal teaching. The time scale, at least in the rudimentary form of past, present and future is probably acquired by most hearing children through language; the difficulties deaf children have in this field are more than merely linking words to pre-established concepts. Similarly children may, in effect, be taught the conceptual framework of family relationships through hearing how the terms for relatives are used.

Re-shaping of concepts

It is debatable whether or not all abstract concepts have an origin in the 'real world' but it is clear that once formed they can be manipulated to form concepts which have no basis there. We may learn the number scale from watching our teacher count out marbles or buttons but at no time are we likely to see her count out 12,642,568 buttons; and yet before long we may be able to handle such a concept quite adequately. Similarly we may be taught the notion of three dimensional space with illustrations from cubes and rectangular blocks but the more advanced mathematical notion of four, five, six, etc. dimensional space can never be illustrated in this way.

This ability to refabricate and manipulate concepts is not confined to abstract concepts. Concrete concepts are sometimes 'rebuilt' by taking parts from various natural concepts and putting them together: the ancient Greeks' idea of a centaur was a creature that was half man and half horse. The unicorn is another mythical animal being a horse with a single horn and the cloven hooves of goats.

Before discussing how the various types of concept and other meanings are linked to words we shall devote the next chapter to the words themselves – how they are built up and how they are put together into phrases and sentences.

3 The tools of language

The words which we use to convey meanings, although they are merely tools to do a job, have an interest in their own right. In this chapter we shall examine the efforts which have been made to describe the structure or patterning which appears not only within words but in the arrangement of words within phrases and sentences. These types of study have been developed within the field of linguistics but, because language is an important part of behaviour and mental processes recent years have seen psychologists taking an increasing interest in the ideas developed by linguists. In these branches of linguistics, as in others, efforts have been made to make theories and principles apply to all languages. Here we shall be concerned mainly with English but the ideas described are fairly general. This is a large and rapidly expanding field of study; what follows is something of a thumb-nail sketch.

The lowest or most fine-grained level of description is called phonology and, since it is a relatively uncontroversial field we shall describe it briefly before dealing with higher levels.

Phonology

Phonology should not be confused with *phonetics*. This latter is concerned with describing precisely the sounds which are made and how they are made in speaking English and other languages. A very large number of different speech sounds have been recognised and a system of recording them has been developed called the International Phonetic Alphabet. The purpose of this Alphabet is to enable phoneticians to record in written form any sound or subtle variation in sound which a speaker of any language might produce.

Clearly, a great many small variations in speech sounds have no significance for recognising words or the meaning of speech. Someone from Yorkshire will pronounce the word 'bath' in one way which would be different from how a Londoner or Scotsman would pronounce it and yet we recognise it as the same word. One person is unlikely to pronounce a given word in exactly the same way on any two occasions but we still recognise it as the same word.

Certain sound contrasts are, however, very important for identifying words. Such contrasts are seen between the beginnings of the words 'pat', 'cat', 'fat', 'mat', 'bat', etc. Thus we can see that speech sounds can be divided into zones such that variations of sound within a zone are of no importance for distinguishing words but variations of sound which cross the boundaries between zones are important. The zones are known as *phonemes*; various sounds falling within one phoneme are called *allophones*. The study of phonemes and their arrangements is called *phonology*. To illustrate the distinction between phonemes and allophones consider the sounds 's' and 'sh'. In English it is important to distinguish them because they differentiate such words as 'sew' and 'show' (thinking of the sounds and ignoring the spelling). Apparently in Japanese there is no important distinction between them and they may be used interchangeably in a word. The phonemes which are commonly recognised in English are shown in the table in Appendix I with sample words to illustrate them and symbols taken from a simplified version of the International Phonetic Alphabet.

If one looks at electronically produced 'pictures' of speech (see Plate 1) the boundaries between successive phonemes and indeed successive words are not marked in any obvious way. It is therefore sometimes thought that the concept of a phoneme is a necessary fiction to aid discussion. This view is no more justified than the supposition that the segmentation of speech into words is a mere fiction. Both words and phonemes are identified not by any physical boundaries but by the fact that they are the elements in the speech stream which repeat themselves in spite of varying permutations while other divisions do not. More will be said about this in Chapter 6.

Grammar

The second and third levels of language description are called morphology and syntax; the two together come under the heading of grammar. This word has rather unfortunate connotations and it might be as well to quote George Miller's (1962) remarks about it:

'I use the term defiantly, for I am fully aware that it is a grim and forbidding subject. It still reeks of the medieval trivium of grammar, logic and rhetoric; it still reminds us vividly of all those endless and incomprehensible rules that our teachers tried to drum into us at grammar school.'

At this stage the reader must take on trust that grammar plays an extremely important part in how language conveys meanings, and some understanding of grammar is essential if we are to unravel how hearing children acquire language and how we might best set about giving language to deaf children. I am not suggesting for one moment that one would necessarily try to teach language to a young deaf child by teaching him grammatical rules. It is simply that we should examine what an understanding of grammar on our part will contribute to teaching methods. We should always remember that a normal five-year-old has a most detailed and sophisticated, if unconscious, knowledge of grammar which he demonstrates every time he speaks. The contrast with all but the most exceptional deaf child is sad indeed. It may appear odd to say a five-year-old 'knows' grammar but the word is here used in the sense that the child obeys the rules in speaking, not that he could state the rules explicitly. The fact that our five-year-old like most normal adults frequently uses what traditional grammar would regard as 'incomplete' and therefore ungrammatical sentences should not detain us; our reasons for rejecting this viewpoint will appear shortly.

In this chapter we shall look first at the difference between 'modern' and 'traditional' approaches to grammar. Then I shall briefly describe some useful ideas in modern grammar and finally I shall outline two modern grammatical theories.

Modern and traditional grammar

Consider the following definition of a sentence used in traditional grammar (this example is given by C. C. Fries (1952)).

'A sentence is a group of words expressing a complete thought.'

If we wish to use this definition to recognise a sentence, it is necessary first to know the meaning of what we are analysing. Although there are apparently more than two hundred definitions of a sentence in traditional grammar these and the definitions of other terms all seem to require that one first knows the meaning of the material.

This may seem reasonable enough but it leads to practical difficulties

For example the following group of words will be generally acknowledged to be a sentence: 'The dog is barking', but the 'complete thought' which it expresses is identical with that in the words: 'The barking dog . . .'. This latter is certainly not a sentence but the 'complete thought' criterion does not tell us so. Difficulties such as these may explain why traditional definitions have proliferated.

The approach of modern grammar is to analyse the arrangements of words and parts of words independently of meaning. It is then possible to see the way in which different arrangements of words signal different meanings. We shall discuss this important aspect of language in the next chapter; such a discussion would not be possible within the frame of traditional grammar.

A further point is that traditional grammar has tended to be concerned with specifying 'correct' usages: it is *prescriptive*. Most modern grammars are concerned mainly with recording the patterns of language which are commonly used and accepted by native speakers of the language: they are *descriptive*. Such utterances as 'over there' (perhaps following the question 'Where's George?') are regarded as quite legitimate material for description. When we say that deaf children's grammar is wrong or bad we mean simply that their language does not follow the commonly accepted patterns of normal speakers. In case this point is not clear the reader should turn to page 51 for an example of the kind of colloquial English which was the subject of one linguistic study. In spite of its breaking many rules of traditional grammar it is acceptable English and thus what we are primarily interested in.

Some terms and ideas in modern grammar

Although terms like 'word' and 'sentence' are very important in modern linguistics, precise definitions are not crucial for our discussion – their 'modern' meanings should become clear later anyway. This section describes a few ideas borrowed from linguistics which will be useful to us. Our first task is to understand the basic problem of linguistics.

The problem

The number of possible sentences is extremely large. One need only thumb through any book to realise that a given sentence almost never occurs more than once. It is fairly safe to say that most sentences are quite new and have never been produced before.

Having said this we should say that although the number of possible sentences is extremely large it is not nearly as large as the number of possible strings of words. If one combined words at random one would quite likely produce something like this: '. . . have street quorum at meaning characteristics they something produce . . .'. Occasionally one would produce a string of words which formed a sentence.

The grammarian's problem is to look at a sample of the language and try to discover patterns and rules governing the arrangement of words in the sample which will enable him to produce new strings of words which are also grammatical. The rules should also enable him to distinguish grammatical from ungrammatical sentences.

A grammar which is sufficiently explicit to enable someone, or even a machine, to construct new grammatical sentences by rule is said to be *generative*. To aim for this high standard of precision and explicitness is something peculiar to modern linguistics and owes much to the work of the linguist Noam Chomsky.

The logical problem is that the linguist can never test all possible sentences since there are so many; there is always the possibility that his rules will lead him to think that a particular string of words is or is not a sentence when a native speaker of the language would disagree. If this happens the rules must be revised.

This logical problem is exactly the same as the problem of induction discussed in Chapter 1. We are constantly using induction and it seems to be very useful but we can never escape from the fact that it is impossible to be completely confident that things will always turn out in the expected way.

Given this unavoidable problem, how can the grammarian discover rules and patterns which will distinguish grammatical and ungrammatical strings of words? Before answering that we must first decide what we mean by saying that a sentence is grammatical.

We have said that modern grammars are concerned with describing the sentence patterns which are commonly accepted and used by native speakers of a language. A point to notice is that we sometimes say things which we ourselves would recognise as ungrammatical if we stopped to think. We might say 'A number of things were on the table' where 'were' should be 'was'. As Chomsky says: 'A record of natural speech will show numerous false starts, deviations from rules, changes of plan in mid-course and so on.'

This distinction between what we would accept as grammatical after some thought and the speech we produce in practice seems to be useful. Notice that we are *not* talking about ordinary colloquial speech with all the features which traditional grammar would regard as wrong. All we are talking about at the moment are slips of the tongue and other 'errors' which the speaker himself, on a moment's reflection, would reject as wrong. Actually slips of the tongue, etc. are not all that common except where the speaker is wrestling with a particularly tough problem of expression. Chomsky develops this distinction between a person's reflective knowledge of a language and his use of it in practice in a rather special way which we shall discuss in the last section of this chapter. For the moment we shall take as our guiding principle that:

The ultimate test of whether a sequence of words is grammatical is whether native speakers of the language would regard it as an acceptable sample of the language after considering it carefully.

We are applying 'acceptable' here only when an utterance is acceptable as a sample of the language regardless of whether it is unacceptable because it is lewd, factually wrong, stylistically bad, illogical, etc. This *acceptability* test is fairly widely used amongst linguists and frequently the linguist himself, as a native speaker of the language, makes the judgment. It overcomes the problem of dealing with the huge number of possible sentences: the linguist does not attempt to list all possible sentences but simply makes a judgment of acceptability of each sentence which he is studying as it occurs. By using his rules to generate a few judiciously chosen sentences from the vast pool of possible sentences and testing their acceptability he can make sure there are no glaring absurdities in the grammar.

It must be admitted that our use of the word 'grammatical' is unorthodox. More usually a sentence is described as grammatical when it obeys rules of grammar propounded by a linguist even if the rules are so crude that they produce many unacceptable sentences. My reason for choosing to use 'grammatical' in this way is to emphasise the fundamental importance of the acceptability test and the principle that the rules of grammar must be revised continually until they match the judgment of native speakers and not vice versa.

We have no sooner propounded our principle than we run into difficulties. We find that native speakers of a language may easily disagree about whether a sentence is acceptable or not. It is perhaps wrong to call this a difficulty. The fact is that the boundary between grammatical and ungrammatical sentences is in fact hazy in exactly the same way that the boundaries between most other concepts are hazy. Here are some illustrations:

The 'sentence' 'A green ships were sail sea' sounds odd to anyone who knows English and would be rejected as unacceptable by almost everybody even if they knew nothing about grammatical theory. By contrast a 'sentence' like 'The banana bites the liberty' seems to obey certain rules of grammar but is nonetheless rather odd. It seems to fall on the borderline between the grammatical and ungrammatical, some people would accept it and others would not. We shall say more about this type of sentence later and we shall find another different example of a borderline case in the section on Chomsky's grammar.

We should add that what is acceptable shows regional variations. Many Welsh people, particularly from the valleys, say and accept as correct, such expressions as 'There's lovely', 'There's nice' and 'Put that by there', 'Shall we go out, is it?', or even: 'Like you know innit see, me mother, see, do always like tell me to do the washing up, innit see?'.

To the English ear these are ungrammatical. Neither the English forms nor the Rhondda forms are more correct than the other. Each are accepted expressions in particular speech communities and should be studied as such. As Roger Brown and Colin Fraser have put it (1963), 'Rules of grammar are cultural norms; like other norms they are descriptive of certain regularities of behaviour within a community . . .' They add that these norms can be prescriptive but only in the sense that anyone joining a speech community from outside will seem odd if he does not follow the accepted patterns.

Morphology and syntax As mentioned at the beginning of this section on grammar, the second and third levels after phonology for describing language, are *morphology* and *syntax* both falling under the heading of grammar. Morphology is concerned with arrangements of morphemes and these are usually defined as the smallest language elements which can carry meaning: the word 'cat' cannot be broken down into smaller elements which can be said to convey meaning so it is also a morpheme. The word 'antechambers' can be broken into 'ante' meaning 'before', chamber' meaning a room and 's' which signals plurality. Each of these are morphemes. Clearly morphemes are often but not necessarily smaller units than words and they may be as small as phonemes. Syntax is concerned with the arrangement of words into sequences.

Form versus substance It will prove useful in later discussion to distinguish the form of a language from the different substances or media in which it may appear. English as a language can appear in the following media:

1. Sound waves produced by a speaker and heard by a listener. We shall call this the oral-aural medium.
2. Written or graphic medium. We still recognise our familiar English even when it is written down. There are various systems of notation:
   (*a*) Traditional Orthography (T.O.). This is the ordinary Roman alphabet in which this book is written.
   (*b*) The International Phonetic Alphabet (IPA). As mentioned earlier this is a system of notation which can be used for any language including English. The table in Appendix I shows a simplified system for English phonemes and below is a sample of English written in this system:

   ði: aul and ðə pusikat went tu si:
   in ə biutifəl pi: gri:n bout.

   FIGURE 15

   (*c*) The Initial Teaching Alphabet (i.t.a.) or Augmented Roman Alphabet. This is a system of notation invented by Sir James Pitman. It is specially designed to reproduce the phoneme structure of English while at the same time being visually similar to T.O. It is designed as a starting medium for teaching reading to hearing children who later transfer to T.O. We shall have more to say about it later.

   Here is our same passage in i.t.a.

   ſhe oul and ſhe pωssycat went tω see
   in a buetifωl pee green bœt

   FIGURE 16

   Notice how easy it is to read with only a knowledge of T.O.
   (*d*) English can also be transmitted as Morse Code which substitutes sequences of dots and dashes for the letters of the Roman alphabet, see Fig. 17 opposite.
   This can be written down or transmitted as radio waves.

3. Manual media. The various manual alphabets used by some deaf people are also examples of media or substances by which English can be transmitted. Examples are given in Appendix II.

```
– • • • • •   – – –   • – –   • – • •   • – – • –   – • • • •   • – – • • –   • • • • •   – • – –
T   H     E     O     W       L       A   N   D   T   H   E     P     U     S     S     Y


– • – • • – – • •   • – – • – • –   – – – –   • • • • • –   • – – – • •   • –
C   A   T     W   E   N   T   T   O     S   E   A     I   N     A


– • • • • • – • • – – • • • • – • • • – • – • •   • – – • – • • –   – – • • – • • • • – •
B   EA   U   T   I   F   U   L       P   EA     G     R   EE   N


– • • •   – – – • – –   • – • – • –
B     O     A   T     •
```

FIGURE 17

Clearly there is no end to the different media which may be used. We could if we liked invent a system using lumps of clay of different shapes. The important thing is that whatever the system we must retain the pattern of contrasts between the different phonemes, morphemes and words of the language. To represent the form of a language it is only necessary to ensure that these significant elements can be distinguished from each other, i.e. that they contrast with each other. The actual physical substances and physical shapes of the elements is not important except in relation to particular uses of the language. In this book the term speech will be reserved for spoken language perceived through the ears (oral-aural language). The general term is 'language' which refers to the patterns of contrasted elements (phonemes, morphemes, words) used for communication regardless of what medium it is in.

Isomorphism For a given language the patterns of contrasted elements will be largely the same from medium to medium but sometimes there are variations. The degree to which two media have the same system of contrasts is called isomorphism.

In the strictest sense two media, say speech and some visible representation, are only isomorphic if every tiny feature of the one has a corresponding element in the other. There are ways of showing speech in a visible form so that all variations of pitch, intensity and timbre for every phoneme are reproduced. But we might still speak of two media being isomorphic even if their phonemes, say, had no resemblance to each other at all. So long as there is a one-for-one correspondence between the phonemes of the first medium and those of the second we can say that they are isomorphic down to the phoneme level. Again we may not be able to find any one-for-one correspondence between phonemes but we can between the morphemes of the two media or even the words only. In these cases isomorphism would exist down to the morpheme and word levels respectively.

The most notorious case of two media not being isomorphic is that of English spelling; it is only approximately isomorphic with the phonemes of spoken English. Here is an illustration:

THE OWL AND THE PUSSYCAT WENT TO SEA

ði: aul and ðə pusikat went tu si:

IN A BEAUTIFUL PEA-GREEN BOAT

in ə biutifəl pi: gri:n bout

FIGURE 18

A given phoneme may be represented by several different letters or groups of letters, for example in English the sound o: may be represented by 'our', (four, pour, court), 'or' (for, porter), 'au' (nautical), 'ough' (ought), 'augh' (naughty). Each of these groups of letters contain single letters and smaller groups which represent other phonemes in other situations, e.g. in the group 'ough', 'o' may in other contexts represent the phoneme o (pot) or the phoneme i (women); 'u', 'g' and 'h' all have other sound values in other contexts. The group 'ough' is itself notorious for the eight different phonemes it may represent and is especially confusing to foreigners. Sir Richard Paget once suggested as an illustration of the lack of logic in English Spelling the word 'ghoti' which is a possible spelling of 'fish', 'gh' as in 'enough', 'o' as in 'women', 'ti' as in 'nation'.

Fortunately, written English in T.O. is isomorphic with spoken English at the word level and largely at the morpheme level. Even at the phoneme level there is a large measure of correspondence. If there was no association at all between the sounds of a word and its spelling then each written word would have to be learned as an arbitrary symbol in the way Chinese characters have to be learned.

Two approaches to linguistics

Modern linguistics is dominated by the theories of Professor Noam Chomsky. In 1957 he published a book, *Syntactic Structures*, which is a major landmark in the science. The theory put forward there has since been expanded and modified somewhat but continues to be very important if controversial.

It is, however, but one of a number of theories all built on a common ground of research and a common 'modern' approach to linguistics. This foundation of fact and agreed theory is perhaps best illustrated by the work of Professor C. C. Fries. His views and the results of an extensive study of natural conversations are set out in his very interesting book, *The Structure of English*, which was published in 1952. I shall outline these views and those of Chomsky without, I hope, doing too much violence to either.

The Structure of English   C. C. Fries

Although Fries's ideas may in some ways have been superseded by later developments I think they are probably still fairly directly relevant to thinking about how deaf and hearing children may acquire language. I have attempted here merely to pick out the main ideas which will be useful to our later discussion. Fries's book deserves to be read in the original. The whole study is based on tape-recordings of actual telephone conversations. Ostensibly Fries is describing the language as it is actually used in practice but a good deal of his own judgment is added, as a native speaker of English, especially in the deciding how to classify words into different parts of speech. Generally speaking we can regard it as a grammar of colloquial English.

Parts of Speech – the principle of substitution Traditionally, parts of speech like nouns, verbs, adjectives etc. have been defined in ways which are ambiguous and inconsistent. A pronoun is commonly defined as 'a word used instead of a noun'. But, Fries asks, 'which of the following substitutes are "pronouns"?'

Wednesday ⎫ is the time to see him
Tomorrow ⎪
Today ⎪
Next week ⎪
Later ⎬
Now ⎪
When ⎪
This ⎪
That ⎪
It ⎭

Clearly the definition does not tell us everything we use to identify conventionally recognised pronouns. Similarly an adjective is often defined as 'a word that modifies a noun or pronoun'. Plenty of words act as modifiers without being adjectives, e.g. 'a hat sale', 'a sofa cushion', etc.

The outstanding feature of all modern grammars is that definitions of parts of speech are based on the principle of 'distributional equivalence' or '*substitution*': Fries chose three short sentences as 'test frames' and systematically substituted words in different positions to see whether they would still make grammatically acceptable sentences. Test frame A was:

'The concert was good'

– and such forms as 'The concerts were good', 'coffee is good' and others were treated as variations on this one sentence frame. The second word in the test frame can be replaced by such words as 'food', 'coffee', 'taste', 'container', 'difference', 'privacy' and many hundreds of others all of which would be grammatically acceptable to a native speaker of English.

By contrast such words as 'quickly', 'kicked', 'afterwards', 'beautiful', 'slovenly', 'fought', etc. will not fit in the 'slot' and make an acceptable sentence. A part of speech defined on the principle of substitution is *a list of the words which may be substituted one for another in a given position in a given sentence without making that sentence grammatically unacceptable.*

These words are obviously the same in many cases as traditional nouns. The other three major parts of speech recognised by Fries also resemble 'verbs', 'adjectives' and 'adverbs' but they by no means always coincide with traditional categories, so Fries has called them Classes 1, 2, 3 and 4.

Words of Class 1, as identified in sentence frame A, may also be substituted in sentence frames B and C in the positions shown:

Sentence frame B: The *clerk* remembered the *tax*.

Sentence frame C: The *team* went there.

The principle of substitution may be used to 'generate' new sentences such as 'The lady was good', 'The pianist was good', 'The singing was good', etc., etc., and Class 1 words recognised in frame A may be substituted in the appropriate slots in frame B: 'The lady remembered the tax', 'The pianist remembered the tax'.

The reader will now have seen that this is not going to work as simply as this all the time: 'The singing remembered the tax' is an odd sentence as are 'The privacy remembered the taste' or 'The banana bites the liberty', which could be formed by substituting indiscriminately. With these latter sentences it is not obvious whether they break rules of grammar or whether they break rules for combining the meanings of words. This uncertainty is reflected in the fact that in linguistic writing they are sometimes described as 'syntactically anomalous' and sometimes as 'semantically anomalous'. In Chapter 7 it will be suggested that they highlight a basic similarity in the processes at work in the learning of both syntax and meanings.

At all events these sentences seem to lie on the borderline between being acceptable or unacceptable since some people might regard them as examples of English sentences and others might not. The fact that there are borderline cases of this kind which are not definitely acceptable or unacceptable, is an important feature of language which will be discussed again later.

Class 2 words are illustrated in these examples:

Frame A	Class 1	Class 2	
(The)	*concert* ———s	is/was are/were seems/seemed seem sounds/sounded sound feels/felt feel becomes/became become	good

Frame B	Class 1	Class 2	Class 1
(The)	*clerk* ———s	remembered (the) wanted saw discussed *etc.*	*tax* ———s

Similar examples apply to Frame C. Words of Class 3 and 4 are illustrated here:

Frame A	Class 3	Class I	Class 2	Class 3	Class 4
(The)	latest	concert	was	good	there
	large			latest	here
	new			large	always
	best			*etc.*	upstairs
	etc.				then
					generally
					etc.

Notice that Class 4, in particular, contains words, like 'upstairs', which would not be recognised conventionally as 'adverbs'. Class 3 words have two distinct locations, one following the Class 2a word in sentence frames of type A and the other between the word 'the' (discussed shortly) and the Class I word which always follows it.

Another point to notice is that a great many 'words' belong in more than one part of speech e.g. wash, list, paint, march, print, etc. etc. can all be used as Class I or Class 2 words. In a sense, although meanings are usually related in the two uses, a word used in these two ways is better thought of as two words just as much as any homonyms would be treated as separate words. It is usual to consider a cobbler's 'last' as a different word from 'the last in line'; an ecclesiastical 'see' as different from the verb 'to see'; a fisherman's 'cast' as different from a playwright's. Whether one defines 'word' as a particular form or as a form with a particular meaning or syntactic use is purely a matter of convenience.

Function words The four major parts of speech make up the vast bulk of different word types in English. Each of the four classes contains thousands of different words. By contrast Fries identifies a mere 154 different 'function words' which do not fit into any of the four classes. But what they lack in variety they make up in sheer bulk of use; they may constitute nearly half of the words in a typical sample of English.

Group A of the function words are all those words which may be substituted for the word 'the' in the sentence frame A:

Group A	Class 1	Class 2	Class 3
The	concert(s)	was	good
		were	

no, a/an, your,
every, one, two,
all, both, *etc.*

Fries points out that the fact that some of these words may occur in the position of Class 1 words and that 'all' and 'both' may occur before 'the' is irrelevant to the classification of these words as function words of Group A. It means simply that these two 'words' can occur in more than one class or group and to that extent they are different words as we have said.

The best examples of this are the words 'not' and 'there'. 'Not' is used in two quite distinct ways:

Group A	Class 1	Group B	Group C	Class 2	Class 3
The	concert	may	not	be	good

Here 'not' forms part of a construction which includes a Class 2 word and served to modify this Class 2 word. This 'not' is classed by Fries in a Group C by itself. 'Not' may also be used in the ways illustrated here:

Group A	Class 1	Group E	Group A	Class 1	Class 2	Group E
The	concerts	not	the	lectures	are	not

Class 2	Class 3	Group E	Class 3	Class 4	Group E	Class 4
were	interesting	not	profitable	now	not	later

This use of 'not' puts it in Group E with the words 'and', 'or', 'nor', 'but', 'rather than' which can stand between words of the same part of speech and serve to indicate that the words connected in this way have the same structural function.

The two uses of the word 'there' appear in this sentence:

Group	Class	Group	Class	Class
H	2	A	I	4
There	is	no	student	there

The first 'there' appears in a characteristic pattern with words of Class 2b and Class 1 or in questions: 'Is there a man at the door?'. As distinct from the second 'there' it is a word which is never given stress in speaking. The second 'there' is a typical Class 4 word.

There is a total of fifteen groups of function words and these should be examined in Fries's book at first hand.

Features of word groups and classes The definition of word classes is purely in terms of the principle of substitution. However words of a given class often share common features and this very probably helps children when they are learning to recognise words and the classes they belong in. Here are a few of many examples given by Fries:

Class 1	*Class 2*
arrival	arrive
refusal	refuse
denial	deny
acquittal	acquit

Class 1	*Class 3*
activity	active
complexity	complex
equality	equal
falsity	false
purity	pure

Class 2	*Class 3*
brighten	bright
cheapen	cheap
darken	dark
deepen	deep
freshen	fresh
harden	hard

etc.

It is worth adding that the correlation of most common Class 1 words with objects, Class 2 words with actions and Class 3 words with qualities probably helps in a similar way.

The indeterminancy of grammar – subgrouping and diminishing returns We defined a part of speech as a list of words which could be substituted acceptably for each other in *a given position* in *a given sentence*. The two qualifiers are rather important as is shown here:

The concert was good
    taste
    liberty
    lady
    cashier
    etc.

All the Class 1 words listed can be substituted acceptably in the given sentence. In Fries's second sentence frame some of these can be substituted acceptably and others are doubtful cases:

The clerk remembered the tax
taste	taste
liberty	liberty
lady	lady
cashier	cashier
etc.	*etc.*

In the first 'slot' taste and liberty look very ill at ease when they are followed by 'remembered'. Oddly enough they fit reasonably well in the last slot.

The Class 2 words listed for frame A (p. 45) do not fit very well in frame B.

The clerk remembered the tax
    is/was
    seems/seemed
    sounds
    becomes
    etc.

The usual solution to this problem is to develop sub-groupings of the main parts of speech. Whereas the pattern of frame B was characterised as: A 1 2 A 1, it might be refined to: A 1a 2a A 1 where

1a refers to a sub-group of Class 1 words which excludes 'taste', 'liberty' and other 'inanimate' Class 1 words, while 2a refers to a sub-division of Class 2 words which excludes 'is', 'becomes', 'seems', etc.

As a general rule word classes or parts of speech developed with reference to a particular sentence frame or position in a sentence frame often require repeated sub-division when applied to another location or special situation. What tends to happen is that the largest bulk of sentences can be described as arrangements of the major parts of speech, but sub-grouping of various kinds are required for a minority of sentences and sub-divisions of these sub-groupings may be required. An example here is the construction '. . . got to the ——'. The usual pattern is illustrated by such sentences as 'I am going to the party', 'I am going to the shops', 'I am going to the theatre'. A very large number of Class 1 words may be substituted in the last slot including such words as 'home', 'school', 'tea', 'dinner', 'bed'; the related construction '. . . go to ——' will only take 'school', 'tea', 'dinner', 'bed', which, with others, constitute a sub-group of Class 1 words. Again such words as 'abroad', 'upstairs', which can be used as ordinary Class 1 words in other constructions can only be used here in the form 'I am going abroad', etc. Curiously, we can say 'I am going home' where 'home' can also be used in 'I am going to the home' but we would not be likely to say 'I am going to the abroad' or 'I am going to the upstairs'. Always where major patterns have been found there are likely to be special cases and exceptions of various kinds. John Lyons (1968) writes: '. . . sooner or later, in his attempt to exclude the definitely un-acceptable sentences by means of the distributional subclassification of their component words, the linguist will be faced with a situation in which he is establishing more and more rules, each covering very few sentences; and he will be setting up so many over-lapping word-classes that all semblance of generality is lost. This is what is meant by the principle of 'diminishing returns': there comes a point (and where this point is might be a legitimate matter for dispute) at which the increase in the complexity of the rules is too 'costly' in proportion to its 'yield', a relatively small increase in the coverage of acceptable and unacceptable sentences.

This is one sense in which grammar is essentially indeterminate; the complete generative grammar which specified every exception and special case might conceivably be written but it would have to be extremely bulky.

There are however two other related features of the grammar problem which indicate that the notion of a full set of rules which can specify language patterns with absolute precision is something of a chimaera. The first is the problem of induction already touched on: we can never test our rules against every sentence because there is, in effect, an infinite number of possible sentences. The second is the fact that the boundaries between the acceptable and the unacceptable in sentences is actually hazy. People disagree over borderline cases, so that our acid test of acceptability will not allow the grammarian with his rules to squeeze the last drop of syntactic juice out of the language. This latter point is discussed more fully at the end of this chapter. The suggestion is made in Chapter 7 that disagreements over acceptability are in fact a result of the induction problem because each individual induces his own personal grammar from a unique sample of the language, different from anyone else's.

None of the foregoing should be taken to suggest that the exercise of trying to write grammars is a waste of time. The main patterns can be specified relatively easily and unambiguously as can the major variations on these patterns. Up to a certain limit we can choose how much precision our grammar gives us according to how much time and effort we are prepared to devote to its construction.

Types of 'sentence' A sample of the colloquial English which Fries analysed (ibid. p. 24) is given below. Notice that most of it (apart from the odd Americanism!) is acceptable to the English ear. Slips of the tongue, etc., are not much in evidence and it seems reasonable to assume that the speakers were using expressions which were also acceptable to themselves. In this sample punctuation is omitted to avoid prejudging what the sentences are.

1. A I don't know whether you let B go out during the week do you suppose he could come over tonight while we go out to dinner
2. Well the difficulty is J that he got back in his lessons
3. Oh oh
4. And in his last report about two weeks ago he was down in two subjects his father hasn't been letting him do anything
5. Well that's a good idea
6. I'm awfully sorry
7. Well that's all right thanks A to tell you the truth I don't want awfully badly to go you know what I mean
8. M hm

9. Well how's the garden
10. Oh it's much worse than yours I imagine the only thing that looks decent at all is the strawberries
11. Yes I know but you know they're not going to be any good unless they get some sun and dry weather
12. No well there's still time for them isn't there
13. Yes I know
14. I've got strawberries started have you
15. What
16. Some of the berries have started on my plants.

Fries's exact method of isolating 'sentences' from this material need not concern us here, but it is well to note some distinctions which he made. He used the term 'utterance' as a more general expression than 'sentence' to mean any passage of speech; he distinguished those utterances which were used to start conversations ('situation utterance units') from those that were used later which he called 'response utterance units'.

From utterances of the first type he isolated 'sentences' of two types which correspond roughly with the traditional classification of *simple* and *complex* sentences. (Fries called them 'single minimum free utterances' and 'single expanded free utterances'. We shall stick to the simpler traditional terms but ignore the distinction in traditional grammar between complex and compound sentences.) The important point is that a fairly limited range of simple sentence patterns were identified as sequences of word classes and these patterns could be used for analysing complex sentences as expansions and variations on the simple sentence patterns. These 'situation utterance units' are all 'correct' full sentences as would be recognised in traditional grammar.

Fries then went on to examine the 'response utterance units' and found that a lot of them used the same basic patterns as the 'situation' units but that many did not. An example was given earlier of the response 'over there' following the question 'Where's George?'. This is one type of response which does not fit the full 'correct' 'situation utterance' pattern but it can be recognised as a contraction of the pattern 'George is over there'. Another type of response utterance includes things like 'Oh oh' or 'M hm' which Fries recognised as merely signals to show the speaker that one is still listening. Where a conversation is held face to face these are likely to be nods of the head or other visual gestures. We shall have more to say about the functions of different types of utterance and sentence patterns in the next chapter.

Expansion of simple sentences There are two overlapping principles by which simple sentences can be made into 'expanded' or 'complex' sentences. The first is the use of modification structures and the second is the use of included sentences.

'Modification' structures In keeping with the principle of analysing sentence patterns according to their form or structure rather than by their meanings Fries rejects the traditional definition of a modifier as 'a word or group or words that adds to the meaning of another word'. This is because a lot of structures can be found which 'add to the meaning of another word' but are not modifiers.

Rather, 'modification' is a structure of connection, but it is a connection of a particular kind. It must be emphasised that 'modification' is here defined purely in terms of patterns of words and not by the fact that it often signals a modification of meaning. It is unfortunate in some ways that a new term was not used but Fries emphasises the special use of the word by putting it in inverted commas.

Each of the four major parts of speech and some function words may act as the 'head' or 'nucleus' of a 'modification' structure. Thus in the sentence:

2-ng   1
A *burning fire* is in the fireplace

The Class 1 word 'fire' is the 'head' of a 'modification' structure with the Class 2 word 'burning' and is distinct from the similar two words in the sentence:

1   2
A *fire burns* in the fireplace

The features which in this case distinguish the 'modification' structure from the second form which is not are these:

1. The '-ing' form of the Class 2 word ('-ed' forms behave similarly). The second arrangement, which forms an integral part of the sentence pattern, is distinguished from the first arrangement in that the Class 1 word and the Class 2 word 'agree' in their inflexions; usually in a sentence pattern a Class 1 word without an '-s' is followed by a Class 2 word with an '-s'.
2. The position of the Class 2 word before the Class 1 word.
3. The structure can stand alone only as a response to a question.

4. The modification structure may be replaced as a unit in exactly the same way as the Class 1 word which forms the 'head'. The term 'head' is itself defined purely formally as that word in the structure which can be substituted for the whole structure without making the sentence ungrammatical.

For 'modification' structures with a Class 1 word as head Fries gives examples of how other classes of word or groups of words may act as 'modifiers'.

1. Class 2 – example given above.

$$\overset{3}{} \quad \overset{1}{}$$

2. Class 3 – 'an *excellent address*'.

$$\overset{1}{} \quad \overset{1}{}$$

3. Class 1 – 'a *paper knife*'.

$$\overset{1}{} \quad \overset{4}{}$$

4. Class 4 – 'The *food there* . . .'

5. A structure with one of the function words of Group F – 'The

$$\overset{1}{} \qquad \overset{F}{}$$

carnival   over on the fair grounds'.

6. An included sentence usually with one of the function words or Group J (who, which, that, etc.).

$$\overset{1}{} \qquad\qquad\qquad \overset{mod.}{}$$

They are the very *ones   that should be invited*

Similarly, there are 'modification' structures which have as heads Class 2 words, Class 3 words, Class 4 words and certain function words. In each of these cases the 'modifiers' may themselves be drawn from any of the four classes or be groups of words formed with Group F function words or be included sentences.

It is clear that the common idea that 'modification' is the preserve of 'adjectives' and 'adverbs' does not hold water.

A rather improbable but quite acceptable example given by Fries of how one Class 1 word may be simultaneously 'modified' by a large number of different structures is this:

'Almost all/the/twenty-five/very famous/Army/*officers*/of the United States/listed in the catalogue/who are still in active service/ . . .'

The importance of his studies is in showing how purely formal, structural devices can serve as signals of the connection between the head of the structure and its 'modifiers'. Once this is established one can then examine the effects of these different connections and structures in terms of different meanings. We shall look at this in the next chapter.

Included sentences We have seen how a sentence may be included in another sentence and act as a 'modifier' of a word of any class, for example (ibid. p. 212):

	I	J	included sentence	
'The	*day*	*after*	*you left*	he came in'.

An included sentence may also replace one of the words forming the basic sentence pattern. Thus the italicised section of this sentence is effectively replacing a Class 1 word (ibid. p. 255):

'*Whatever you decide to do about the place of the dinner* will be all right with us'.

In other cases the included sentence does not form part of the structure of the other sentence at all but is linked to it for convenience or perhaps because of a common topic:

'I washed my face and I brushed my hair'.

The importance of these two methods of expanding the simple sentence patterns is that they lead to a huge variety of possible sentences. The facility of substituting different words in the basic patterns gave a fairly large number of possible sentences but this additional facility makes the number astronomical.

Immediate constituents One aspect of grammar about which we have said little is the notion of immediate constituents. Most linguists recognise that sentences can be divided up into smaller groups of words the members of which somehow belong together. In the sentence:

Poor John ran away

there seem to be two groups 'Poor John' and 'ran away'. Each of these groups are themselves divided into two parts. This can be marked thus:

(Poor John) (ran away)

or thus:

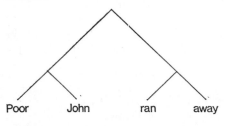

FIGURE 19   *Based on Lyons 1968*

The two systems of marking are equivalent. Here is another example:

(My friend) ((came home) late) (last night)

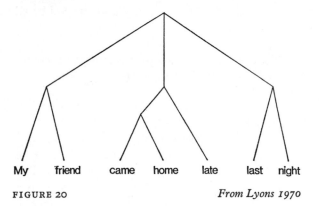

FIGURE 20   *From Lyons 1970*

This second example illustrates quite nicely some of the problems of immediate constituents analysis:

1. It is not altogether clear whether this sentence should be represented as three groups of words with equal status ('my friend', 'came home late', 'last night') or not. Some linguists maintain that every sentence contains only two immediate constituents at the first level and both of these are divided into two parts and these

again into two parts until one reaches individual words. On this scheme our sentence would be analysed in this way:

(My friend) (((came home) late) (last night))

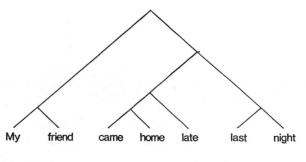

FIGURE 21

2. Another difficulty is that there may be alternative groupings of words which look satisfactory. Most people would agree that 'friend home' or 'late last' do not form coherent groups in quite the same way as 'my friend' or 'last night'. But the words 'late last night' seem to belong together in a group almost as well as 'came home late'. Here is an alternative analysis:

(My friend) (came home) (late (last night))

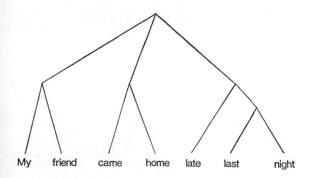

FIGURE 22

or again we may adopt the binary grouping:

(My friend) ((came home) (late (last night)))

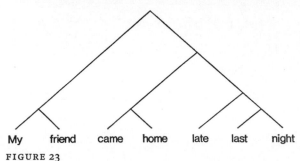

FIGURE 23

There are many examples to be found where the precise grouping of words is open to dispute but there are also other cases where there is no room for argument:

1. ((an examination) (of the students)) (which is thorough)

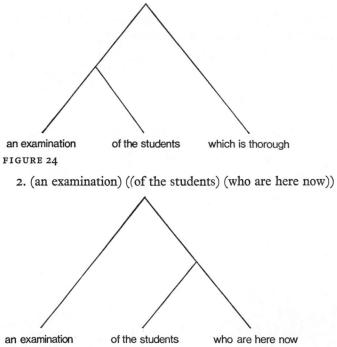

an examination   of the students   which is thorough

FIGURE 24

2. (an examination) ((of the students) (who are here now))

an examination   of the students   who are here now

FIGURE 25

These two examples are in fact 'modification' structures. In these cases there are clear signals of which groups belong together. In the first case the words 'which' and 'is' correlates with 'examination' but not with 'students' so that 'which is thorough' must be the 'modifier' for the group containing 'examination'. In the second case 'who' and 'are' correlate with 'students' but not with 'examination' so that 'who are here now' must first be linking to 'of the students' and then the whole group is linked to 'an examination'.

In general we can think of sentences and parts of sentences as built up in 'layers' or 'chunks' of structure with small ones grouped into larger ones and the larger ones grouped into still larger ones and these in turn forming whole sentences. In many cases the groupings are clearly signalled by formal features but in many others the precise grouping is not completely clear and there is room for argument.

The 'tree' diagram for showing immediate constituents shows most clearly the hierarchy of layers of structure in sentences. The words 'hierarchy' and 'chunks' have been introduced deliberately at this point as a reminder of the possible way in which the organisation and the production of language resemble the organisation of other types of behaviour (see Chapter 1). We shall meet these ideas again in Chapter 7.

In this section on Fries's approach to grammar I have tried to bring out his emphasis on analysing sentences purely by the pattern and forms of words and not by meaning; we have described the principle of grouping words into four major parts of speech and function words according to whether they can be substituted for each other in a sentence without making the sentence ungrammatical. Also illustrated is how a fairly limited range of simple sentence patterns can be recognised which may be expanded in various ways into more complex patterns. We have sketched the notion of immediate constituents.

These ideas are fairly widely accepted in modern linguistics. Chomsky's grammar, discussed briefly in the next section, is built on these ideas but he has made some fairly fundamental alterations.

Chomsky's grammar

It is, perhaps, a little unfair to give Chomsky all the credit for the innovations described here. Other linguists such as C. F. A. Hockett and Z. S. Harris have developed similar ideas but Chomsky's theories are best known. The three features of language described below are the principle seeds of Chomsky's grammar.

Our discussion of immediate constituents might have suggested that when a sentence had been successfully divided up into its different layers of structure then we could make a simple step from the structure to the meaning. We would be mistaken because it happens quite frequently that a 'chunk' or group of words which can be bracketed in only one way can have two quite distinct meanings.

An example is the expression: 'The love of God' which would be bracketed like this:

(The love) (of God)

'of God' modifies 'The love' but it can do it in two different ways:

1. The loving is being done by God as in: 'God loves Mankind'.
2. God is being loved by someone else as in: 'Mankind loves God'.

Another famous example given by Chomsky is '(flying) (planes)'. As it stands it is ambiguous and the word 'flying' could be the head of the structure as in the sentence 'Flying is dangerous'. In this case 'planes' modifies the word 'flying' to make clear what kind of flying.

Alternatively 'planes' could be the head of the structure as in the sentence 'planes are dangerous' and in this case 'flying' modifies 'planes' and makes clear what kinds of planes are described.

Another curiosity is the fact that two sentences with very similar structures can have rather fundamentally different meanings as the result of only one word being different. The famous example here is the two sentences:

'John is eager to please'

and

'John is easy to please'

In the first case it is clear that John is the person who is doing the pleasing while in the second case John is a person who is being pleased by someone else.

The third significant fact which we have already remarked on is that a given meaning can usually be expressed by several different structures. Fries gave these examples (ibid. p. 204):

1. The committee recommended his promotion.
2. His promotion was recommended by the committee.
3. The recommendation of the committee was that he be promoted.

4. The committee's recommendation was that he be promoted.
5. The action of the recommending committee was that he be promoted.

It was facts such as these which led Chomsky to postulate a 'deep structure' underlying the 'surface structure', which we have described so far.

The deep structure reflects what are thought to be the fundamental structural facts that every sentence has a logical 'subject' or performer of some action, it has a verb which describes the action and it has a logical 'object' or sufferer of the action. In the two sentences:

'The boy kicked the ball'

and

'The ball was kicked by the boy'

the logical subject or actor in both cases is the boy; the action is kicking and the logical object or sufferer of the action is the ball.

In Chomsky's theory both these sentences have the same[1] deep structure which is represented by a sequence of symbols called a 'kernel string'. In simplified form the kernel string would be represented as:

$$NP_1 - V - NP_2$$

where NP stands for 'noun phrase' like 'the boy' or 'the brown football with patches on it'; the first NP is the logical subject and the second NP is the logical object. V stands for verb.[2]

The kernel string is not a sentence itself but is the base from which different types of sentences can be derived. The simple declarative sentence like 'The boy kicks the ball' can be derived from the kernel string with very little change and is therefore sometimes called a 'kernel sentence'.

To form the passive sentence ('The ball was kicked by the boy'), NP_1 ('The boy') has to change places with NP_2 ('The ball') and some words and parts of words ('was', '-ed', 'by') have to be added or

---

[1] Actually this assumption has been modified more recently but the principles which this example illustrates still stand.

[2] The reader may be puzzled that terms from traditional grammar like 'noun' and 'verb' have been introduced again. In fact Chomsky's use of these terms is, like Fries's, based on the principle of substitution. He might just as well have numbered them like Fries did.

substituted. Again, in simplified form, the change would be written something like this:

$$NP_1 - V - NP_2 \rightarrow NP_2 - Aux - V - ed - by - NP_1$$

The symbol Aux (for auxiliary) means 'was' and similar auxiliary verbs.

This change, needed to derive a passive sentence from the kernel string, is called a *'transformation'* and the rule which states what changes to make is called a *'transformational rule'*. There are transformational rules to derive other sentences such as the negative form ('The boy did not kick the ball'), the negative-passive form ('The ball was not kicked by the boy'), question form ('Did the boy kick the ball?'), etc., etc. It will not have escaped the reader that the notion of deep structure is very similar to the idea of meaning or semantics itself. To quote the linguist John Lyons (1968, p. 269): '. . . most linguists who accept the validity of the distinction between deep grammatical structure and surface grammatical structure . . . assume that there is some particularly intimate connection between deep syntax and semantics.' We must reserve further discussion of this point until the chapter where we relate words to meanings.

More about what we mean by 'grammatical' Earlier in this chapter it was suggested that a native speaker's judgment of whether a sentence was acceptable or not ought to be the ultimate point of reference for constructing a grammar. This is a step beyond simply describing what people say; we are describing what people think is acceptable to say. The important point is that we have still retained the principle of *describing* how people use and react to language rather than prescribing how they ought to use it. It is this which makes linguistics interesting to psychologists and anyone else who wants to know about actual use of language.

Chomsky's notion of people's inner, considered knowledge of language, which he calls 'competence', is rather different. In his theories the rules of grammar take on a life of their own so that they are themselves often used for deciding whether a sentence is grammatical or not. Here is an illustration which is based on the following well-known nursery jingle:

'This is the cow with the cumpled horn that tossed the dog that worried the cat that killed the rat that ate the malt that lay in the house that Jack built.'

This sentence, which is normally accepted as grammatical, is built up as a chain of small sentences. Instead of new sentences being added always at the end as in this example they can sometimes be inserted in the middle of a larger sentence:

1. The malt lay in the house that Jack built.
2. The malt *that the rat ate* lay in the house that Jack built.

This is called a 'nested' construction for obvious reasons and would be readily accepted by most people. Chomsky's theory supposes that this nesting process can be used indefinitely like the chain in the original nursery rhyme. The third step in nesting would be:

3. The malt *that the rat* **that the cat killed** *ate* lay in the house that Jack built.

Because it follows the nesting rule this sentence would be regarded by Chomsky as perfectly grammatical as also the last example in this sequence:

4. The malt *that the rat* **that the cat** THAT THE DOG THAT THE COW WITH THE CRUMPLED HORN TOSSED WORRIED **killed** *ate* lay in the house that Jack built.

This last sentence is not likely to be accepted by most English speakers; sentence 3 is probably a borderline case. Chomsky has thus abandoned the principle of using the actual speakers of the language as his guide to the language. His theories are correspondingly less valuable to psychologists and anyone else wishing to know about actual usages.

Incidentally, there have been some interesting speculations, notably by Yngve (1960), about why 'sentences' of the second type are so difficult to follow but these considerations are not directly relevant to the question in hand.

If we look at how native speakers of English interpret grammatical structures we find that even when they consider the matter carefully people do not always agree; this sheds doubt on the idea that grammatical structures are absolute and that there is only one correct interpretation for every structure.

Broadbent (1970) has taken a sentence: 'Learning that John had won the race surprised him' and asked a number of people whether they thought 'him' could mean 'John'. Many thought not but a minority thought that it could. This is in direct conflict with Chomsky's assertion that in this sentence 'him' can never refer to 'John'.

In Chapter 5 are described the results of some tests given to children by Carol Chomsky to see how they interpret grammatical structures. While most are mastered by the age of ten some appear not to be fully agreed even amongst adults. We may say that such adults are simply wrong but equally we may say that our grammar should describe these facts rather than assert features of language for which there is no evidence.

In this book we have borrowed from Chomsky the distinction between a person's considered knowledge of language and his use of it in practice. But we have seen that, for our purposes, Chomsky's idea of competence is less useful to us than the more straightforward idea of acceptability.

The complexity of grammar

What a study of grammar and attempts at writing grammar teach us is how rich and complex is the ordinary person's knowledge of the syntactic relations between words. We can now see that when a language is learned not only the forms of the words and their meanings are remembered but for each word also a range of syntactic contexts in which it may be used. Through long and wide experience we learn the 'natural history' of the types of verbal context in which every word typically appears; for any given context we come to know which words will fit acceptably, which are marginally acceptable and which are definitely not acceptable. Natural history is a good analogy because although someone may know the evolutionary or geomorphological theory of how living things or hills and valleys acquired their particular forms, this knowledge is not directly relevant to how these complex patterns are learned. If we want to know the lay of the land it is best to look and see or at least use a map produced by someone who has done that; the detailed shapes of a range of hills are too complicated and variable to be specified more than approximately by a set of rules.

It is sometimes thought that a child's knowledge of syntax is complete by five but it will be seen in Chapter 5 that this is far from true. Children need to hear and use very large amounts of language for quite a number of years before they attain a reasonably complete mastery. Houses can burn up or down but furniture never burns down (Wooden 1962). We may succeed in a task *with* the help of a friend but *by* a lucky chance. Something may be bought *on* account but something else is *under* discussion. People *make* haste or do things *in* haste but there is no analogic form for doing things slowly. So much of language is usage without any logical reason that it is not surprising that it requires a time to learn.

Fortunately, the broad patterns remain intact in spite of all the special cases and idioms. In some ways language is like a tree in which the main structure of trunk and major branches is clear to see but the smaller branches, the branches off these and twigs require long experience to be fully learned. Children's apparent mastery of syntax by five is deceptive. It is as if they had learned the main branches and a modest selection of side branches and twigs. This is enough for them to produce a reasonably useful range of sentences acceptable to the adult ear. It is not until special tests are devised, such as those used by Carol Chomsky, that the comparative poverty of their knowledge compared with adults is revealed. When one considers that vocabulary grows steadily at the rate of between 1000 and 2000 words a year throughout childhood and that most words have several syntactic uses it is obvious that the details of syntax cannot approach completion until adulthood.

4 Words and meanings

The study of semantics or how words relate to meaning is the subject of this chapter. Because psychological processes are very relevant to this study we shall not attempt to stick to pure linguistic ideas but shall broaden the discussion to look generally at language use.

We can distinguish four elements which contribute to how meanings are conveyed by language. We shall list them first and explain them afterwards:

1. What the Norwegian psycholinguist Ragnar Rommetveit (1968) calls the 'common cognitive domain' of the speaker and the listener (or the writer and the reader).
2. Lexical meanings – the meanings which are attached to single words and morphemes.
3. Structural meanings – the meanings which are conveyed by the order and inflexion of the words, including 'modification' structures.
4. Prosody (in the case of speech).

The 'common cognitive domain' between speaker and listener

This rather unwieldy expression refers to an idea which is fundamentally important to understanding how meanings are transmitted between people and how language helps in this process. I have said that language only 'helps' because language, although it is exceedingly useful, cannot usually do the whole job by itself and not infrequently it may be dispensed with completely.

An example perhaps is the situation where both teacher and her pupils have completed a lesson and all of them know that it is time to pack up and go to another room. In this situation the barest inclination of the teacher's head might be equivalent to her saying: 'Pack up quietly now and lead on from the row by the door; and woe betide any terrible child who pushes his neighbour or jumps the queue or starts running in the corridor', etc. Our teacher need not be as fierce as this but the point is made.

The situation outlined here illustrates the 'common cognitive domain' of teacher and pupils at that time and the idea is clearly very similar to the idea of mental models or schemata discussed in Chapter 1. We shall treat the two ideas as identical.

Even where language is a necessary part of the message it frequently depends on unspoken understandings. The other day my wife greeted me in the evening with the words 'He came and mended it today'. We had been expecting someone to come and mend the gas stove for some days so the meaning of both 'he' and 'it' were clear from this common knowledge.

The shared schema may be derived from the physical situation as in these examples but it is often built up by language itself. This is the rule with any lengthy piece of speech or writing. Although novelists sometimes start a story deliberately without doing this they will fill out the picture later of who an initially unspecified 'he' or 'she' may be.

Most words only develop their full meaning in the context of a particular situation. Some words like 'he', 'it', 'there', 'here', etc., depend a great deal on context to realise particular meanings in particular situations. They are called *deictic* words.

Where speaker and listener do not share the same schema then misunderstandings, tragic or humorous are likely to occur. The bearded man who asks the barber to 'shave it all off' could conceivably find himself bald as well.

Quite often the shared schema is so powerful that it overrides the clues to meaning given by other features of the language. The sentence 'There are no chairs here' would normally be regarded as a statement of a fact. However, as Rommetveit points out, if it is said by someone in authority who is talking to a caretaker about chairs in a room then it may very well be interpreted as a command: 'Please get some chairs for this room'.

Not only does it enable communication to occur with minimal language but this shared schema, the background to all language, can help in conveying subtleties and nuances of meaning. A wink may be enough to show that the intended meaning is the opposite of what the language itself seems to convey. A raised eyebrow or certain variations in intonation, pause or stress may alert the listener to some innuendo or other implication below the surface of the words.

It is fortunate for many deaf people that these processes work like this. It means that they can usually convey simple meanings to other people even if their language is very imperfect or they are using relatively crude gestures or mimes. But the limitations of simple gesture and mime, if not the more sophisticated sign language of many deaf adults, is illustrated in this tragi-comic report from *The Times* of 21st August, 1971:

> *Roast Poodle, Sauce and Bamboo Shoots*
> Zurich, Aug. 20 – A Swiss couple who went on holiday to Hong Kong have returned with the sad story of how their pet poodle Rosa was accidentally cooked as their main dish in a Chinese restaurant.
>
> They told the newspaper *Blick* that they asked a waiter over to their table and pointed to the poodle while they made eating motions to show they wanted it to be fed.
>
> Eventually the waiter appeared to understand and took Rosa off into the kitchen. About an hour later he came back with their main dish and when they picked up the silver lid they found their poodle roasted inside, garnished with pepper sauce and bamboo shoots. – '*Reuter*'.

It is clear that communication at this level never approaches the richness, subtlety and precision which language makes possible. This point should be emphasised because people are sometimes misled into thinking that it is not really necessary for deaf children to master even plain English let alone the finer points of style. But without language deaf children are denied the huge reservoir of common knowledge and ideas which is a hearing child's birthright and they are denied the means of articulating their thoughts, hopes and fears with their friends and families.

Lexical meaning

There are a number of ways in which individual words may be said to carry meaning. In all cases we are adhering to our definition of meaning as the communicative work or function which a word does:

1. Words can act as 'labels' for concepts. We shall look at this in a moment.
2. Words or small groups of words may serve merely as greetings: 'Hello', 'How do you do?'. These act like handshakes and salutes

in acknowledging the other person's existence and perhaps conveying some attitude of respect or affection, etc.

3. Certain words: 'Hi!', 'You there!', 'George!' serve to attract another person's attention; they are calls.
4. Some 'words' are simply signals of an emotional state and may be produced involuntarily: 'Ouch!', 'Gosh!', 'Well, I never!'.
5. As we noted in the last chapter, short expressions may be used to signal that one is still listening to the speaker: 'M hm', 'Uh huh'.
6. Certain words, particularly the function words discussed in the last chapter serve to signal certain grammatical structures which themselves signal particular meanings. These structural functions will be discussed in the next section on structural meanings.

It is the rule rather than the exception for a given word or a group of words to have more than one of these functions and for the function to vary from occasion to occasion; if we say 'It's a lovely day' we may intend this primarily as a greeting but we would not say it, except as a joke, if there was sleet and freezing fog. Words like 'in', 'on', 'under', etc., can be said to label certain situations but they also have important structural functions.

Words as labels for concepts – referential meaning

It is sometimes said that a word 'refers' to something. Here we mean that the word acts as a label for a concept and I have tried to stress that reference of this kind is only a part of meaning.

The basic idea is simple enough that the word 'orange' refers to the complete set of objects which are designated as spherical, of an 'orange' colour, having a skin and edible juicy flesh, etc. There are two refinements in the notion of reference which are important:

1. First is the fact that most concepts, or, more strictly, the words which label them, have an extensive range of associations or '*connotations*' which are not really part of their designative or distinctive features but are regularly associated with the concept or with the word which stands for the concept. These connotations usually have a strong emotional colouration.

   Thus the word 'snake' not only signifies a legless reptile with dry scaly skin but also suggests to most people something sinister and rather horrible. The word 'kitten' not only means a young cat, it also suggests something cuddly, playful and lovable, if a bit naughty at times.

Clearly the connotations which any person attaches to a concept depend on their individual experience. While the connotations of snake and kitten are fairly uniform for most people it is possible for an individual to have connotations for a word like 'kitten' which differ from the usual ones perhaps through some tragic experience, caused by a kitten, which that person suffered.

To return to our 'balloons' as a way of representing these ideas, the concept may be pictured as an envelope with an outer zone to represent the connotations:

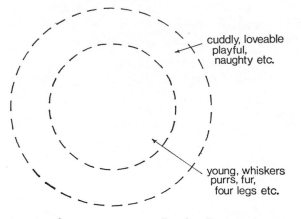

cuddly, loveable
playful,
naughty etc.

young, whiskers
purrs, fur,
four legs etc.

FIGURE 26   *Based on Rommetveit 1968*

2. The second point is that it is only right to think of a word as a label for the whole area of the concept and its connotative border when we are looking at it as a word by itself, out of context as we would find it in a dictionary. Whenever a word is used in practice it almost invariably has a more restricted meaning than the whole range of possible meanings. An example given by Rommetveit is the word 'craft'. Ignoring for the moment the meaning in terms of woodwork, etc., this word can refer to boats (usually small ones), aeroplanes and airships, in fact any man-made device for travelling on water or in the air. In the sentence 'He sails his craft skilfully' the restricted meaning is similar to 'boat'. In the sentence 'The pilot accelerates and lifts his craft off the runway' it is clearly an aeroplane. Sub-regions of a concept can be shown as illustrated in Fig. 27 opposite.

Overlap is shown because some crafts like sea-planes can be thought of as both boats and aeroplanes.

In these examples the different uses of the word 'craft' do not suggest any particular connotations – they are free from emotional colouration or associations. But in a poem about a thirsty sailor the

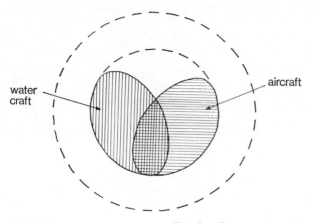

FIGURE 27   *Based on Rommetveit 1968*

word 'water' would not only designate water but would also suggest connotative associations of its life-giving, thirst-quenching and refreshing qualities. This is in contrast to the use of the word in a chemistry textbook where it would have a certain designative meaning but its special chemical properties, not strictly part of the definition, would be uppermost in the reader's mind. Rommetveit pictures this example like this:

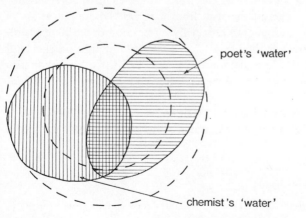

FIGURE 28   *Based on Rommetveit 1968*

Sometimes words are used purely for their connotative associations. Students of advertising will find plenty of examples there, but again Rommetveit's example is:

'And the leader of the surviving soldiers had really shown that he was a *man*'.

He pictures the meaning of 'man' in this example as shown here.

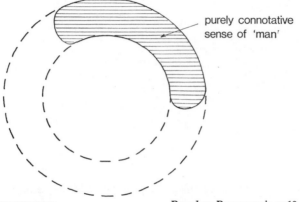

purely connotative
sense of 'man'

FIGURE 29   *Based on Rommetveit 1968*

To summarise this section, words which are functioning as labels for concepts rarely have one single meaning. More usually they can act as labels for a cluster of overlapping and closely related concepts all falling roughly within one envelope. The Oxford English Dictionary lists forty-nine district meanings of the word 'water' with numerous sub-divisions. They range all the way from a verb: 'To supply water as aliment to (a plant, crop, etc.) especially by pouring or sprinkling with a watering can, hose or the like . . .' to a noun: 'The transparency and lustre characteristics of a diamond or pearl. The three highest grades of quality in diamonds were formerly known as *first*, *second* and *third water*. . . .'

Most dictionary meanings are designative but, in addition, words may be used with a variety of connotations or metaphorical uses in particular situations.

Structural meanings

We have seen that linguists and psychologists have, until recently, tended to study language independently and in rather different ways.

Generally speaking the linguist has been concerned simply to find economical ways of describing language structure without asking whether the laws and rules which he discovers tell us how people learn and use language in practice. The problem is that we have two rather different theories of language structure and they seem to say rather different things about how the structure signals meanings. As before we shall examine Fries's views first.

He, of course, was only studying 'surface structure' and was concerned to find objective observable features of the structure which signal particular meanings. Three main types of structural meaning are usually recognised and Fries describes certain definite cues which show which type of utterance one is dealing with:

1. *Statements.* Characteristically these have a Class 1 word followed by a Class 2 word and these words are 'tied' together by the fact that their forms 'agree':

       1 — 2
   'The leader is here'
   'The leaders are here'

   The singular Class 1 word has a singular Class 2 word and the plural Class 1 word has a plural Class 2 word.
   A statement is an utterance which merely conveys information without requiring any particular response by the listener.

2. *Questions.* When the Class 2 word is the word 'be' and its various forms, then a question is signalled by the fact that the 'tied' Class 1 word and Class 2 word have reversed their order:

       2 — 1
   'Is the leader here?'
   'Are the leaders here?'

   The meaning or function of a question is to seek information and the appropriate response is a verbal answer.

3. *Requests or Commands.* These are usually signalled by the fact that the Class 2 word which comes first is in an unmodified form and does not usually 'agree' with the Class 1 word:

       2   1
   'Have the man paid'

The unmodified form of the Class 2 word is sometimes the same as the plural form and this can lead to ambiguous sentences:

2 — 1

'Have the men paid'

Here the Class 2 word may or may not be 'tied' to the Class 1 word and so the sentence may be either a question or a command. Which it is may be decided by the context (cognitive domain) or by the prosody. We shall return to this point.

The meaning of a request or command is that the listener should do something and the appropriate response is this action.

Fries discusses a number of exceptions to these basic patterns and each case is marked by a clear structural device. The 2 — 1 pattern for questions used to be general in Elizabethan times but these days it is more or less confined to forms of 'be'. We usually form questions with forms of the word 'do'.

G — 1 2 1

'Do you like coffee?'

This word 'do' is not the same as the form of the word 'do' in 'The boys do their paper rounds', either in its meaning or in its structural position. In fact this is one of the few words like 'there' (function word H), which cannot be said to have any lexical meaning: it functions purely as part of the structural pattern; in this case it signals a question. It is classed in a function group G by itself.

There are other structural patterns which signal other meanings and these are bound up with the traditional notions of 'subject', 'direct object', 'indirect object', etc. Although Fries uses these terms he puts them all in quote marks and makes very clear that he is using the terms to mean parts of sentences which are recognised only by their positions in the sentence pattern and not by their meanings. As we saw in Chapter 2 traditional terms are all defined by their meaning and this leads to contradictions.

This limited range of major sentence patterns with their associated features which signal particular types of meaning are only the most prominent patterns of English. There is a wealth of detail waiting to be documented of just how meanings are shaped by variations in word order, the varying effects of optional additions to sentences at various loci and the complexities of modification.

Chomsky's views on semantics are not simple but, as we saw in the last chapter, structural meaning and 'deep structure' are very similar ideas in his theories – so similar that it is difficult to distinguish them. Without arguing the point in detail the view which I have adopted is that in deriving deep structure from meaning Chomsky has fallen into the trap which Fries so carefully avoided. In case this seems a rather large claim it is as well to look again at the examples which have been used to illustrate why the idea of deep structure was developed in the first place.

We have seen that the expression 'The love of God' can be interpreted in two different ways. The question at issue is whether every meaning has to have a corresponding structure or whether this might be a case where a single structure has two possible meanings which are simply left unspecified by the structure. Taking the latter view the word 'of' simply indicates some kind of modification link between 'love' and 'God' without saying exactly what. Which of the two possibilities applies simply cannot be deduced from the structure. Fortunately, as we saw at the beginning of this chapter, whenever language itself is not fully efficient in specifying all the details of meaning we have a kind of semantic 'putty' which we can use to fill in the cracks and smooth over the rough spots. This is of course the common schema of understanding or cognitive domain of speaker and listener. The context of discussion usually makes clear which of several possible meanings is intended and, as we saw earlier, it may actually override a meaning signalled by the structure ('There are no chairs here'). The fact that language may be ambiguous now and then and may require interpretation does not invalidate what was said earlier about not relying too heavily on unspoken understandings.

The second type of construction ('John is eager to please', 'John is easy to please'), which has been adduced as evidence for deep structure, is different. This is not an example where the meaning is unspecified by the language. It is quite unambiguously clear that 'John' is the actor or agent who is to do the pleasing in the first case while in the second case he is the one who is pleased by someone else. The question we must ask is whether we have to postulate two different deep structures simply because there are two different meanings. By deducing structure from meaning we run into all the difficulties and pitfalls which Fries has so carefully described and avoided. In this and similar examples it seems at least as reasonable to say that the structure signals part of the meaning but that the final interpretation depends on particular words used. In short, these would be cases where structural meanings and lexical meanings interact. The fundamental ambiguity of the structure is revealed in the sentence:

'John is nice to please'

In this case John may be either the agent or the sufferer, and we depend on context to make clear which. In the first two examples the ambiguity is resolved entirely by the lexical meanings of 'eager' and 'easy'. Words like 'eager', 'clever', 'foolish', 'happy' are always used to denote features exhibited by people or animals. Words like 'easy', 'difficult', 'impossible' are always used to describe actions or events and the accepted convention is that if such words are used in this pattern (1 is 3 to 2) then the Class 1 word is not the performer of the action.

Some further entertaining examples of these types of construction and the way children interpret them will be given at the end of Chapter 5.

It may be thought that this is a hair-splitting argument and that it does not matter whether we use the term 'deep structure' or 'structural meaning' because we are talking about the same thing. This would be a fair comment if we were only looking for a way of describing language patterns and this is indeed the linguist's main concern. The difficulty is that some linguists and others have claimed that Chomsky's grammar is not merely an elegant way of describing language patterns but that it also describes the psychological processes which produce those patterns. There have been a lot of experiments to try to decide whether or not we produce sentences by rearranging (transforming) a kernel string – the dust has not settled yet; some of the more recent experiments have shown up weaknesses in earlier ones and cast doubt on the notion of transformation as a psychological process.

One of the most important psychological problems in language is how we learn it in the first place. This is the subject of Chapter 6 where we shall say a bit more about ideas based on Chomsky's theories and the main alternative.

'*Modification*' structures

Finally, in this section we should say something about 'modification'. This term is put in inverted commas to emphasise that it is a structure which is recognised by the arrangement of words and not by its meaning. Nonetheless most 'modification' structures have an important effect on meaning, namely modification (without inverted commas).

'Modification' structures signal *some kind* of link between the lexical meanings of the words in the structure. Usually the particular kind of link is left unspecified and the listener infers it from the context or from his past experience of what the phrase usually means: 'A flying bird' is a bird which is flying; 'a dancing girl' might be a girl who is dancing but most people would understand it as a girl who does dancing for a living and need not be dancing at the moment referred to; 'a working hypothesis' is not a hypothesis which works but one which someone uses when they work; 'a parking ticket' is not a ticket which parks or even one which someone uses when they park but is usually a ticket given when you park in the wrong place. The reader should have no difficulty in finding other examples of 'modification' structures where very similar structures have widely varying meanings.

Notice that a great many 'modification' structures have acquired their meanings through convention in exactly the same way, presumably, as words acquire their lexical meanings. In a sense these conventional meanings of phrases are a form of lexical meaning.

For example, everyone knows the meaning of a 'hard worker' and how it differs from a 'hard rock'. In these examples the relationship between the head and the modifier is different (the worker works hard but the rock does not do anything let alone in a particular kind of way); also the lexical meanings of 'hard' in the two cases are related but different. We can only assume that the meaning of 'hard worker' has developed over the years by common usage. It is a cliché, idiom or figure of speech. Although clichés are generally frowned upon they do in fact constitute a very large part of our language and fulfil a function very similar to that of individual words. Some common idioms are listed here:

'He got up at the —— of dawn'
'It's a case of swings and ——'
'A tall order'
'A tall story'
'It rained cats and ——'
'The boat sank like a ——'
'As quick as greased ——'
'To throw a party'
'A straight answer'
'To give short shrift to'
'To put up a case'

There is no sharp distinction between clichés and common expressions whose meanings are established by convention. We 'set the pace' or 'make the pace' but we could just as logically 'put the pace'. In referring to some other part of a text we speak of 'below' or 'above' but, in accounting, money is 'brought forward'; in fact this expression could as logically be 'brought backward'.

The importance of word order for meanings is that without some consistency these many patterns and their meanings will be destroyed. Where variations in word order and optional additions and omissions are allowed as grammatically acceptable it becomes even more necessary to follow the rules. Without this the interrelationship of words is upset, particularly in modification structures. As an illustration here is Fries's 'modification' example from the last chapter but with words in random order: 'still catalogue twenty-five very States officers of Army in who listed the the famous the United are all active almost service in.' This might conceivably be read as: 'The very active officers in service of the famous Army who are almost twenty-five listed all United States still in the catalogue.' or in dozens of other ways. The immediate constituent structure and thus the modification effects of words on each other depend crucially on word order.

Prosody

Any student of speech and drama will know how much can be contributed to speech by variations in pitch (intonation), by pause and by stress. A given sentence may be endowed with many nuances of meaning by changing the emphasis on different words or by raising and lowering the voice in different places. Much of this is concerned with emotional colouration: surprise, joy, anger, disappointment, etc., which enriches the speech but is not strictly necessary from a functional point of view. The popularity of writing as a language medium in which nearly all prosody is eliminated testifies to this view.

But, certain intonation patterns, for example, can have a powerful effect on the functional interpretation of a sentence. The best known example is the intonation pattern which signals a question. The effect of this is sometimes to convert something into a question which is structurally a statement:

'You want to go $\sqrt{\ }$ out?'

Although a sentence with this intonation must be a question it is by no means true that all questions must have this intonation pattern. If the reader will speak the following sentence aloud he will find that it is quite possible to say it in a neutral kind of way which allows it to be either a question or command:

'Have the men paid?'

In general the link between intonation and what we may call the 'straight' meaning of a sentence (as opposed to emotional or connotative meaning) is rather loose and written language is not usually considered to be markedly impoverished compared with speech. There are just a few cases where alternative structures are marked exclusively by intonation:

'The discussion afterward proved the success of the talk' (Fries, p. 216)

In this example there are two quite distinct intonation and pause patterns according to whether 'afterward' modifies 'discussion' or 'proved'. Even in cases such as this the context usually resolves any uncertainty which may arise from the written form.

The importance of this for our present purpose is that we may feel reasonably confident that a deaf child will not be greatly handicapped if he cannot register prosodic patterns. A hearing child may get some assistance in identifying e.g. questions by having clues both from intonation and from structure but if we consider how often questions are asked without the appropriate intonation and how many other context clues are available we can be fairly sure that it plays only a minor part.

The complexity of semantics

What this chapter should have shown is how very intricate is the relation between words and the meanings they are used to convey. Referential meanings of those words which are used as labels for concepts have a location, range and degree of vagueness in 'semantic space'. Different sub-regions of a word's semantic space are activated in different situations. Many connotations of words are common to all members of a speech community but there are individual variations produced by individual differences in experience. The meanings of different syntactic constructions are usually unambiguous but there are borderline cases as with Broadbent's 'Learning that John had won the race surprised him.' Structural and lexical meanings can interact.

What all this means is that, as with syntax, it is almost impossible to make a record of all this material. A large dictionary is a reasonable account of lexical meanings but connotations and the change of meanings in different contexts is rarely covered. The study of structural meanings is in its infancy.

A child's knowledge of meanings may develop far enough in his first few years for everyday communication but the process of enriching and expanding the 'natural history' of semantics continues throughout life.

5 The sequence of language development

At least in the early stages it is relatively easy to describe how speech and language develops in normal hearing children. What is much less clear is how this remarkable feat is achieved, as there seems to be a tremendous amount to be learned and it seems to be absorbed quite effortlessly and in quite a short time. Of course learning of any kind is still poorly understood, but there are at least some laws and patterns which seem to hold for other kinds of learning; one of our tasks in the next chapter will be to see how relevant these may be to language learning. Our aim in this chapter will be to paint a picture of how language grows before we think of possible explanations.

A point to be made at the beginning concerns terminology. One is apt to talk about 'stages' of development. In this book there is no suggestion that language development is usually anything but a process of continuous growth and the word 'stage' is not meant to suggest sudden breaks or changes in the process; it is simply a convenient way of marking off periods. Where some aspects of development are thought to change quite suddenly this will be made clear.

The chart overleaf shows the main landmarks in the way young children learn to produce and respond to vocal sounds. Right from birth a baby cries and this is usually taken to mean that the child is uncomfortable in some way – hungry, wanting to be picked up, etc. Crying seems to be a distinct vocal pattern which persists even into adulthood.

In these early days it is always more difficult to be sure of the effect of speech and other sounds on a child than it is to record what sounds he himself makes. If a child makes no response to a sound (unless it is very loud) we cannot therefore say that he is not perceiving it. None the less it is accepted that babies come quite soon to appreciate human voices, usually as a form of reassurance that someone is close by.

Like most new developments at this time cooing starts quite suddenly. It is generally agreed that landmarks like this appear as a result of the

Behaviour	0	6	12	18	24	30
First noted vocalisations	xxxxxxxxx					
First responds to human voice	xxxxxx					
First cooing	xxxxx					
Vocalises pleasure	xxxxxxxx					
Vocal play	xxxx					
Vocalises eagerness and displeasure		xxx				
Imitates sounds		xxxxxxxxx				
Vocalises recognition		xx				
Listens to familiar words		xxxx				
First word		xxxxxxxxxx				
Expressive sounds and conversational jargon		xxxxxxxxxxxxxxxxxxxxx				
Follows simple commands			xxxxxxxx			
Imitates syllables and words			xxxxxxxx			
Second word			xxxxx			
Responds to 'no' and 'don't'			xxxxxxxxxxxxx			
First says more than 2 words			xxxxx			
Names object or picture				xxxxxxxxxxxxx		
Comprehends simple questions				xx		
Combines words in speech					xxxxxxx	
First uses pronouns					xxxxx	
First phrases and sentences						xxxx
Understands prepositions						xxx

From D. McArthy 1946

FIGURE 30

maturing and growth of the child's nervous system rather than as a result of learning.

The sounds which are produced are almost all vowel sounds at the beginning when the baby 'coos' with no respect at all for the phoneme categories of adult speech. Gradually, from six months, consonants appear as cooing changes to babbling and the proportion increases steadily even until the child is speaking in relatively mature ways at five or six. Again, at this stage, many of the sounds have no counterpart in the parents' language and perhaps not in any language at all. They seem to be 'discoveries' or 'inventions' by the child himself without the benefit of imitation. Apparently even deaf children coo and babble in their first few months.

The function of cooing and babbling is not altogether clear. Babies 'talk' to themselves quite happily when they are alone and so the function cannot be social. We can say at least that it is a form of generalised activity like the kicking of the baby's legs or the waving of his arms which may serve to keep the 'machinery' ticking over and in working order until it is mature enough to serve its main function. It may serve to teach the child what his speech organs are capable of and this may help in later learning of adult phonemes.

At the same time as these non-social vocalisations are developing babies also show a steadily increasing use of their voices socially. Quite early they develop gurgles and a proper laugh which they may produce when they are being played with. By about eight months they may shout (rather than cry) if they want attention.

Perhaps the most significant development from our point of view is when a baby starts to imitate sounds after about nine months. Up to the age of two or three and to some extent beyond, young children tend to echo new speech patterns which they hear. They may repeat sounds over and over almost as if they were echoing their own speech – 'baba-baba', etc. This imitation is an important landmark because it shows that the oral (speech) system is beginning on that long and fruitful partner-ship with the aural (hearing) system which makes speech development possible. A profoundly deaf child will not imitate speech.

The development of meaning

It is not long before the baby begins to respond appropriately to a few words like 'no' and 'don't' spoken by adults. It is often said that com-prehension develops earlier than speech production although a lot depends on how one assesses comprehension. As we discussed in the last chapter a great deal of communication depends on a common understanding of the situation; the very barest signals, linguistic or of some other kind, may convey a message. A mother may say 'Come away from the fire or you will burn yourself' and her crawling baby may appropriately stop playing with the fire-guard. It is most unlikely that he has understood this sentence in the full adult sense, but he perhaps knows from past experience that the fire is forbidden territory and so he is alert for anything that may be construed as a warning. If we are to test a child's comprehension we should really eliminate all clues from context so that the child depends entirely on the devices of language. In her developmental language test, Dr Reynell (1969) has attempted to do this. It is interesting to notice from her norms that on average, girls first comprehend a simple six-syllable sentence (with minimum clues from context) at two years-two months and that expressively, girls first use sentences of four or more syllables at the same age. Boys are a little slower. While this is only a rough guide it does suggest that if one's definition of comprehension is fairly strict the receptive and expressive sides of language develop much more closely than is usually thought. I should emphasise again that we can easily get a falsely inflated idea of how much a child understands and deaf children in particular may be credited with a better receptive grasp of language than is in fact the case.

The 'first word' is not any sound which has the same form as an adult word. What is usually looked for is any sound which has at least approximately the same form as an adult word and which is also used in an appropriate context. It would be unrealistic to expect the child to grasp the full adult range of lexical and structural uses which a given word has or, in the case of reference, for the child to know the exact range and vagueness of the concepts involved. We expect merely some understanding of the word as a functional unit and not just a sound: we would forgive the toddler for saying 'pussy' to denote a dog if his use of the word was clearly restricted to animals with some resemblance to cats. In connection with children's first words it has often been remarked that they have a preference for words containing a repeated syllable: e.g. mama, dada, baba. In Dr Ruth Weir's (1962) study quoted later the child's favourite word used far more commonly than any other was Bobo, the name of his toy. There is an obvious connection between this observation and the one that children generally like to repeat sounds over and over. The stage when a child begins to understand the uses of words both receptively and expressively is thus a second major landmark. Although children's comprehension of language and the meanings they attach to their own speech are very important aspects of their language development it is not possible to say much about them because these areas simply have not been explored very much. We shall none the less indulge some speculation in the next chapter!

Much of what follows in the next few months is a consolidation of the learning of new sounds by imitation and the learning of the meanings of sound-patterns. Babbling persists with adult-type forms included in it – it is sometimes called 'jargon'. However those sounds which do not belong in the language seem to disappear gradually and the remaining sounds are steadily shaped to conform to adult phoneme patterns. This is quite a slow process and infantile speech forms often persist in five-year-olds and even in adults.

New words in the sense described above are added rather slowly between twelve and eighteen months, the child having perhaps six words at that time. Thereafter the pace quickens and from the age of two to eight and beyond about 1000 words a year are added to the child's vocabulary. It is difficult to measure vocabulary sizes accurately, but this feature of vocabulary growth is not disputed. There are, incidentally, quite large variations amongst normal children in the age at which this 'take-off' occurs. Another well-recognised pattern is that 'nouns' tend to predominate amongst a child's first words and to grow fastest. 'Verbs' seem to appear next followed by 'adjectives' and then by other parts of speech. Most studies which have revealed this pattern have used the terms of traditional grammar as applied to adult language. There are good reasons for thinking that a young child's syntax is rather different from that of an adult and that from a grammatical point of view we should not use adult parts of speech in describing children's language. None the less children take their words from adult speech even if they use them differently. In spite of the weaknesses of traditional categories this is still a worthwhile observation which we should try to fit into any scheme of explanation.

Word combinations

A third major landmark is shortly before the age of two when a child begins to use combinations of words, usually two together at the beginning. The essential point is that we only say that two or more words are combined if we know that the child uses these words separately or in other combinations on other occasions. From an earlier age children may have expressions like 'cup-of-tea', but it is not until they can use 'cup', 'of' and 'tea' in other ways that we would say that 'cup-of-tea' was anything but one word from the child's standpoint.

This first stage of word combination has aroused much interest in recent years because it seems to be the beginnings of syntax which itself has proved a puzzling problem psychologically. It has also been a focus of interest because there is a manageable amount of material which is not too complicated. At later stages changes are so rapid and the variety of utterances becomes so large that analysis becomes very difficult.

Some of the best-known studies of first word combinations have come from a team at Harvard University headed by Roger Brown. Martin Braine in Washington has got similar results.

Braine's (1963a) samples from three children are taken at the very earliest stage where the great majority of combinations contain only two words; we shall discuss these first. The accompanying charts show all the utterances obtained.

see boy	hi plane
see sock	hi mommy
see hot	big boss
+ *11 more combinations with* see	big boat
	big bus
pretty boat	more taxi
pretty fan	more melon
my mommy	allgone shoe
my daddy	allgone vitamins
my milk	allgone egg
do it	allgone lettuce
push it	allgone watch
close it	
buzz it	mommy sleep
move it	milk cup
	ohmy see
nightnight office	+ *17 more unclassified*
nightnight boat	*combinations*
byebye plane	
byebye man	
byebye hot	
+ *28 more combinations with* byebye	

FIGURE 31a   *Gregory's word combinations, first four months.*

From M. D. S. Braine 1963

Pivotal Constructions

all broke	see baby	boot off
all buttoned	see pretty	lights off
all clean	see train	pants off
all done		shirt off
all dressed	more car[4]	shoe off
all dry	more cereal	water off
all fix	more cookie	
all gone	more fish	airplane by[6]
all messy	more high[5]	siren by
all shut	more hot	
all through	more juice	mail come
all wet	more read	mama come
	more sing	
I see	more toast	clock on there
I shut	more walk	up on there
I sit		hot in there
	hi Calico	milk in there
no bed	hi mama	light up there
no down[1]	hi papa	fall down there
no fix		kitty down there
no home	other bib	more down there
no mama[2]	other bread	sit down there
no more	other milk	cover down there
no pee	other pants	other cover down there
no plug	other part	
no water	other piece	
no wet[3]	other pocket	
	other shirt	
	other shoe	
	other shoe	
	other side	

Other Utterances

airplane all gone	byebye back	what's that	look at this
Calico all gone	byebye Calico	what's this	outside more
Calico all done[7]	byebye car	mail man	pants change
salt all shut	byebye papa	mail car	dry pants
all done milk	Calico byebye	our car	off bib
all done now	papa byebye	our door	down there
all gone juice		papa away	up on there some
all gone outside[8]			more
all gone pacifier			

[1]'Don't put me down.' [2]'I don't want to go to mama.' [3]'I'm not wet.'
[4]'Drive around some more.' [5]'There's more up there.' [6]'A plane is
flying past.' [7]Said after the death of Calico the cat. [8]Said when the
door is shut: 'The outside is all gone.'

FIGURE 31b *Andrew's word combinations, first five months.*

From M. D. S. Braine 1963

Pivotal Constructions

want baby	get ball	beeppeep bang[5]
want car	get Betty	beeppeep car
want do	get doll	
want get		that box
want glasses	see ball	that Dennis
want head	see doll	that doll
want high[1]	see record	that Tommy
want horsie	see Stevie	that truck
want jeep		
want more	whoa cards[3]	here bed
want page	whoa jeep	here checker
want pon[2]		here doll
want purse	more all	here truck
want ride	more book	
want up		bunny do
want byebye car	there ball	daddy do
	there book	momma do
it ball	there doggie	(want do)
it bang	there doll	
it checker	there high[4]	
it daddy	there momma	
it Dennis	there record	
it doggie	there trunk	
it doll	there byebye car	
it fall	there daddy truck	
it horsie	there momma truck	
it Lucy		
it record		
it shock		
it truck		

Other Utterances

bunny do sleep	baby doll	find bear	eat breakfast
Lucy do fun	Betty pon	pon baby	two checker
want do pon[6]	byebye car	pon Betty	Betty byebye car
want drive car	Candy say	sleepy bed	Lucy shutup Lucy shutup Lucy

[1]'Put it up there.' [2]'Put on' or 'up on' or both. [3]'The cards are falling.' [4]'It's up there.' [5]'The car that goes "beeppeep" is falling.' [6]'I want (you) to put (the jeep) on top.'

FIGURE 31C *Steven's word combinations, tape-recorded sample at end of fourth month*

From M. D. S. Braine 1963

The most obvious thing to notice is that certain words are used repeatedly in combination with different other words and Braine has arranged them in groups to make this clear. Braine gave the name 'pivot words' to these overworked words which are relatively few in number, but are used very frequently. They seem always to occupy a fixed position, first or last, those coming first being most numerous. All the rest of the words, including those used singly Braine called 'open class' words. A point which is not illustrated by the chart is the fact that utterances containing a given 'pivot' word tend to be introduced together within a relatively short space of time. The child then moves on to elaborate utterances using another pivot word.

It can be said with some confidence then that these young children are not combining words in any random way. Words occurring within the same class are very rarely combined and, as we have said, the word orders seem to be relatively fixed. These things are reminiscent of adult grammar and it is for this reason that Braine and others have suggested that young children have a definite if primitive grammar of their own.

Having said this we are immediately confronted with the problems of saying exactly what this grammar is. Can we safely state as a rule of the grammar that any pivot word can be combined with any open class word? Andrew said 'I see', 'I shut' and 'I sit'. He also said 'hi Calico', 'hi mama' and 'hi papa'. The pivot words are 'I' and 'hi' but can we predict that the child should on some occasions say e.g. 'I mama', 'hi shut', etc? The other extreme is to treat all the words occurring with a given pivot word as one class and all the words occurring with another pivot word as another class, etc., and to have as a rule the grammar that a given pivot word can only be combined with words of its special class. This is unduly restricting and does not allow the child scope to invent or discover combinations which he has not used before.

If we were dealing with an adult language the method of approach would be, as we saw in Chapter 3, to ask a native speaker of the language to tell us which combinations were acceptable and which were not. This approach simply does not work with young children because it is almost impossible to convey to them what you want them to do. There is, however, some indirect evidence that young children, at least at later stages of development, do have fairly definite notions of what is acceptable to say and what is not even when their ideas seem wrong to adults. Two examples will be described on page 97 and page 112 of how children can stick very dogmatically to their own childish utterances even when an adult is trying to correct them.

In the next chapter it is suggested that the processes which produce the distinction between pivot class and open class words are rather different from true grammatical processes which come into play at later stages. At this very earliest stage it is probably meaningless to think of the child as having a notion of acceptability. Only when he has begun to apply generalisations about the patterns of language should we look for a difference between what a child may say in practice and what he regards as acceptable. Even at these later stages we shall assume that slips of the tongue and other 'errors' are a relatively minor part of language use and that in everyday relaxed conditions what children and adults actually say is a very good guide to what they regard as acceptable to say.

We are still left with the unavoidable problem of predicting, from a limited sample, what other utterances would be regarded as acceptable.

It is worth observing that this logical problem of induction which confronts the grammarian is not essentially different from the problem of the child himself who must discover the patterns of adult language by listening to a finite, though admittedly large, sample of adult language. There is a facetious parallel to be drawn between the dogmatism of some grammarians who ignore the fact that their own pet rules are not always acceptable by native speakers of the language and the curious obstinacy sometimes shown by children themselves in sticking to their current notions of acceptable sentences.

Before we leave the pivot/open class stage of development there are a few other points to be noted.

Many of the utterances have no counterpart in adult speech ('more high', 'see pretty', 'allgone shoe', 'want up', etc.). This fact has led some people to suppose that language cannot be learned by imitation. This important point will be discussed in the next chapter.

Although Braine's pivot and open classes of word are probably not parts of speech in the adult sense, it is worth comparing them with adult parts of speech. The pivot words cover a range of adult classes: 'want' (Class 2), 'it' (Class 1), 'there' (Class 4 or function word H), etc., and there are some which are unclassifiable ('beepbeep', 'allgone'). Similarly the open class words cover a range of adult parts of speech. Here and there are suggestions that particular adult parts of speech are being used for preference e.g. Class 2 words with 'it' in Gregory's speech: 'do it', 'push it', 'close it', 'buzz it', 'move it'.

Longer utterances

After the first start on word combinations at about two the length of children's utterances and their variety gradually increases – and their character changes.

Although he did not give many examples, Braine commented that the pivot/open class distinction becomes less clear and children begin to combine words which previously fell in the same class and were thus 'forbidden' from being combined. At about five months after the first word combinations the children he was studying were saying such things as 'man car' and 'car bridge'.

The samples of children's speech recorded overleaf by Roger Brown and Colin Fraser (1963) are taken from about this period. Because there is a much greater variety only a selection were published which are shown in the accompanying chart. We can see that some of the utterances look like pivot constructions but the pivot words are used in more than one way. At the same time we can see some utterances which are perfectly grammatical in the adult sense ('There it goes', 'Leave that block here', 'Come here', etc.). In between fall most of the utterances which are not grammatical in the adult sense but seem to be better than the primitive combination of words in pairs many of which have no counterpart in adult language. The term which has been used to describe these kinds of utterance is 'telegraphic' which quite nicely underlines the way they seem to capture the basic adult word order but omit certain words or morphemes much as in a telegram. Other examples from Brown and Fraser's records are shown here:

'two boot'
'a gas here'
'hear tractor'
'see truck Mommy'
'there go one'
'put truck window'
'Adam make tower'

A few oddities still occur with no apparent counterpart in adult speech: 'me see', 'now here'. It seems a reasonably generalisation that the words or morphemes which are omitted are the ones which usually carry least emphasis in adult speech (e.g. *put* the *truck* by the *window*). We have already noted the preference for 'nouns', 'verbs' and 'adjectives' at this stage.

MUM

Here it is, Mum.
Here, Mum.
Here (the) coffee pot
  broken, Mum.
More sugar, Mum.
There it is, Mum.
What's that, Mum.
Mum, (where is the cards)?
Mum, (where's the rags)?
WANT COFFEE, MUM.
Want apple, Mum.
Want blanket, Mum.
Want more juice, Mum.
I want blanket, Mum.
I want (it), Mum.
I want paper away, Mum.
(The) pan, Mum.
I want apple, Mum.
I want blanket, Mum.
I want blanket now, Mum.
I want juice, Mum.
Mum, I want some, Mum.
Popeye, Mum?
I wants do, Mum.
I wanta help, Mum.

I found, Mum.
I do, Mum.
I don't, Mum.
I get it, Mum.
(Gonna) dump, Mum.
Fall down, Mum.
Fall, Mum.
An apple, Mum.
Apple, Mum.
Again, Mum?
Out, Mum?
Salad, Mum?
SEE, MUM?
Coffee, Mum?
Turn, Mum?
No, you see, Mum?
No help, Mum.
Won't help, Mum.
Coffee, Mum.
HI, MUM.
Ok, Mum.
Here, Mum.
Mum, over here.
Enough, Mum.
Silver spoons, Mum.

DAD

See paper, Dad.
WANT COFFEE, DAD.
I want cream, Dad.
SEE, DAD?
Dad, want coffee?
Some more, Dad?
Work, Dad?
HI, DAD.

HERE

Here (a car).
Here all gone.
Here (block).
Here brick.
Here chairs.
Here coffee is.
Here comes Daddy.
Here flowers.
Here goes.
Here is.
Here it goes.
Here it is.
Here it is, Mum.
Here's it here.
Here light.
Here (mail) more paper.
Here more.
Here more bricks.
Here more blocks.
Here more firetruck.
Here more toys.
Here more truck.
Here Mum.
Here Mummy.
Here my bricks.

Here not a house.
Here stars.
Here (the) coffee pot
  broken, Mum.
Here the card.
Here the cards.
Here the cheese.
Here (the) flowers.
Here the paper.
Here (we go).
See the bolt here, see?
That block here.
That one here.
That one right here.
I put bucket here.
Come here.
Do here.
Leave that block here.
Put it here.

Right here.
Over here.
Mum, over here.
Now here.

THERE

There goes.
There (he) goes.
There is.
There it goes.
There it is.
There it is, Mum.
There kitty.
There more block.
There more truck.
There more nails.
There Mum.
There my house.
There my nails.
There Noah.
I wanta put (it) right
  there . . . (under)
  the couch.
Me see (in there).
Blanket in there.
In there.
Right there.

SMALL CAPS identify contexts common to *Mum* and *Dad*.
Italics identify contexts common to *here* and *there*.

FIGURE 32   *From Brown and Fraser* 1963

It is now a much bigger task to analyse children's language and we shall reserve fuller discussion of grammar and possible processes at work until the next chapter. A fairly safe generalisation is that the 'grammaticality' of what children say steadily improves so that by four or five it sounds largely acceptable to adults apart from occasional oddities.

Play

A feature of children's language which we touched on when describing cooing and babbling is the prominent role of play. In case anyone should doubt that children do play with language here is another quotation from Brown's records:

Adult: 'That's the tattooed man'.
Child: 'Tooman. Tattoo man. Find too tattoo man. Tattoo man. Who dat? Tattoo. Too man go, Mommy? Too man. Tattoo man go? Who dat? Read dat. Tractor dere. Tattoo man'.

Perhaps the most striking evidence that children use and experiment with language for its own sake quite independently of any need to communicate is the observation that they will often talk to themselves when they are alone. Dr Ruth Weir of Stanford University has produced a most interesting book, *Language in the Crib* (1962) based on tape recordings of her son Anthony, aged two and a half, talking to himself before he went to sleep at night.

Here is a typical record (ordinary spelling is used except where words are unrecognisable when the IPA is used):

1. That's office ($\times 2$)
2. Look Sophie
3. That Sophie
4. Come last night
5. Good boy
6. Go for glasses
7. Go for them
8. Go to the top
9. Go throw
10. Go for blouse
11. Pants

12. Go for shoes
13. Powder
14. S'not dry
15. Get powder on
16. Shoe fixed (×2)
17. And me shoe
18. Some powder
19. On the leg
20. Anthony's leg
21. Put in Daddy's legs
22. Put some Mommy's legs
23. Mommy's legs (×2)
24. Mommy get some (×2)
25. Soap
26. Mommy take a shower
27. Take some soap
28. Down

The different utterances are marked off from each other by pauses.

This sample of Anthony's 'soliloquies' illustrates a number of features of the whole set of recordings. Dr Weir suggests that the first three items illustrate a general tendency to play with and repeat sounds in different context; the [sof] sequence in the first item is mimicked in the second and third. Other examples occur elsewhere in the records:

[bink]
[let boubo bink]
[bink ben bink]
[blu kink]

[boubo] is the name of the child's toy but [bink], [ben] and [kink] do not appear to have any meaning. Anthony seems to be merely articulating the [nk] sounds for their own sake in different contexts and combinations.

Another feature is the way the child seems to take a short sequence of words and form variations on it, replacing various words but keeping some the same. Items 6 to 10 and 12 illustrate this. Notice the two phonemes [go] at the beginning of item 5 which are the same as the first two of item 6 – a further example of sound repetition perhaps.

There are a great many examples in the whole record of sequences of utterances which retain certain words in common but substitute others. Here is a sequence illustrating a few:

1. Alice (calling)
2. Mommy (4× – calling)
3. Mommy's too weak
4. Alice strong
5. Alice too weak (×2)
6. Daddy's too weak
7. Mommy's too weak
8. Too weak with Barbara.
9. Be careful Barbara
10. Barbara can broke
11. Careful broke the [rami]
12. Careful broke Anthony
13. Careful broke it (×2)
14. Careful broke the
15. Broke the finger
16. Broke the Bobo
17. Broke the vacuum clean
18. The broke
19. [begi phu]
20. Get some broke
21. Broke the
22. Alice broke the baby fruit
23. Alice almost dropped
24. It's David fruit
25. Look (×2)
26. All right
27. Lady
28. Mama

The impression one gains from these and other samples is that the child is recalling snippets of speech heard perhaps during the preceding day and also constructing variations of his own on them. He also seems to be recalling other snippets heard containing features in common with the first one or with one of the variations. Thus 'Mommy's too weak' is apparently a sentence Dr Weir used when she did not feel like giving Anthony a ride. After an item ('Alice strong'), apparently related through semantics rather than form, Anthony produces a number of variations using 'too weak' some of which may have been actually heard and others probably not (e.g. 'too weak with Barbara').

There is direct confirmation of Anthony mimicking phrases heard earlier, in one sequence in which the parents were in his room during the recording:

	Mother present
	Do you want me to close this one for you or leave it open?
Open	
Want to listen (×2)	To what?
Daddy want to listen	To what?
[dankis] closing the door	
Listen to one	Tomorrow we'll listen to records. Daddy will have his dinner now.
	Mother leaves
	Father comes
Listen to blue one (×2)	I'm going to have my dinner now, Anthony
	Father leaves
My dinner	
closed	
leave it open	
closed	
[danki] curtain	
[m m m]	
etc.	

The thread of similarity running through sequences is often similarity of sound or similarity of words but quite often it seems to be similarity of the situation in which the phrases may have been heard originally. In the first sequence quoted above there is a series of items starting at about item 11 which seems to be related to nappy changing and dressing. Other examples occur elsewhere. In addition to play some of what Anthony said might class better as practice:

[bak] please
[beriz]
not [bariz]
[bariz] (×2)
not [bariz]
[beri:z]
[ba] (×2)

this looks suspiciously like practice of the phoneme contrast between [a] and [e] in 'berries'. Dr Weir remarks that Anthony was never corrected by adults except for unintelligible speech.

Later developments

By the age of four or five most of the gross differences between children's and adult's grammar have disappeared. It is far from being the case however that language learning is complete at this stage. One's vocabulary continues to grow almost throughout life and the rate of growth is steady and fast well into the teens. Studies of written language have shown that children use an increasing proportion of compound and complex sentences right up until adulthood.

Roger Brown and Jean Berko (1960) have revealed some interesting differences between adults and children of six and older in the way they give word associations. A word association test simply requires the person to say the first word that enters his head after the tester has said another word. Brown and Berko found that children tend to give a word of a different part of speech from the stimulus word such as might follow or precede the word in a sentence. Adults tend to give a word of the same part of speech. Thus if the stimulus word is 'dark' children tend to say 'night' but adults tend to say 'light'. If the stimulus word is 'man' children tend to say 'work' and adults tend to say 'woman'. This difference between adults and children is not at all obvious from casual observation. It suggests a progression of sorting and classifying of words continuing throughout childhood.

Another study of six- to eight-year-olds by Jean Berko (1967) shows up the imperfections in morphology which persist in children of these ages. She tested their use of irregular plurals and past tenses by presenting a picture and saying 'This is a mouse'. She then presented another picture and said 'and now there are two mice'. Then she asked the children to tell her what the pictures were. In many cases the children's plurals were 'mouses', 'mouse', 'meeces' or 'mices' in spite of the fact that she had given them the correct version only a moment before! Similarly the children's versions of 'rang' were in many cases 'ringed' or 'rung'. 'Song' often became 'sing', 'singed', 'sung' or 'sanged'. 'Geese' were often 'goose' or 'gooses'. The proportion of children giving these kinds of responses decreased in older age groups so that most eight-year-olds got most of them right.

It is not uncommon for children to exhibit their own (wrong) notions in this way and to resist correction, but we are not justified in concluding that children do not learn language by imitation, as we shall see.

As a further illustration of the fact that children's language continues to develop, not merely in vocabulary growth, long after the age of five, we shall outline the results of a very interesting study of children's syntax between the ages of five and ten (1969).

This is the work of Carol Chomsky. While she is wedded (both literally and metaphorically) to Noam Chomsky the study is intrinsically interesting irrespective of its theoretical foundations.

The first test was designed to find out how children of these ages interpret sentences of the two forms:

John is eager to see
John is easy to see

To this end a blindfolded doll was presented to the child who was asked 'Is this doll easy to see or hard to see?' and 'Would you make her easy/ hard (according to the child's previous answer) to see?' Here are some examples:

ERIC H. (5.2)
Is this doll easy to see or hard to see?
– *Hard to see*
Will you make her easy to see.
– *O.K.* (He removes blindfold)
Will you explain what you did?
– *Took off this.* (pointing to blindfold)
And why did that make her easier to see?
– *So she can see.*

Again,

CHRISTINE M. (5.1)
Here's Chatty Cathy. Can you tell me whether she's easy to see or hard to see?
– *Hard*
Could you make her easy to see?
(*removes blindfold*)
Can you tell me why she was hard to see in the beginning?
– *'Cause she had this over her eyes. 'Cause she had the blindfold on.*

'Cause she had the blindfold on. And what did you do? Explain what
you did.
- *Take it off*
And what did that make her?
- *ch* . .
Did that make her easy to see?
- *Yes*
Can you say that? Say 'I took the blindfold off'
- *I took the blindfold off her.*
And it made her. . . .
- *See*

It is quite clear that these five-year-olds are interpreting this construction as if 'easy' and 'hard' were equivalent to 'eager' in 'John is
eager to see', i.e. that the person doing the seeing is John (or the doll)
not someone else.

As might be expected the adult interpretation is more frequent
amongst older children thus:

ANN C. (8.8)
Here's Chatty Cathy. Can you tell me, is she easy to see or hard to
see?
- *Easy*
Could you make her hard to see? Can you think of a way?
- *In the dark*

None the less wrong interpretations can persist up to the age of nearly
eight-and-a-half which may come as a surprise even to those with much
experience of children.

The second test was concerned with the contrasted interpretations
of the two forms:

John promised Bill to shovel the driveway
John told Bill to shovel the driveway

In the first case adults will agree that John is to do the shovelling. In
The second case it is Bill. To test children's understanding of this
contrast Carol Chomsky used puppets of the Walt Disney characters –
Donald Duck and Bozo:

PETER F. (6.9)
Donald tells Bozo to hop across the table. Can you make him hop?
- (*making Bozo hop*) *Bozo, hop across the table.*

Bozo promises Donald to do a somersault. Can you make him do it?
– (*making Donald do a somersault*) *I promised you you can do a tumble-*
sault.
Would you say that again?
– *I promised you you could do a tumblesault.*

The intention of the third test was to discover whether and how children observed the two interpretations of:

I asked him what to do.
I told him what to do.

In the first sentence 'I' is to 'do' something while in the second 'him' is to 'do' the task. This test proved more complicated than the others because there are in fact four constructions in which 'ask' and 'tell' require varying interpretations. What emerged was that some children always treated 'ask' as 'tell', others observed all adult interpretations but the majority had mastered the use of the two words in some constructions but not in others. While the construction described earlier showed a steadily increasing mastery with age there was a very wide variation with 'ask' and 'tell' so that some five-year-olds did better than some nine-year-olds. The 'stages' of learning seemed always to come in the same order however. Curiously enough children's mastery of these constructions did not appear to correlate with classroom ability at least as assessed rather informally by the children's teachers.

The interesting suggestion is that the interpretation of some ask/tell constructions may remain unlearned even in some adults. Carol Chomsky observes, with respect to the construction 'Ask L what to feed the doll.' that: 'We found nine-year-olds and ten-year-olds who could not, even with prodding, respond with the correct answer: *What should I feed the doll?*'

'The question we wish to raise is whether these children are still in a process of acquisition with respect to this structure and will at some future time be able to interpret it correctly, or whether perhaps they may already have reached what for them constitutes adult competence. We have observed from informal questioning that this structure is a problematic one for many adults, and that there are many adult speakers who persist in assigning the wrong subject to the complement verb. This seems to be a structure that is never properly learned by a substantial number of speakers.' She adds an example from the language of a group of Indian tribes on the St Lawrence river in which some speakers distinguish one form of 'he' when talking about a man and another form when talking about a second man who enters into the same account as the first man. Many speakers of Menomini apparently ignore this distinction altogether.

The last test was designed to discover whether children realised that in the sentence: 'He found out that Mickey won the race,' 'he' cannot be the same person as Mickey. By contrast with the other constructions this one appears to be mastered consistently by all children older than five-and-a-half.

The interest of this study is in showing how late some interpretations may be learned. Another point of interest is that the 'stages' of acquiring a structure seem to come in a fixed order but the ages at which a particular structure is acquired may vary quite a lot; some structures are more variable than others.

Learning to read

Our description of language learning has been devoted exclusively to how language is normally first learned through the aural-oral medium. Deaf children may have to use another medium or media for this first learning of the phonological, morphological and syntactic patterns of language, but whatever the medium we shall call it a *primary medium* for language learning.

When the basic patterns have been laid down children may learn to recognise them in other media which we shall call *secondary media*. The most commonly mastered secondary medium is, of course, written language.

To anticipate the next two chapters in which the mechanics of language learning is discussed I shall pose and answer a question here on the processes at work in learning to read: 'Are the psychological processes involved in learning to read basically the same or different from those involved in primary language learning?' The answer, without any doubt, is that they are 'different', the crucial difference being that a normal hearing child learning to read already has the patterns of language laid down and this is a great assistance to him.

The reader will recall the principle of economical coding described in Chapter 1 where I suggested that whenever we can recognise a new pattern as basically the same as one we already have in memory store then maximum use is made of this fact to avoid storing the same pattern twice.

It is a tremendous help to a child learning to read to discover that there is some correspondence between the speech sounds and the letters: 't' almost always stands for [t], 'p' for [p], 'b' for [b] and many other speech sounds have typical spellings. Instead of the patterns of letters having to be learned as arbitrary sequences, the child's prior knowledge of sound patterns will help him. The problems of putting words in the right order is solved at once through the child's knowledge of spoken language.

It was fashionable at one time to suggest that children should be taught to recognise written words without any use of the correspondence between letters and speech sounds. If children taught by this 'whole word' method learned to read they did so in spite of the method not because of it: if letters and sounds did not correspond at all then learning to read English would be as hard as learning the Chinese idiographic system in which each character for every word has to be mastered as an almost completely new pattern.

Having said this it should be emphasised again that the reading and writing of English would be even easier to learn if the correspondence between letters and sounds was better than it is. (In Chapter 3 was described how a given sound may have several different spellings, a given spelling may stand for several different sounds and occasionally – as in the word 'one' – it is impossible to match the sounds and the spelling at all.)

The proof of the assertion is to be found in the results of trials with the Initial Teaching Alphabet (e.g. Warburton and Southgate, 1969). Children taught to read on i.t.a. learn very much quicker than children taught on T.O., at least when they are tested in the medium in which they were taught, which is all that matters for the present point. Sir James Pitman designed i.t.a. to give, as far as possible, a one-for-one correspondence between the i.t.a. written characters and the phonemes of speech. This can be seen in the example given in Chapter 3. When children have become fluent at reading in this medium, it is intended that they transfer to T.O. They do this quite well although perhaps not as easily as was hoped for originally. The reader unacquainted with i.t.a. will find that he can cope quite adequately with the sample shown here, and this will give him the feel of how children taught on i.t.a. do the reverse. Children will find it harder no doubt because of their relative inexperience in reading compared with adults.

Two things help the transfer: firstly, the characters are specially designed so that words spelt in i.t.a. have a visual resemblance to the

ᚦhe man lꝏkt around, and ᚦhær woʂ ᚦhe pig wiᚦh hiʂ feet in ᚦhe creem. hee ran at ᚦhe pig, but ᚦhe pig ran about ᚦhe rꝏm until ᚦhær woʂ creem aull œver ᚦhe flor. at last ᚦhe man pꝏt ᚦhe bæby doun and ran ᚦhe pig out ov ᚦhe dor wiᚦh a stick. but aʂ ᚦhe pig went out, ᚦhe man fell œver ᚦhe stick and bumpt hiʂ hed on ᚦhe dor.

hee rubbd hiʂ hed and went back tꝏ ᚦhe bæby. bie ᚦhis tiem ᚦhe bæby woʂ in ᚦhe creem, tꝏ. hee had tꝏ ᚳhænj her clœᚦhʂ.

"ꟗhot a tiem ie am haviŋ!" hee sed tꝏ himself. "ᚦhær iʂ mor tꝏ dꝏ nou ᚦhan when ie started ᚦhis morniŋ."

FIGURE 33

same words spelt in T.O. Secondly, use is made of the gap-filling and distortion-correcting capacities of an established schema. Illustrations were given in Chapter 1 of how we can recognise patterns with which we are familiar in spite of omissions and distortions provided these are not too great. By giving children fluency in the written medium first, i.t.a. enables them to recognise words written in T.O.

It is often thought that the use of i.t.a. will make for bad spelling later. If anything, children taught to read on i.t.a. seem to be better spellers later than those brought up on T.O. One of Attneave's principles for economical coding may be invoked again: it is easier and more economical to code a pattern as a variation on a similar regular pattern already known than to encode it from scratch.

The principles outlined here, especially the distinction between primary and secondary language media will prove important in discussing how best to present language to deaf children.

Second language learning

The learning of a secondary medium for a given language is not the same as learning a second language, say French or Russian for an English child. And the processes involved in learning a second language will be rather different again from either learning a first language or learning a secondary medium. These points are made to avoid unnecessary confusion but it is not proposed to discuss second language learning in any detail. The fact that one language is already known will undoubtedly affect how the second one is learned, not necessarily in a favourable sense, and it could be exceedingly difficult to unravel the details.

Testing a child's language abilities

Earlier we touched on the problem of testing a child's grasp of language and the issue has been implicit elsewhere in the chapter. We are now in a better position to make some general points about the problem.

If we want to test someone's ability to drive a car we ride around with him watching how he performs in various situations and perhaps creating some specially (e.g. an emergency stop) to explore his range of skills. Within half-an-hour we should have seen most of what he can do although we may miss a few things like the handling of the car in a slide.

If we listen to someone talking we will quickly observe the common words in his vocabulary but we might wait days, months or years to hear every word in his repertoire. To make a comprehensive assessment we not only want to find out what words he knows but for each one the range of meanings and syntactic uses. In addition we should observe the various syntactic constructions and the meanings they are given. As with the word forms there are a limited number of word uses and constructions which are used very often but many more only appear comparatively rarely. The fact that most five-year-olds have reached a stage where most of what they say is grammatically acceptable to adults disguises the fact that they do not have the range or depth of expression of most adults.

Unlike the driving test our test of language must take samples. To ensure that the picture we get from these samples is fairly complete, we should cover the different types of skill, and we may be misled by tests which do not. For example, vocabulary tests in which children match words with pictures or give the meanings of words verbally should be treated for what they are and not full language tests. Actually they are a surprisingly good guide to other language skills, but in normal children only. Deaf children commonly 'know' quite large numbers of words but have little idea of their syntactic uses.

There is no test on the market which covers all facets adequately. The Illinois Test of Psycholinguistic Abilities (Kirk *et al.*, 1968) might be thought to be such but in fact it attempts to assess the processes which are thought to underly language rather than linguistic knowledge itself. No test has yet attempted to explore the ranges in addition to the locations of word meanings. Tests of syntactic structures and meanings aim merely at a global measure without probing deeper.

What this means is that we have to be very careful in interpreting test results lest we assume that because one thing is known, others are also. Carol Chomsky's pioneering work demonstrates how 'blunt' are the usual instruments of assessment, including casual listening. It is only when one starts asking the right kind of question that hidden strengths and weaknesses are revealed. This comes out in a study by D. F. Moores (1967) in which he employed a method of measuring control of syntax known as the 'Cloze' procedure.

A word is omitted from a prose passage at regular intervals (say every fifth word) and the task is to put a suitable one in each gap. It need not be the same as the one that was omitted but should be of the right grammatical class (Fries's classification). A group of deaf children were tested, average age sixteen years nine months, and also a group of hearing children aged nine years ten months, the two groups having the same average score on a conventional reading test. Ostensibly they had the same linguistic abilities but in fact the hearing children were significantly better at the 'Cloze' task.

The biggest trap is not to assess language at all. Time and again one is told by parents of children whose speech development is delayed that they 'understand everything', only to find in many cases that they understand very little speech. People are misled by the fact that the instructions 'Come and sit down and have your dinner', or our earlier example about the fire warning, frequently occur in situations where context and past experience effectively tell the child what to do. Sir James Pitman describes how his dog not only obeys the command 'sit down' but also 'asseyez-vous' and 'sitzen Sie'. He points out that it is not a multilingual dog but merely one sensitive to the voice of command.

Dr Reynell has partly but not completely eliminated these influences in her test. The instruction 'put the doll on the chair' when the child is faced with a small set of toys including a doll and a chair can be and sometimes is followed correctly when only 'doll' and 'chair' are recognised because this is the obvious way to relate the two things. If it was 'put the chair on the doll' or 'put the chair in front of the doll' one could be more certain that a correct response meant full understanding.

The range of possible responses is always restricted to some extent by context and if one is merely interested in making a comparison with 'normal' or some other standard this does not matter. Occasionally tests are not used like this and the result can be misleading. If a deaf child is asked to choose single objects from, say, a dozen or so objects in a lip-reading test, he will probably do quite well. But normally the range of possibilities is very much larger and lip-reading correspondingly harder. It becomes harder still when a sequence of words rather than a single word is to be understood.

6 An explanatory scheme

There are too many unanswered questions in this field for anyone to claim a full explanation of how language development occurs. At present arguments centre on what types of process occur and the learning of syntax is the chief bone of contention here. This scheme is a personal view which is intended mainly as a frame of reference to put the issue in perspective.

Learning is itself a disputed subject and much discussion still, for example, revolves round the question of whether learning can occur without rewards and punishments. For our purpose I have adopted two principles which are fairly widely accepted and we shall see how helpful they may be in explaining language learning.

1. The importance of pattern

In Chapter 1 we saw how one can think of the stimuli of light, sound, touch, etc. as a collection of 'events' occurring together or in sequence. If all these events were completely random we would live in a world where our eyes only saw a kind of speckled soupy fog and our ears only heard a crude kind of hissing sound like the background noise on a cheap radio. We could never hope to register the vast amounts of information in this random stimulation and there would be little point because past experience or learning would never enable us to anticipate the future. Fortunately, as we saw in Chapter 1, most stimulation is very redundant and our nervous systems have a very marked tendency to seize on any kind of regularity or pattern (redundancy) in the stimulation and to use it as a means of storing the information economically. The various devices for doing this which were described earlier all seem to be based on one principle: wherever two or more 'events' regularly occur together they form a pattern which can be recognised as the same in two or more parts of a larger pattern of one, two or more different occasions;

the pattern need only be recorded once in detail and whenever it occurs again it is only necessary to record that the new pattern is the 'same' as the old one.

If we can find regularly recurring patterns in language we would expect the same processes which are so clearly at work in other forms of perception and learning to be able to deal with the learning of these patterns.

As a general rule, *the greater the redundancy or pattern in the stimulation the more salient and easily learned it should be.*

Small patterns, having a smaller information load than large patterns should be learned earliest and most easily.

2. The law of frequency

This is the familiar fact that we are more likely to learn something if we see or hear it often than if we see it only a few times. *Other things being equal we would expect those features of language which occur often to be learned earlier than the rarer features.*

Actually the Law of Frequency is only a special case of our first principle. If a pattern is repeated it is, in effect, simply a larger pattern (distributed in time) with internal regularities or redundancy. The more repetitions there are the more redundant is this large pattern.

The term 'the Law of Frequency' originates in behaviourist learning theory and the use of the term may suggest that I am adopting this theory. To forestall any misunderstanding I should emphasise that this approach is not behaviourist in the usual sense.

On average the small elements in language recur more frequently than the larger patterns. Certainly most of the 44+ phonemes occur more frequently than most words. The commoner words which form the bulk of our language probably occur more frequently than particular phrase or sentence patterns. Here then is a second factor helping to explain why children tend to progress from the small elements in language to the larger patterns.

I have said nothing about rewards and punishments. Some learning theories maintain that nothing can be learned without one or other. The difficulty is that a lot of learning seems to be its own reward. Children often seem to get a lot of pleasure from acquiring new words and phrases in the same way that they have a tremendous urge to explore new objects and situations apparently just to know what is in them; the desire by a young child to find out what is in a lady's handbag, say, is sometimes mistaken for 'original sin' (oddly enough when all the objects have been removed and examined they will then frequently be replaced meticulously one by one and the bag carefully closed).

Regarding rewards and punishments we can say at least that something is more likely to be learned when there is an obvious incentive than when there is not. It is not safe to assume that learning will not occur when there is no obvious incentive. Before looking at the sequence of development there are some general points to be made about the learning and use of language which will help us in later discussion.

Receptive and expressive language

We should remind ourselves first of our model of perception and action discussed in Chapter 1. We saw how our sensory systems seem to work in a series of stages with the sensory information being analysed and reorganised at each successive stage. In recognising a complex pattern we seem first to process details, then collections of these recognised details are grouped as larger patterns and complete objects or words are recognised as arrangements of these larger patterns. We also saw the powerful effect which the largest stored patterns (schemata) could have on recognition: there is quite a strong tendency to see and hear what we expect to see and hear. If some details do not quite fit in we tend to ignore them.

Our actions also seem to be controlled at a series of levels ranging from the overall strategy down to fine control of muscles. While the perceptual systems seem to be able to work by themselves the motor systems cannot. Most actions are guided by feedback: our perceptual systems constantly gather information about the effects of our actions and thus guide them. Because receptive language is in a sense simpler than expressive language we shall discuss it first.

Receptive language – recognition and understanding

The main focus of attention in this chapter is not processes like recognition as such, which were discussed in Chapter 1, but how children learn to recognise or reproduce patterns of various kinds.

Recognition is a process of comparing incoming stimulation with stored patterns and deciding which stored pattern fits the data best. Frequently we pay attention to only a few features and ignore the rest. We tend to be guided by our overall schema or expectations for a situation and we are particularly prone to ignore details which do not fit in. It is only when the incoming data simply will not fit with existing stored patterns that we are forced to adapt our stored patterns or to store new ones. This is perceptual learning.

It is often said that children's recognition and understanding of speech tend to develop earlier and grow faster than their ability to produce speech. As we have seen this statement needs to be qualified because a lot depends on the attention to detail demanded. To take an obvious example, it is much easier to recognise a bird amongst a collection of animals including a cat, a fish, a centipede and a lizard than to recognise a Willow Warbler in a collection of birds including a Chiff-Chaff, a Reed Warbler, a Garden Warbler and a Wood Warbler. We have already seen how a predictable situation can make it seem as if a young child has a better understanding of language than he really has. In a similar way it is common experience that we can recognise an object far more quickly and with far less attention to detail than if we wish to produce an acceptable drawing of it. We might identify the object in half a second as a vase with flowers in it but be unable to say anything about the pattern on the vase or the shapes of the leaves and petals on the flowers. The same would not be true after we had attempted to draw it.

As a general rule, recognition often requires less attention to detail than reproduction. The reason for this is probably that most entities (objects, actions, etc.) have far more distinctive features than are strictly necessary for identification. This make identification easier because we can quickly find one or two distinctive features when there is a large number to choose from. We are therefore spoiled and demand a similar wealth of detail in drawings and speech productions. It is only when the range of entities to be distinguished from each other differ very slightly that the amount of attention to detail needed for recognition becomes as great as that needed for the production of a pattern. By suitable emphasis or exaggeration a skilled cartoonist can make recognition easy using only a few distinctive features.

A corollary of this rule is that *the attempt to reproduce or imitate a pattern focuses our attention on the details and thus helps to make recognition more accurate and reliable.*

This is not to say that recognition is impossible without production.

Occasionally children are born whose speech apparatus is paralysed but who none the less learn to understand language. Christy Brown is a cerebral palsied man whose excellent language proves that a child need not produce speech in order to learn to recognise and understand speech patterns. The only part of his body that he could control properly was his left foot. He learned to read and to write with this foot and thus to give expression to language which in the first place he had acquired through passive listening. His autobiography (1954) makes fascinating reading.

We can note these aspects of recognition and understanding and at the same time admit that relatively little is known of the details of how this side of children's language develops. This is because it requires systematic testing whereas the expressive side of children's language can be recorded more directly. Most of the discussion in this chapter is thus necessarily focused on expressive language.

An addendum to this section on receptive language concerns 'competence' and 'acceptability'. Whereas Chomsky's special notion of competence does not fit into the scheme presented here 'acceptability' does. In this context 'acceptability' is merely a particular form of recognition: recognition of grammatical patterns as distinct from ungrammatical ones.

Expressive language – imitation

Again, our emphasis here is on learning. As we have said the motor side of the nervous system cannot usually work alone; it needs the perceptual system. When a child learns to produce speech he not only has to learn what to do with his tongue, lips, teeth, breath etc. to produce particular speech patterns but he has to be able to distinguish these different sound patterns perceptually.

It is usual to assume that children learn language by imitating adults. Before proceeding we should clarify what we mean by 'imitate' because it has been a source of misunderstanding. The word is used here to mean that children learn language by progressively modelling their own speech to resemble the forms which they hear other people using. Sometimes 'learning by imitation' has been taken to mean that the actual act of producing a replica of heard speech is necessary for learning. This is not at all true as Christy Brown's case shows.

Jean Berko has suggested as a result of her study, already described, that imitation cannot play a big part in language learning. Susan Ervin

(1964) has also found that children can be remarkably slow to model their speech on adult lines as is shown in this example:

Child: Nobody don't like me
Mother: No, say 'Nobody likes me'
Child: Nobody don't like me
       (eight repetitions of this dialogue)
Mother: No, now listen carefully: say '*Nobody likes me*'
Child: Oh! Nobody don't like*s* me.

These two authors seem to be assuming that imitation is a copying process like printing or photography in which there is a direct point-for-point transfer from the original to the copy. They also seem to be assuming that the actual act by the child of trying to produce a copy is necessary for children's speech to become progressively more like adults'.

A moment's reflection will show that it would be surprising if children could immediately reproduce adult sentence forms; a graphic artist may take years to develop the skills necessary to make a 'photographic' drawing of something. In a similar way, part of the process of learning speech and language will be development of the skills of imitation. Actual practice in mimicking adults is not necessary for this. Two well recognised processes are described here which may well be sufficient explanation of the inaccuracies in children's imitations and other speech.

1. *Imitation as a hierarchy of sub-skills* The quality of an imitation can never be better than the elementary perceptual and motor skills from which it is built. A child who knows how to say [ʃ] may not be able to hear that [s] is a different sound; he may be able to hear the difference but does not know how to alter the position of his tongue to make the difference; he may not be able to do either. In all three cases he is always likely to say [ʃ] when he should be saying [s] as, perhaps in the word 'yes' which he would pronounce 'yesh'. (If, in general, children hear differences between sounds before they learn how to pronounce them this may account for the observation that correct pronunciations of particular sounds often appear 'across the board', all at once, in all the different words in which the sounds were previously wrongly pronounced.)

We can think of imitations as mosaics built up of the elementary skills which the child possesses. If a particular type of coloured glass is missing the imitation will be a distortion of the original. The particular element is either omitted or a similar one is substituted. Adults who try to learn a foreign language may have some experience of this. The vowel sound in the French word 'du' is not part of an English speaker's repertoire. Consequently the novice speaker of French may at first substitute the nearest English equivalent, perhaps [u:] (as in 'do') and amuse his French friends in doing so. Other French phonemes like [m] or [e] which are the same as in English cause no difficulty. English attempts at 'Llanelli' often illustrate the same effect.

The fact that complex skills of recognition and production are built from sub-skills seems to offer a third reason why children start with small elements in language and build up to larger ones.

These effects are no different in principle from the deficiencies in the drawing of an artist who does not know, for example, the techniques of showing perspective, of modelling or of suggesting lines without actually drawing them.

In this section we have treated perceptual and motor skills together. Where omissions or substitutions occur one ought to ask whether the deficiency is in perception, execution or both. Very few studies have attempted to separate these two factors.

2. *Exploration, experiment and exercise* To produce a complex pattern successfully, all the necessary skills are brought into play together at a variety of different levels. It is the general rule amongst artists, musicians, gymnasts, jugglers, etc. that large and complicated projects are not attempted until the necessary sub-skills have been mastered. It is for this reason that exercises of various types are commonly practised, many of which are not obviously related to the ultimate project. An artist may spend much time drawing eggs or cylinders as a means of discovering the most effective way of showing their three-dimensional quality. He may experiment with different kinds of pencil and paper or with different kinds of shading, stippling or cross-hatching. He expects that the skills he develops in these experiments and exercises will help in producing portraits, landscapes, etc.

The complex skill of producing language is not likely to be mastered by the child simply applying sub-skills directly. Some of the effort must go into experimenting with his speech apparatus and exploring the different things that it can do; he must develop the sub-skills before he can use them.

As we suggested before, it is likely that babbling and vocal play does just this: the child seems to be exploring what different sounds are produced by different speech actions and the different ways these sounds may be combined. Against this it has been said that children sometimes have difficulty in imitating sounds which previously they pronounced during babbling. But then it can be argued that the child will not have learned the oral–aural link for all the sounds which he produced during babbling. Clearly more work needs to be done here. Examples of how children play with language were described in the last chapter.

To recapitulate, there are now four riders which we can add to our two main principles:

1. We should expect children to learn the small patterns in language before the larger patterns because they have a smaller information load, they tend to recur more frequently and they form the building bricks needed to recognise and produce the larger patterns.
2. Recognition and understanding of language patterns usually requires less attention to detail than the production of language. It is probably true that attempts to imitate and produce language patterns help receptive language learning but they are not necessary for it.
3. We should expect children's early imitations to show distortions of adult patterns because the necessary sub-skills are not fully developed. A child's incomplete mastery of speech sounds shows itself for some time in his pronunciation of words. Distortions in large patterns will not be corrected until the necessary sub-skills have been developed.
4. Together with imitations we should also expect to find children saying things which are essentially discoveries or inventions of their own.

Armed with these ideas we are now in a position to look at the developmental sequence to see how well they apply.

The sequence of language development

1. *First imitations*

We have already said something about cooing and babbling so we can turn straight away to the child's first attempts at imitation.

It is often remarked that children's first words and other imitations are often sounds like 'dada', 'baba', 'mama' (and in Weir's study 'Bobo') in which a syllable is repeated. It has been suggested that 'Mummy' and 'Daddy', 'Mama' and 'Papa', have in fact been chosen by adults to accommodate infants.

The fact that most infants are already producing such sequences in their babbling (dadadada, mamamama, etc.), seems likely to assist them; they have merely to match these pre-established sounds with similar elements in adult speech.

We have suggested that at this stage the child is building up a repertoire of speech sounds, small elementary parts of the speech stream, which form the building blocks or mosaic elements for constructing the larger patterns, words and phrases.

At this stage the child's elementary speech sounds are probably not the same as the phonemes recognised by adults (Appendix I). Whereas [b] and [d] are recognised as separate phonemes by adults the child is more likely to use [ba] as a single element.

It is well to ask on what basis young children select elements from the speech stream for use as units for constructing larger patterns. It is possible, using electronic apparatus, to represent speech sounds visually as a sound spectrogram. If we examine the spectrogram shown in Plate 1a we see that there are some sharp boundaries and markings but the boundaries of many phonemes at least have no clear marking at all.

Our two principles suggest that two processes will operate in the selection of speech sound elements:

1. We would expect those elements marked off by sharp, salient boundaries to be isolated. This seems to be generally true of consonants with an accompanying vowel. But while these consonants have a sharply defined boundary they also have a relatively low volume compared with vowels. Until there is an accurate means of measuring salience this point cannot be settled. Vowels are probably harder to differentiate than consonants because they are so very variable in adult speech. Not infrequently five and six-year-olds are still failing to distinguish a number of vowels but the adult ear does not detect this in their speech. This is probably one of the factors contributing to reading failure; if a child cannot for example distinguish the vowels in 'cat', 'cart' and 'cut' then he cannot learn to associate these sounds with their common spellings. For him English spelling looks even more irregular than it is already.
2. Those elements which recur frequently are more likely to be isolated than those which do not. Since phonemes are the elements which retain their identity (or similarity) in a variety of combinations

we would expect a tendency for infants to recognise phoneme boundaries on this basis; elements which bridge the boundaries between phonemes will be less likely to be isolated.

Of course this is all very speculative but it can at least be said that there is no evidence against this view. It is a difficult field in which to obtain positive evidence either for or against such hypotheses. The question of how words are isolated as units from the continuous speech stream is a similar one on which some work has been done. This will be described in a moment.

Generally then, children seem first to learn a limited range of the more obvious and frequent speech sounds which may or may not be the same as adult phonemes; they certainly ignore many of the subtler distinctions in adult speech for some time.

With this limited set of building blocks, to be refined and perfected in the following months and years, the child starts to try his hand at words. Because he is still struggling with the smaller elements it is not surprising that the rate at which children learn words at first is rather slow. We remarked previously that about six months after the first word the rate of progress begins to increase quite sharply and new words are then learned at a steady fast rate for some years. It seems likely that this acceleration occurs when the child has mastered enough speech sounds for him to be able to cope with most of the common words and he can concentrate on learning the order of the speech sounds rather than the details of how the individual sounds are recognised and produced.

The final identification of all phoneme contrasts is probably not completed until the child has quite an extensive experience with language: even some adults may fail to make certain phoneme distinctions which most other people would recognise. Thus a young child might easily use [d] and [b] interchangeably in the phrase 'a —ig one'. It is not until an adult says to him 'Not "dig", say "big" ' or until he hears the word 'dig' used in appropriately different contexts that he has any reason to make a distinction between [d] and [b]. Phonemes, or the contrasts between phonemes, have been defined as the contrasts needed to distinguish different words and it is likely that this plays an important part in how children learn the phoneme structure of the language.

The segmentation problem

A question which arises is how the child isolates words from the stream of speech. If we look at the sound spectrogram (Plate 1a) we can see that there is no gap to mark off different words as there is in writing. In the following sentence both the word boundaries and another possible grouping are marked:

↓   ↓   ↓   ↓

GEORGEMAKESHIMSELFSOMETEA

 ↑   ↑   ↑   ↑

The question is how do children come to recognise the words 'George', 'makes', 'himself', etc. as the important elements and not 'elfso', 'metea', etc. This question of how we come to recognise words as the elements in the continuous stream of speech is a neglected problem but one interesting, recent experiment throws some light on it.

John R. Hayes and H. H. Clark (1970) wished to settle the question of whether segmentation could occur when the 'words' had no kind of stress or pause to mark their boundaries and when there was no possibility of their being recognised simply because they were regularly used in association with some object or event. These are both theories which have been put forward from time to time.

It was decided to have a nonsense language with no meaning so that the second theory could not apply, and because they thought a human speaker might unwittingly put in pauses or emphasis to mark off the 'words', they programmed a computer in connection with a loudspeaker to produce a set of nineteen completely artificial 'phonemes' which could be produced in any order. In the main experiment four 'words' were constructed six or eight 'phonemes' long, and the computer produced them one after the other in random order for as long as was wanted.

Volunteers were asked to listen to this 'talk' for forty-five minutes and then they were tested. In the test they listened to two short sequences but with pauses introduced. In the first sequence the pauses were placed at the boundaries between the 'words' and in the second sequence the pauses were placed in the middle of the 'words'. The task was to decide which sequence marked the same 'words' as could be heard in the original forty-five minute sample.

The results showed clearly that people could pick out 'words' simply by the fact that they were repeating patterns whereas other combinations of phonemes were not. This does not mean, of course, that the other two processes play no part in how children isolate words. It simply means that they are not essential.

An interesting feature of this study was an account by the experimenters of what it felt like to do the task themselves:

'In the experimenter's subjective view the process seems to proceed roughly as follows. At first, the sound stream seems quite amorphous and featureless. After perhaps a minute of listening, an event – perhaps a phoneme or part of a phoneme – stands out of the stream. When the event has recurred several times, the listener may notice that it is typically preceded or followed by another event. The combination of events can in turn be related to events that happen in its neighbourhood. Recognition of a word, then, seems to proceed from perceptually distinctive foci outward in both directions towards the word boundaries. Presumably the process would tend to stop at word boundaries because the correlations across the boundaries are weak.'

To illustrate the last point consider the word 'George'. The sequence of letters GEORG is almost invariably followed by E. In other words there is a very high correlation between GEORG and E. But the sequence of letters GEORGE can be followed by a great variety of different letter sequences – there is a low correlation between it and anything which follows. Hayes and Clark suggest that a 'clustering mechanism' may be operating which can recognise intercorrelations between speech sounds and thus identify word boundaries by the relatively low correlations across them. They cite a theory of Z. S. Harris which describes how a linguist, confronted with an unfamiliar language which he wishes to divide into words, might use this principle. Here is a brief description of an exercise I have undertaken to test this idea:

A sample of English was punched on to computer cards but with all punctuation omitted and no spaces between words. The computer was programmed to make a count of all twenty-six different letters in the text and for each one count up what letters followed it. A given letter, say T, is followed most often by H, next most often by O and next most often by I. T is hardly ever followed by G or K or N, etc. When these counts had been made the high correlating pairs were picked out and added to the list of letters of the alphabet. The letters and the pairs now added to the list were termed 'elements'.

The next step was to do the same thing to a new sample of English but this time to make counts for all the elements, new and old alike. Thus a T followed by an H would be counted as unitary TH and the programme would record whatever element followed it. (Most frequently E.) A T followed by anything other than H, O or I would be counted still as T. At the end of this run all the high correlating pairs of elements were extracted, as before, and added to the list of elements. This time the new elements would again include pairs of letters but also triplets (where a pair was joined with a single or a single with a pair) and quartets (where two pairs were joined together). The programme was then run again in the same way using a new sample of text and the process repeated as many times as necessary.

In successive 'cycles' the elements grow bigger but after a time they cease to grow because they have reached word size and the low correlations at the boundaries prevent any increase. This is true of most words but a number of the small words (e.g. 'in', 'on', 'to', etc.) tend to be used as building bricks for making bigger words. It is not possible in this programme to recognise that IS is a word but IK is merely part of a larger word; preliminary trials with a fairly simple adaptation show that this problem can be overcome.

In the example shown, using books 8a and 9a of the Ladybird Reading

Cycle 1					
AM	AN	AS	AT	AY	DA
HA	PA	SA	DA	DO	LD
ND	ER	ES	ET	HE	ME
HA	HE	HI	HO	SH	TH
WH	IM	IN	IS	HI	LI
KE	NK	LD	LI	OL	ME
AM	IM	ND	NK	NT	AN
EN	IN	ON	OL	ON	OO
OU	OW	DO	HO	TO	PA
PE	RE	ER	OR	ST	SU
AS	ES	IS	YS	YE	TH
TO	AT	ET	NT	ST	OU
SU	WE	WH	OW	YS	AY
EY					
Cycle 2					
JAN	AYS	SAY	SAYA	ETER	ETER
PET	THE	THE	HIM	SHE	THE
HIM	HIM	HIM	JAN	PETE	ETER
SAYS	TER	PETE	THE	ETER	PET
SAYS	AYS	SAY			
Cycle 3					
JANE	PETER	PETER	PETER	JANE	PETER
PETER	PETER	PETER	PETER	PETER	

FIGURE 34

Series and a modification of the above programme which records both backwards and forwards correlations, the first cycle produces seventy-nine high correlating pairs of letters including most common two letter words. The second cycle produces 'say', 'says', 'the', 'she', 'him' and bits of 'Peter' and 'Jane'. The fact that they are produced several times reflects the way they have been built up via several different routes. The programme was set to accept only relatively common elements to avoid a situation where a chance occurrence, once, of, say, Z and T or other unusual combination would result in a spuriously high correlation. This explains why only the commonest words have been isolated. For the same reason nothing is produced after Cycle 3 and the programme stops.

The process is called a 'redundancy net' because it always sifts out the big fishes, big in the sense of highly redundant. This strong tendency to exploit redundancy for efficient coding is one respect in which the process models the activity of the nervous system. The elements are built up in a hierarchical structure just like the immediate constituents structure of a sentence. The possible significance of this will be discussed in the next chapter.

The process is also in tune with another aspect of brain function – our undoubted tendency to learn contextual probabilities. This in turn suggest an adaptation to the process which may turn out to mimic another feature of brain organisation: retrieval from memory store on the basis of contextual probability. In case this is not clear I should explain that the original version of this programme had a very inefficient method of finding whether or not an element had been stored – it had to search through the whole list of stored elements in sequence. It would obviously be much quicker if, for example, the programme having identified PET in the text and 'knowing' that ER is the most probable next element in that context, it checked that first. This programme is now organised to work in this way with a ninety-fold increase in speed. In effect the programme uses the principle of induction or 'going beyond the information given'.

One respect in which the model does not imitate what happens in practice is that the function words, which are by far the commonest words in adult speech, are not particularly abundant in a child's first vocabulary. We said earlier that they are often mumbled by adults and not emphasised. Many of them are short and rather similar and thus not salient or easy to distinguish. Steven, one of the children whom Martin Braine studied had a short [a] or [da] sound which seemed to serve for 'a', 'is' and 'to'. More important perhaps is the fact that many function words do not have a very obvious lexical meaning since their function is mainly structural.

In the next section we see that words which do have obvious correlates in the real world are likely to be more readily isolated and recognised than those which do not.

The learning of meanings

Our second landmark which coincides approximately with the 'first word' is the child's first understanding and production of language with meaning.

It is almost invariably assumed that the learning of meaning (particularly the 'labelling' of a concept by a word) can be explained as a simple associative link between the word and the concept, through the child learning the word regularly in association with the object or concept. Whatever the details of the process it is obviously similar to the way Pavlov's dogs learned to produce saliva in response to a bell rather than the sight and smell of food. (See any textbook of psychology, e.g. Woodworth and Schlosberg, 1954.) They had learned that the bell 'meant' food. Whereas the reward of eating the food has been thought necessary for the dog to learn the association, infants learn the names of things without obvious rewards of this kind.

Associative learning does not seem to be essentially different from other forms of pattern learning involving the isolation of redundancy and constancy. The regular correlation of a word and its concept is a form of redundancy quite parallel with the correlation of black clouds with rain or smoke with fire. We may say, further, that all forms of lexical and structural meaning described in the last chapter seem to be learned in the same way. All that is apparently necessary is for a given pattern of sounds or words to occur regularly in association with particular objects, qualities or situations for them to become signals or means of identifying these entities.

As we saw before, the different basic sentence patterns have certain characteristic meanings, not in the sense of reference but in the sense that a question requires an answer, a request requires an action, 'modification' structures alter meanings in certain ways; all these forms and others are signalled by formal cues from the arrangement or inflexion of words.

Even the special cases discussed in connection with transformational grammar (John is easy to please, etc.) can be adequately accounted for as a form of associative or pattern learning. The fact that a particular structure may be interpreted in a certain way only when certain words are used is not different in principle from the fact that 'throw' has the meaning 'give' only in the context of the phrase 'to throw a party', or that deictic words like 'here', 'there', 'this' and 'that' take on particular meanings only in use in particular contexts.

An association or correlation cannot usually be established from one co-occurrence of word and relevant situation. The reason for this is that the particular feature of a situation to which a word applies is almost invariably accompanied by others. Unless the naming convention (described in a moment) is used, there is no means of knowing to which feature the word applies. Normally a child will hear a word – 'milk', say – in several different situations, which will enable him to identify milk as the element common to them all. This may be called *rotation* of meaningful situations.

Structural patterns are amongst the largest patterns in language and are likely to be learned late. Consequently most function words, which are only meaningful in the context of a structure, can only acquire their meanings when the structural patterns of which they form a part, have been learned. Thus in the early stages the child is confronted with some words having obvious correlates in the world of objects, events and situations and others which do not. Our first principle of salience would suggest that the first type of word should be most easily isolated.

The majority of commonly used 'nouns' denote objects and this may explain why such words are amongst the first which children learn. The obvious correlations of many 'verbs' with actions and 'adjectives' with qualities may explain why these types of words tend to be favoured by young children in contrast to most function words. To work out this hypothesis fully we should need an accurate method of measuring salience and we should need to take account of word frequencies. Without these tools and detailed information, it is not possible to test these speculations properly.

To summarise these ideas it is suggested that the 'telegraphic' quality of young children's speech and the preponderance of 'nouns', 'verbs' and 'adjectives' in their vocabularies can probably be explained partly from the fact that adults tend to emphasise these words and partly because, unlike function words, they correlate simply with features of the real world. While the majority of meanings are probably learned in this way there are other processes at work also.

When a child has acquired quite a lot of language the language itself takes on some of the functions which the physical world has, in illustrating the meanings of words. Instead of the speaker and listeners' common cognitive domain being entirely the result of the common physical situation, they may create another schema out of words. They may talk and think about things which happened yesterday or will happen tomorrow or in some other place. If a child hears a new word in such talk he may piece together its meaning from the way it is used in the general conceptual schema:

'I was watching farmer Pritchard try out his new widge-driggler the other day. He had a bit of trouble with the engine at first and when it got started there were clouds of smoke but it really did the job. It was a treat to see it chugging across the field stacking up packets of sprouts ready for the shops and dumping the old plants in neat bundles ready for composting. Of course it's meant some other changes. . . .'

In a similar way children can ask the meaning of a new word and have a direct explanation in words rather than by examples.

The idea of things having names seems to emerge very early even before explanations are possible. Adults may deliberately name things for a child. In this case the association between the name and the concept is made artificially strong. The adult's pointing finger reduces a great deal of the uncertainty about which object is being named and his emphasis of the important word helps the child identify it.

An axiom of pattern learning which fits with ordinary experience and which we shall assume but not try to justify [1] is that a correlation between two 'events' is more easily observed when they occur close together than otherwise. Pavlov's dogs learned that a bell 'meant' food when the food followed within a few seconds. It is most unlikely that they would have learned as well or at all if the delay had been minutes or hours.

In the early stages of the learning of meanings, where meanings are derived from the physical situation, the link between speech and relevant objects and events is very close. When children know enough language to be able to grasp the 'cognitive domain' of a discussion of things in some other place or at some other time the link is just as close. Any unknown word which occurs leaves a hole in the schema which can be filled from context: this teaches the meaning of the new word.

[1] The explanation is likely to be along the same lines as the suggested explanation of why the smaller elements of language are learned before the larger ones.

Referential meaning The details of how children learn the names of concepts is an interesting field which is not much explored. In Chapter 2 we saw how a concept can be said to have a range and a degree of vagueness. Most concepts also have a set of connotations which are not strictly part of the concept but are regularly associated with it.

When, for example, an adult first names an object for a child the child has no direct means of knowing any of these three things. The object in question, perhaps a red leather lady's shoe with low heels and laces, could be grouped in a great variety of ways. It might belong with other red objects, leather objects, footwear in general, things found in cardboard boxes, things with laces, things which come in pairs, etc., etc. In Chapter 2 it was suggested that some groupings are more natural, obvious or salient than others and, as it were, invite themselves to be recognised. If this is the case we would expect the child to take the newly learned names as applying to the concept which is most salient in his view. Where the adult application of the name coincides with this grouping we should find that very few examples will serve to teach the child the word's correct usage. Where the grouping is more artificial or where the concept is essentially strange to the child we will expect to find the child using the word correctly in situations which are very similar or identical to the original one but to make mistakes on other occasions. The correct use of the word may take quite a long time to learn as the child hears it used in a wide variety of situations. In such a case it would be fair to say that the language has taught the child a concept which he did not otherwise recognise. In a sense this is a second way in which 'rotation' of meaningful situations is necessary to establish meanings.

The case of Sam, which we have described, seems to illustrate the distinction between natural and artificial concepts and the need for caution when dealing with words applying to concepts which perhaps he does not possess. In Chapter 10 we shall look again at what these ideas may mean for deaf education.

There has been little work on groupings of naturally occurring entities but there have been some studies using artificially contrived situations to see the kind of approach people use to discover concepts. Bruner, Goodenow and Austin (1956) used cards with patterns on. They did not actually use playing cards but their procedure can form the basis of an amusing game which can be played using playing cards. In one type of experiment all the cards were laid out and the volunteer chose cards singly; on each occasion he asked the investigator whether or not it was an example of the concept which the investigator had in mind e.g. odd-numbered cards of the suit clubs and diamonds. The investigator would say 'yes' or 'no' and the volunteer would form some hypothesis about what the grouping might be and choose the next card appropriately, trying to arrive at the concept in as few choices as possible. These and other experiments gave some useful insights into the kinds of strategies people use for discovering artificial concepts.

The application of such findings to conceptualisation of the 'real world' is likely to be a complicated business but we can get glimpses of young children's thought processes just through hearing them talk. One two-and-a-half year old boy I know learned the word 'pattern' one day as the pattern on some material was pointed out. Later, when asked about another pattern, he felt able to pronounce with great authority that it was not a pattern and was unwilling to be persuaded otherwise. This charming arrogance about his first generalisations will surely disappear with increasing experience. Pattern is probably a rather artificial concept which cannot be abstracted immediately from the variety of different individual patterns.

This is an example of the child applying the word too narrowly. On other occasions he would apply a word too broadly, e.g. he would talk about cows' 'shoes' (meaning hoofs). Children of this age often do not wait to be corrected in their use of words but question adults quite systematically: 'Is that a loaf?' 'Is that a loaf too?', etc. They exhibit active exploration in this field of learning as in many others.

For normal hearing children the process of acquiring concepts and of language probably interact: the recognition of salient natural concepts will help the learning of their verbal labels which the learning of verbal labels for artificial and abstract concepts and observing their range of application will facilitate the learning of these concepts.

While we must profess ignorance about the details of how different particular concepts are learned and generalised, these observations should alert us to possible problems in deaf education when we may be trying to teach language to handle concepts which the child does not have. In this case one is faced with the problem of teaching the concept as well as the name for it. Learning the names of common objects and colours is usually very simple for deaf children; learning time expressions and the lexical meaning of 'propositions' is notoriously difficult and the absence of appropriate concepts may be part of the reason.

Rather than words acting as labels for single concepts they more usually apply to clusters of related and overlapping concepts. In addition many words acquire a 'halo' of connotations or associations, usually of an emotional character. 'Cat' in the strict sense means *felis domesticus* but it may also apply to lions, tigers, leopards, etc.; it has an almost purely connotative use when applied to a certain type of women and it finds related application in such expressions as 'cat-nap', 'cat-suit', 'cat-walk', etc. Most words and expressions in our language gather this enriching patina or moss of related and connotative meanings in each person's experience as new associations are learned throughout life. This is an important feature of language which contributes valuably to its richness and ability to express subtleties of meaning.

7 The acquisition of syntax

Our third main landmark after first imitations and first recognition of meanings is when children start to put words together. This is obviously an important stage on the road to talking in full sentences or other utterances which are acceptable in adult speech. In Chapter 3 we saw how native speakers of a language can easily distinguish acceptable sequences of words from unacceptable sequences (except in some border-line cases) and that they can often do this without being able to give a reason for one sounding 'right' and the other sounding 'wrong'. We also saw that the number of acceptable, 'correct' sentences is gigantic; the vast majority of sentences which a child hears are new to him and, quite probably, new to the world, never having been produced before.

This fact has puzzled linguists and psychologists because on a simple theory of learning by imitation one would expect children to learn to speak in sentences by repeating sentences which they had heard. If this was the case they would have to learn all but a very few sentences after hearing them only once; the number of different sentences to be learned would be huge and they would never be able to produce sentences which they had not heard someone else say. This simple theory is obviously false.

Another theory supposes that children build up sentences word by word by learning, for each word, what other words are likely to follow it. The result can easily turn out something like this:

'rough sea on the most of my word to go for a small thing will you and when was not. . . .' *etc.*

This theory is obviously false as it stands, and variations on it also fail to produce acceptable sentences reliably. This is not to say that children do not learn what words are likely to follow what or that this learning does not help them to form acceptable sentences.

Two features in particular of syntax development have been the focus of attention: the speed at which syntax is mastered and the fact that infants' syntax seems to be rather different from that of adults. Many word or morpheme combinations produced by infants have no counterpart in adult speech ('allgone shoe', 'more high', 'outside more' and the interesting oddities demonstrated by Jean Berko).

Before accepting uncritically that the child's learning of language is in fact very fast in comparison with other forms of learning, we should remember that there is as yet no sure means of measuring the quantity of material learned either in language or other learning. Language is thought to embody a comparatively large amount of material because a linguistic description of language such as Chomsky's involves an extremely bulky and complicated body of rules in spite of the fact that the principle of transformation is basically a very simple idea.

Taken with the apparent failure of a simple imitation theory for learning of grammar these ideas have led Chomsky and his followers to suppose that the principles of learning which have been established in other fields cannot apply to language. It has been proposed, in fact, that children are born with a special Language Acquisition Device (LAD) already present in the brain which has the principles of transformational grammar already built into it. Clearly, the details cannot be present at birth and must be learned because children always learn the language of their environment. The LAD can only have those features of grammar wired into it which are common to all the 1500 languages of the world.

Before accepting this idea we should try to see how far our two principles and their 'riders' may carry us in explaining syntax learning.

Pivot constructions

At this level, by contrast with the phonological level, language is already becoming a useful instrument of communication for the child. Apart from producing single words for non-social reasons the eighteen-month-old child may use words to convey that he wants something ('Teddy') or to point something out ('pussy') or in a very general way to share the pleasure of recognition ('car'). Although a lot of adult guesswork goes into deciding what is intended, single words are very much more useful than undifferentiated cries.

By the same token, two words together add a whole new dimension of possibilities and a corresponding addition to the potency of the child's powers of communication. If a child has a vocabulary of ten words the discovery that they can be used in pairs could in theory produce an immediate addition of forty-five new elements with corresponding refinements of meaning. If we are looking for incentives for language learning and experimentation this is surely one of them. The word 'no' which is fairly useful by itself becomes quite a sensitive tool in the combinations 'no bed', 'no down', (which in this example from Braine's study was used to mean 'Don't put me down') 'no fix', 'no home', etc.

The child need only recognise that adults use word combinations for him to try out his own combinations. We have seen exploration and experimentation at work at earlier stages. Such expressions as 'there high', 'more high', 'no down', 'no pie', 'allgone shoe', etc., which have no counterpart in adult speech are surely examples of the same process at work at this level.

If it is the case that many utterances at this stage are the result of experimental pairings between words already in the child's vocabulary we should ask why these pairings are not made randomly. The pivot construction itself, in which words from the pivot class and words from the open class are never paired with words from the same class, and the fixed position of the pivot words, first or last, show that pairs are not made up at random. To date these features have been taken as evidence of a primitive grammar. The true explanation may be otherwise.

One possible explanatory factor is economy. Having discovered the possibility of putting a particular pair of words together and remembering this new communication tool, less memory capacity is required for a new combination in which only one word is substituted than one in which both have been substituted. Again, it is more economical to keep words in fixed positions than to change them about. In support of this view is the observation that utterances containing the same pivot word tend to appear one after the other and are then followed by another sequence using another pivot word. This is consistent with a process of systematic substitution.

Another factor may lie in the usefulness of the utterances. The pivot words are all words which can be used meaningfully in a wide variety of situations – the child uses them as primitive modifiers. If the child had hit on an expression like 'car bib' neither of these words would usefully develop into pivot words because they could not be used meaningfully except in very restricted situations. 'All', 'no', 'more', 'it', 'there', etc., are words which are much more generally useful and may explain the child's readiness to use them in as many different situations as possible.

Rather than the pivot construction being a primitive grammar it is more probably a by-product of the way children experiment with word combinations; it probably lacks one characteristic feature of an adult's knowledge of grammar – the capacity to distinguish acceptable from unacceptable utterances.

While many first word combinations are likely to be the products of 'invention' others are obviously straightforward borrowings from adult speech e.g. 'close it', 'all gone', 'I see', 'hi Papa', 'more juice', 'all done', 'what's this', etc. A third category is those which seem to owe something to adult models but in which intervening morphemes, normally small and not emphasised, are omitted e.g. 'see (the) mail('s) come', 'it('s) (a) ball', 'it fall(s)', 'there('s) momma', etc. A fourth category, best illustrated by Steven's speech from Braine's study is those utterances which seem to be imitated from adult speech but which show substitutions. The table of Steven's utterances does not show this but he often included a sound like (a), (ta) or (da) at the beginning or middle of many things he said. Steven's family apparently took these as 'I' before 'want', 'see' and 'get', as 'to' in 'want (-) do', as 'it' in 'want (-) high' or 'want (-) up' and as 'is' or 'of' in other contexts. Sometimes they could not identify the appropriate word.

These third and fourth categories seem to be examples of imitation with insufficiently developed sub-skills which we discussed earlier. Where small insignificant morphemes have not yet been mastered they are either omitted or represented by some generalised morpheme which is used for a variety of similar sounding ones.

Many utterances at this stage seem then to be the result of experimentation and of imitation with or without the omission or substitutions which result from incompletely developed sub-skills.

Children's inventive productions are not in themselves going to teach the child to recognise and produce adult patterns. In the same way that adult speech sounds and sound combinations are gradually selected from infants' early babbling, a selective process operates so that those utterances which are completely at odds with what adults say come to be eliminated gradually. If we compare Braine's records with Brown and Fraser's and other records of later speech there seems to be some support for this view: a given word usually forms an acceptable combination with one of its neighbours even if not both.

Later developments

It is especially true now that very much more simple recording of what children say and understand needs to be done before any theory can be examined in detail.

The pivot construction seems to disappear and combinations of words appear which depart from the earlier established 'rules'. If our understanding of pivot constructions is correct this development is the natural result of an increasing memory capacity (both through the growth of the brain and through the development of sub-skills) and ability of the child to use expressions with restricted and special uses.

At the same time more three- and four-word expressions are being used and the length of phrases is steadily increasing. In general we can say that these phrases tend to be 'telegraphic' ('Eve toy big') and that their grammatical acceptability to the adult ear improves steadily. We have already noted two possible explanations of the telegraphic quality. The way adult grammar patterns may develop requires more discussion.

Our first guiding principle has been that our perceptual systems require pattern in the incoming stimulation in order to store it economically. The more regular or redundant the patterns and the more frequently they recur the easier they should be to learn.

The fact that very few sentences occur more than once is the chief obstacle to applying this principle and has been taken to rule our established principles of learning.

Before we abandon these principles too rashly, we should ask whether there are any pattern elements which are relatively constant in the huge variety of sentences. The answer is 'yes' but in a rather special sense: while it is true that there are no apparent patterns in the arrangements of individual words there are very definite patterns in the arrangements of word *classes*, as we saw in Chapter 3. There is a limited set of major word class patterns and these may be used as they stand or may be expanded and rearranged in a limited number of well-defined ways. (Although the rules governing the expansion and elaboration of the basic pattern may be fairly limited in variety they can in practice enable a huge number of permutations or combinations of pattern elements to be produced.)

This looks like a promising start for applying our two principles but there is a further problem: we defined a word class as a group of words the members of which could all be substituted in a given sentence frame without making the sentence unacceptable. If children were exposed to a succession of sentences identical except for substitutions in one position in the frame one could see how they could learn word classes and thus learn to recognise sentences as sequences of word classes; this does not happen. What is needed is a kind of 'boot-straps' operation whereby word classes are learned by reference to sentences patterns and the sentence patterns are learned as sequences of word classes. A possible solution to this apparent paradox is offered in the following scheme, tied as closely as possible to the observed facts of language development.

A theory of syntax learning

Nothing is new under the psychological sun and the theory outlined here is no exception. It is a summary of a growing consensus on the kinds of processes at work when a child learns syntax although there are many differences of opinion about details.

1. *The formation of word classes*

James Jenkins (1965) of the University of Minnesota describes how word classes may be established simply on the basis of shared verbal contexts which may be smaller than whole sentences. The example he gives is of two sequences of words ABCXD and ABCYD and he suggests that X and Y may be classified together because they occur in the same context. A more realistic example might be that of a child hearing, on different occasions: 'a car', 'the car' and 'your car'. Since 'a', 'the' and 'your' have all been followed by 'car' they should be classified together. (They are in fact all function words, group A, in Fries's classification.) The unit '—— car' can be termed a 'test frame'.

George Kiss (1972) of the Medical Research Council's Speech and Communication Unit in Edinburgh has analysed samples of English in this way (using a computer to do the laborious counting and arithmetic involved). He made the working assumption for the sake of simplicity that each word's context would be taken to be merely the word following. After all the different contexts had been counted up the words could be classified into groups by similarity of context. These groups corresponded rather closely to the parts of speech recognised by linguists. The groups were not sharply defined categories and this is theoretically important as we shall see.

A result like this does not of course prove that this is what children do but it does demonstrate that a rather simple principle is sufficient to explain the phenomenon of word classification. Other factors may operate also. Thus we noted in Chapter 3 that certain suffixes or prefixes of words are typically associated with particular word classes (e.g. these Class 3/Class 1 contrasts: baggy/bag, cloudy/cloud, dirty/dirt, dusty/dust, funny/fun, etc. Many other examples appear in Fries's book). Another thing which probably helps children recognise word classes is the fact that most common Class 1 words are the names of objects, most common Class 2 words describe actions and most common Class 3 words denote qualities. The conceptual distinctions between objects, actions and qualities correlates with syntactic distinctions.

The most striking evidence that children do use snippets of adult speech, smaller than complete sentences, as test frames for establishing word classes comes from Weir's study. Several examples were given in Chapter 5 of such systematic substitutions and evidence was noted that some of the utterances were mimicked from adults. We also observed that utterances were not only related by similarity of verbal context but by similarity of meaning or similarity of situation. Further evidence for classification will be considered in the section on generalisation.

2. *Assembling patterns of word classes – chunking and hierarchical organisation*

Having established, at least tentatively, a set of word classes, the next question is how sentence patterns are built up from these. We have seen already that sentences are unlikely to be built up as a simple chain of words each word associated merely with its immediate neighbours. The same probably applies to word classes.

The most widely accepted alternative, which seems to have been first suggested by Karl Lashley (1951) and Miller, Gallanter and Pribram (1960), is of layers similar to or the same as linguists' immediate constituents analysis described in Chapter 3. The notion of hierarchical organisation is a unifying principle which was discussed in Chapter 1 in connection with non-language skills, in Chapter 6 related to pre-syntax skills of imitation and production and here occurs again as applied to the learning of syntax.

Also in Chapter 1 we saw how the memory store should not be envisaged as a tank which can be filled up until suddenly it can hold no more. We have a limited memory capacity only in the sense that the maximum number of items or parcels of information which we can retain for a few seconds and repeat back is about seven; the amount of detail in each parcel seems to be irrelevant. As George Miller showed so clearly, if we are faced with the task of remembering more than seven items we have to group them into 'chunks' to reduce the effective number of items. These chunks may themselves be grouped into larger chunks and these perhaps into larger ones – a hierarchy of chunks in fact.

In its simplest form the theory may be stated thus: that syntactic patterns are learned by successive grouping or chunking of small units into larger units and these into larger units, the final organisation corresponding to the immediate constituents structure of adult language; the units are to be conceived not as particular words or parts of words but as classes of words or morphemes.

Before considering evidence there is one point to be clarified. It does seem necessary for the twin processes of classification and hierarchical chunking to march hand-in-hand. A simple frame such as 'the ——' can be completed by 'car', 'bus', 'house', etc. (i.e. Class 1 words) but can also be completed by 'green', 'big', 'nice', etc. (i.e. Class 3 words). If 'the ——' was the only frame available for classifying these words then they would all end up in one class. The particular problem, however, is what happens when the child has reached the stage of needing to handle not merely 'the green' or 'the bus' but the arrangement together of 'the', 'green' and 'bus'. What has to be learned is that following 'the', 'green bus' as a unit is equivalent to 'bus' (or 'blue bus' or 'double-decker bus' or 'bus with the engine at the back', etc.) but, following 'green', 'the bus' is *not* an acceptable substitute for 'bus'. In other words it must be assumed that classification operates not merely on words but on larger chunks. It must also be assumed that these larger chunks are registered not necessarily as sequences of particular words (although this may happen) but as sequences of *classes* of words. The concurrent operation of classification and some kind of integration was recognised by Roger Brown and Ursula Bellugi-Klima (1964) in their study of young children's utterances:

'In summary, one major aspect of the development of general structure in child speech is progressive differentiation in the usage of words and therefore progressive differentiation of syntactic classes. At the same time, however, there is an integrative process at work. From the first, an occasional noun phrase occurred as a component of some larger construction. At first these noun phrases were just two words long and the range of positions in which they could occur was small.

With time the noun phrases grew longer, were more frequently used, and were used in a greater range of positions. The noun phrase structure as a whole, in all the permissible combinations of modifiers and nouns, was assuming the combinatorial privileges enjoyed by nouns in isolation.'

As examples they quote such expressions as 'That (flower)' in contrast with 'That (a blue flower)' or 'Where (ball) go?' compared with 'Where (the puzzle) go?' and again 'Put (hat) on' as against 'Put (the red hat) on.' The brackets mark the noun or the noun phrase and illustrate how the two seem to be interchangeable in a given context.

Classification not only operates on elements larger than words but also on morphemes and speech sounds. Jean Berko's study, discussed in the next section, illustrates the classification of morphemes. The terms 'allophone' and 'phoneme' mark the distinction, long recognised, between a particular speech sound and the class in which it belongs.

The main line of evidence for hierarchical organisation is through attempts to show that the immediate constituents structure of sentences is psychologically real. The most striking of several experiments which have provided such evidence is one by Neal Johnson (1965) of Ohio State University. His volunteers learned sets of sentences by rote. When he tested them he kept a record of all the errors and then worked out a figure for each word to show how many times it was wrongly remembered given that the previous word had been remembered correctly. A typical result is shown here:

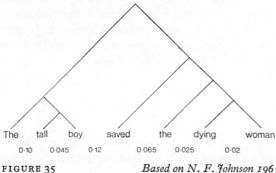

| The | tall | boy | saved | the | dying | woman |
| 0·10 | 0·045 | 0·12 | 0·065 | 0·025 | 0·02 |

FIGURE 35   *Based on N. F. Johnson 1965*

The figures are placed between the words but indicate how difficult the word to the right of each figure was to recall given that the one to the left was correct. The higher the figure, the more the errors. A fairly uncontroversial marking of immediate constituents is shown.

The point of interest is that the chance of an error corresponds very closely with the height of the corresponding 'node' in the tree diagram. Most errors occurred at the 'boy-saved' transition which is the major break in the sentence structure. The error score for the 'dying-woman' transition is smaller than for 'the-dying' and this in turn is smaller then the error score for 'saved-the'. The heights of the corresponding nodes follow the same order. Similarly the error rate for 'the-tall' is larger than for 'tall-boy'. Comparisons between the two major groups ('the tall boy' and 'saved the dying woman') do not show the pattern so clearly, but more of this in a moment.

Johnson's suggested explanation is that before a word can be recalled the parcel of chunk in which it occurs must be unpacked or decoded. Thus 'saved' cannot be retrieved until the whole 'saved the dying woman' unit has been decoded, but to retrieve 'dying' only 'dying woman' has to be decoded. The bigger the unit to be decoded the greater is the chance of an error during decoding.

Although it is not immediately relevant to the present issue it is appropriate to mention here another study on phrase structure which has a bearing on our earlier observation that immediate constituents analyses are not always as clear cut as they might seem. Edwin Martin (1970) of the University of Michigan questioned whether there was not room for variation in the degree of 'compactness' of word groups of of a given 'level'. His experimental subjects were asked to examine several sentences and mark what were to them the intuitively natural groupings of the words. Martin then applied a formula to the results which, for each sentence and for the whole group of sixty subjects, enabled him to draw a phrase structure diagram in which the heights of the nodes showed the compactness of the groups – the lower the node the more compact the group. This study is not in itself evidence for hierarchical structure because the formula could only be applied on the prior *assumption* that grouping was hierarchical.

One set of sentences, the members of which would be given identical phrase structures in a linguistic analysis, was these:

1. Children who attend regularly appreciate lessons greatly.
2. Waiters who remember well serve orders correctly.
3. Pupils who read slowly teach laymen now.
4. Men who arrive hurriedly give donations also.
5. Carpenters who build competently command ransoms nowadays.

The phrase structures obtained from the results are shown in the diagram below. Notice that even when two sentences have the same overall structure (e.g. the first and fourth sentences) the compactness of corresponding groups can be quite different. Thus 'give donations' in the fourth sentence seems to be much more compact than 'appreciate lessons' in the first. Another thing to notice is that when two or more adjacent nodes have the same height then, in effect, they become one node with three or more branches; this is a possibility which we noted in Chapter 3.

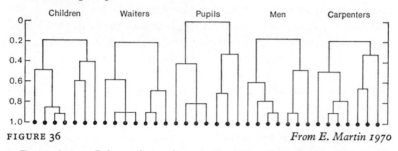

FIGURE 36   *From E. Martin 1970*

Returning to Johnson's study we may speculate whether his transition error counts might not also give a measure of compactness. The assumption was that 'tall boy' and 'dying woman' were both not only lowest level groups but also equally compact groups. The results suggest that 'dying woman' is in fact the more compact of the two groups. This observation does not alter the fact that the overall structure remains the same as a conventional linguistic marking. It would be interesting to know whether structure and compactness measures derived by Johnson's method for a given sentence were the same as those derived by Martin's method for the same sentence.

The proposed combination of a classification process with a hierarchical chunking process seems fairly straightforward at first sight but the logical implications are extremely complex. To find out whether such processes are in principle capable of reproducing the major features of syntax learning it will probably be necessary to use a computer to carry out the logical manipulations involved. The redundancy net described in Chapter 6 is almost the simplest possible version of a hierarchical chunking process and it seems to be a useful preliminary model of segmentation. Whether it can be used in conjunction with a classification programme to reproduce the segmental structure of sentences rather than words remains to be seen.

The two processes are rather similar in their initial stages. In both, counts are made of what elements follow what. Then, in both, these counts are converted into transition probabilities and finally, in both, all transition probabilities below a certain level are discarded. In any theory one should avoid postulating two processes when one will do. These two processes may prove simply to be two facets of one basic process.

3. *The generalisation of syntactic patterns*

To understand and produce language a child must necessarily do more than store a record of what he has heard. As has been said, the vast majority of sentences are new combinations of words which have never been produced before. Brown and Bellugi-Klima write: '. . . a child's linguistic competence extends far beyond this sum total of sentences [which he has heard]. All children are able to understand and construct sentences they have never heard but which are nevertheless well formed, well formed in terms of general rules that are implicit in the sentences the child has heard. Somehow, then, every child processes the speech to which he is exposed so as to induce from it a latent structure. This latent rule structure is so general that a child can spin out its implications all his life long. . . .'

The key word is 'induce'. As with all other kinds of perception we are able to extrapolate or generalise from a finite set of examples and predict or expect future examples following the same pattern.

The mechanism of classification is also the mechanism of inductive inference. In our earlier example 'a', 'the' and 'your' were classified together because they all occurred in the frame '—— car'. If the child now hears '. . . a bus . . .' then his previously established classification will allow him to infer that 'the bus' and 'your bus' are acceptable combinations without actually having heard them.

Martin Braine (1963b) has conducted experiments with ten-year-old schoolchildren learning a simple 'language' of nonsense syllables and has demonstrated that generalisations of this kind can occur. Most of the children made correct generalisations of the patterns but very few could give reasons for their choices of 'words': the pattern learning was unconscious.

A more real life piece of evidence is Berko's study described in the last chapter. The children produced such forms as 'ringed', 'singed' and 'cutted' obviously by analogy with regular verbs such as 'kicked', 'batted', etc. Similarly 'mouses', 'leafs', 'gooses', 'knifes' and 'halfs' have been generalised from the common pattern of adding '-s' to make a plural. Other responses showed an awareness by the child that something was odd about the words but they did not quite know what. Some irregular words like 'sheep' do not add '-s' in the plural. This may explain some children's failure to add '-s' to 'mouse' and 'goose'. Interestingly enough the children who failed to pluralise 'mouse' by adding '-s' were also the ones who did not add it to 'goose'.

These observations illustrate another point. Children not only generalise their classifications, they *over*-generalise them. In other words they do not wait until their classification scheme for morphemes, words and phrases has been refined to an adult level of detail before applying it. They pitch in straight away, however crude their classifications might be, trying out new combinations of elements, inventing new forms. Invention, recombination or reconstruction is at work from the very beginning in speech sounds, words, pivot constructions and larger constructions. The examples given earlier from Brown and Bellugi-Klima's study illustrate this point: 'That (a blue flower)' seems to have been constructed by analogy with 'That (flower)'. 'Put (hat) on' seems again to be formed as an analogy of 'Put (the red hat) on'. As with pivot constructions the large majority of the larger utterances can be viewed as imitations of adult speech with or without omissions or substitutions (reflecting incompletely developed sub-skills), with or without inventive combinations of elements:

'*D*ats your / a car.'
'*D*ats a / your car.'
'A / *d*at's cheese.'
'Fast / the car.'
'The car / fast.'
or possibly: 'The car (is) fast.'
'*D*is hammer / other one.'
'Why not / cracker can't talk.'
'Why / I didn't see something.'
'Why not / you are looking / right place.'
'No want / stand head.'
'No more / sharpen it.'
'Book / say no.'
'That / no / Mommy.'
'There / no squirrels.'
or, perhaps, 'There (are) no squirrels.'
'You didn't / caught me'.

These are just a few 'ungrammatical' examples from the records of Roger Brown's team. Supposed substitutions have been italicised, possible omissions bracketed and obliques used to mark the probable division between the elements being combined.

Where an utterance has to be divieed into more than two parts one may ask whether it has been constructed all at one level or whether some of the elements had been previously joined and then such larger units combined with others. Thus 'Where / milk / go?' and 'Where / horse / go?' appear to have been formed as 'Where / (milk / go)?' and 'Where / (horse / go)?' because 'Ball go' was recorded as an isolated construction.

Semantically and syntactically anomalous sentences – again It will be recalled that certain kinds of sentence falling on the borderline between the grammatical and the ungrammatical are sometimes said to be semantically anomalous because they are thought to break rules of semantics or else they are described as syntactically anomalous because they seem to break rules of grammar. To construct such a sentence it is only necessary to take a common sentence pattern, as expressed in terms of the major word classes, and scan the word class lists for words which make 'odd' combinations like these:

The	boy	kicks	a	ball.
A	I	2	A	I
The	table	shoots	a	democracy.
The	freedom	flies	a	dog.
The	bicycle	walks	a	suspicion.

The purpose of introducing this matter here is to point the parallel with children's ungrammatical utterances and also to suggest why such sentences should be described both as semantically and syntactically anomalous.

George Kiss's study underlined the fact, already recognised in the necessity for sub-grouping of word classes, that word classes (and this no doubt applies to classes of phonemes, morphemes and phrases) are not sharply defined categories but have a gradation at their boundaries. In the 'core' are those words which belong firmly in the class and round the core are concentric zones having progressively less of the contextual qualities defining the class. Every word has a special set of words with which it is commonly combined, a further set which it may be combined with in exceptional cases and the remaining words with which it is most unlikely to be combined. If an adult deliberately chooses words from the latter two categories he will produce odd sentences much in the same way that a child does when his classification system is still only crude.

The fact that there are regularities in the world of objects, actions and qualities, etc., means that corresponding regularities are partly but not completely reproduced in the language which is used to describe that world. The physical nature of tables is such that we most commonly wish to say that a table 'is' or a table 'stands' or a table 'bears', etc. Because tables are not normally constructed in such a way that they can shoot means that such an expression as 'the table shoots . . .' is semantically odd. But the very fact that such a combination of words rarely occurs means that it is also syntactically odd. 'Table', 'chair', 'sink', 'piano', etc., share many contexts (e.g. 'is', 'stands', 'bears', 'supports', etc.) and are thus grouped into the major Class 1 group. But the physical nature of, say, a sink is such that we can say that it 'fills', 'empties' or 'gurgles'; we would not be likely to say this about a chair or a table.

This general concordance between semantic and syntactic rules is quite often broken as many semantically odd expressions have come to be accepted by usage as syntactically correct. Examples are 'to shoot a question', 'to buy time', 'to get ploughed in an examination', etc.

The 'creativity' of language It is sometimes thought that people's ability to construct a large variety of sentences stems from a mysterious, metaphysical 'creativity'. While there is certainly cause for wonder at the marvellous productions of creative genius through the ages it would be wrong to class ordinary sentence productivity with them. An astronomical variety of sentences can be made simply from permutations of elements within the constraints imposed by morpheme, word and phrase classes. Using optional elements, one basic sentence like 'The man chopped wood' can be expanded in many different ways:

1. The *tall* man chopped wood.
2. The tall man chopped wood *in the garden*.
3. The tall man *who was wearing a flat cap* chopped wood in the garden.
4. The tall man who was wearing a flat cap *on his head* chopped wood in the garden. *etc.*

Substitute 'boy' for man or 'curly haired' for tall, or both, and a whole new set of sentences becomes available.

In a sense our ability to produce a large variety of sentences is not more mysterious than the ability of a kaleidoscope to produce an infinite variety of patterns from a finite set of coloured chips.

In this chapter and the last one we have followed a few explanatory principles through the different stages and aspects of language learning.

At all times we meet the strong tendency to sift out redundancy or pattern in language. The small elements tend to be isolated first and then used as building blocks for assembling larger patterns. These in turn are used in the recognition and recording of still larger elements. At the same time these elements at all levels are grouped into classes mainly on the basis of shared contexts, verbal or conceptual.

Such classification affords the means to generalise the observed patterns to new constructions. The tendency for children to produce new inventive combinations of elements within the constraints of their classification scheme is present from the earliest stages. Ultimately it is responsible for the rich productivity of adult language.

Part Two

8 The problem of deafness

The main concern of Part Two is to examine various ways in which the harmful effect of deafness on language development may be overcome, drawing, where appropriate, on psycholinguistic principles as discussed in the first part. As a preliminary it is as well to give a sketch of hearing, deafness and speech perception in elementary terms and some account of the history of the education of the deaf so that we may see what past thinking on this subject has to offer. Those who are familiar with these matters are invited to give this chapter sufficient attention to see where emphasis has been laid: certain points are picked up again in later chapters.

Hearing and speech perception

The figure shows in a diagrammatic form the view one would get of one ear if someone's head was cut in half by a vertical cut passing

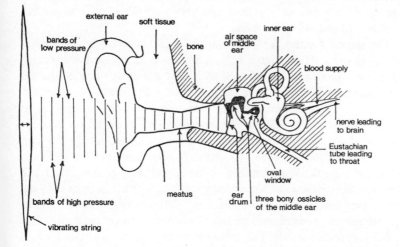

FIGURE 37   *Based on Davis and Silverman (eds.) 1947*

through both ears! To one side is shown a source of sound, say a violin string. The sound is produced by the rapid backwards and forwards motion or vibration of the string. Every movement towards the ear compresses the air on that side of the string and a band of compressed air travels towards the ear. Every movement away from the ear produces a band of low pressure which follows the high pressure band. The flaps on the sides of one's head may help to trap these pressure waves a little and feed them towards the ear 'hole', or meatus. The eardrum, a thin piece of skin stretched across the bottom of the meatus responds to the pressure waves so that each high pressure band pushes it in and it moves out to accommodate each low pressure band. The three small bones in the middle ear transmit these backward and forward movements to an 'oval window', similar to the ear drum, which is the beginning of the inner ear.

The details of the inner ear need not concern us except to say that the backwards and forwards movements are changed to corresponding nerve impulses in the auditory nerve which travel to the brain where they are analysed and interpreted. The mechanism of the inner ear is quite complicated and delicate and it is surprising that things do not go wrong with it more often than they do. There are three main features of the sound wave which are detected and transmitted to the brain.

The first is the frequency with which the high and low pressure bands follow each other. Rapid vibrations, say at 4000 oscillations or cycles per second, are heard as high pitched sounds. Slow vibrations, say at 250 cycles per second (c/s or Hertz (Hz)) are heard as low pitched sounds – Middle C is 261.6 c/s.

The second feature is the size of the oscillations or the amount of energy in them. High energy sounds are heard as loud and low energy sounds are faint. The decibel (dB) scale of sound energy levels, which is in common use is shown in the chart opposite with illustrative examples.

The third very important feature of sound is what we hear as its quality or timbre. By this is meant the difference one can hear between an oboe and a violin, a woman's voice and a boy's individual voices, or, say, different vowels spoken by one person all of the same loudness and pitch but none the less sounding different. Differences in timbre result from the fact that few sounds are simple oscillations at one frequency but are varying mixtures of sounds of many different frequencies. Usually one frequency predominates which allows one to recognise the pitch at which say, someone sings but there are many other frequencies too.

The sound spectrographs shown in Plate 1 are made by a

Plates

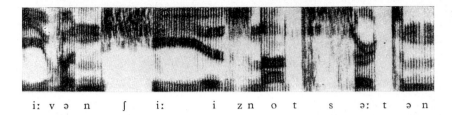

i: v ə n   ʃ   i: i   z n   o   t   s   ə: t   ə n

1. (*a*) A sound spectrograph of the sentence 'Even she is not certain'.

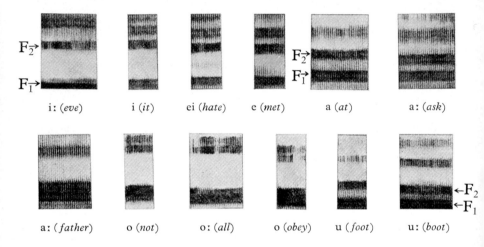

i: (*eve*)   i (*it*)   ei (*hate*)   e (*met*)   a (*at*)   a: (*ask*)

a: (*father*)   o (*not*)   o: (*all*)   o (*obey*)   u (*foot*)   u: (*boot*)

(*b*) & (*c*) A selection of vowel patterns produced by sound spectrography.

Note: The American pronunciation of the vowel in 'ask' is, unlike the southern English pronunciation, mid-way between 'at' and 'father'.

 [g]

 [b]

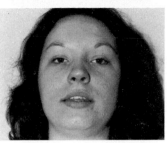 [j]

 [p]

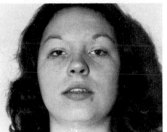 [n]

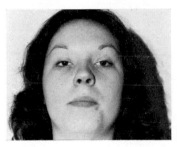 [m]

Group 1

Group 2

2. The lip-patterns of speech phonemes (excluding dipthongs and affricates). A phoneme in one of groups 1–3 is very similar to others in the same group.

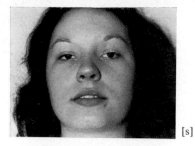 [s]

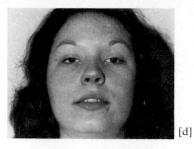 [d]

 [ʃ]

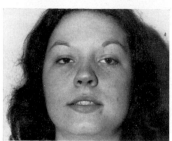 [z]

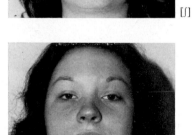 [t]

2. *Group* 3

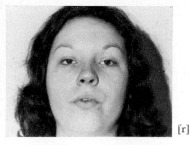

[r]

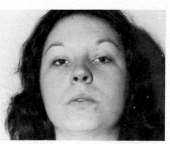

[u:]

[u]

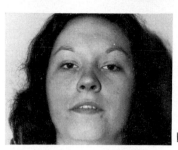

[v]

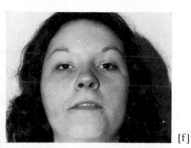

[f]

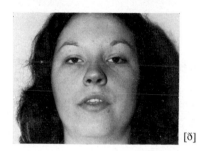

[ð]

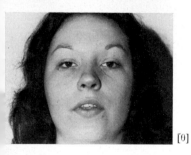

[θ]

2. *Group* 4

 [i]

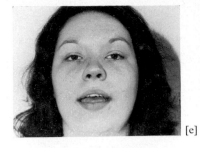 [e]

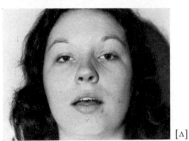 [ʌ]

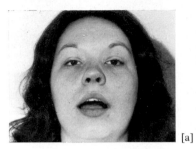 [a]

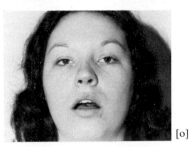 [o]

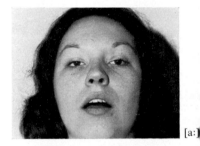 [a:]

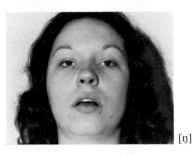 [ŋ]

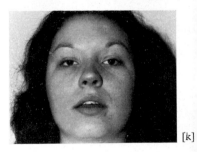 [k]

 [h]

2. *Group 5*

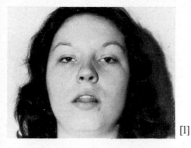

[l]

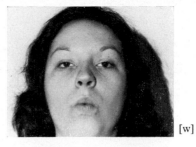

[w]

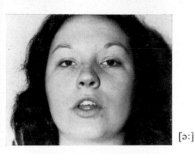

[ə:]

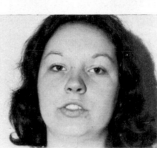

[ʒ]

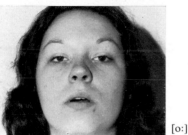

[o:]

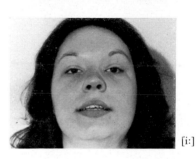

[i:]

2. *Others*

Bad

Bed

Big

Bird

Boat-Cruise

Bored

3. Manual Signs.

machine which can separate out the different frequencies and show how much of each is present by the density or blackness of the marking. High frequencies are shown at the top passing through middle to low

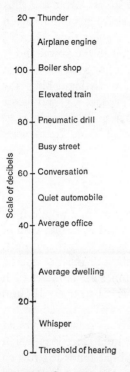

FIGURE 38
From Stevens and Davis 1936

frequencies at the bottom. These spectrographs have been extremely useful in studies of how we recognise speech sounds and perceive speech generally. It is not appropriate to give a full account here of this interesting work but we can briefly indicate that the two lowest predominant frequencies of speech sounds play an important part in distinguishing these sounds. The two lowest and most pronounced bands are marked by arrows on the spectrograph and labelled F_1 and F_2, meaning formant 1 and formant 2. The relationship between these formants distinguishes the vowels. Thus in the vowel [iː] as in *eve*, F_1 is low frequency and F_2 is high frequency; in the vowel [a] as in *at* F_1

and F_2 are close together and both relatively high frequency; in the vowel [uː] as in *boot* they are both close together again but at a relatively low frequency. Other vowels have the two formants at intermediate positions. The plosive consonants [p, b, t, d, k, g] which are formed by blocking the air stream and then releasing it are in fact silent and thus identical at the moment they are formed. As the air begins to flow again and the following vowel is pronounced there is a short time when F_2 has not yet taken up the frequency corresponding to the vowel and is moving from another higher or lower frequency. It has been shown that this brief transition is critically important for distinguishing the plosive consonants. Fricative consonants [r, h, f, v, s, z, ʃ, ʒ] and nasals [m, n, ŋ] do not usually have formants but their frequencies are spread over a wide zone. The particular distribution of these frequencies enables us to distinguish these various sounds.

Deafness and audiometry

As we have said the ear and particularly the inner ear is a wonderfully delicate apparatus. It is just as well that it is packed in a solid case of bone. Many different things can go wrong, some commoner than others. Occasionally a child may be born without ear flaps or meatus leading to the ear drum and middle ear. Provided the inner ear is intact such a child can hear moderately quiet sounds (as quiet as 50 to 60 dB) and it is not too difficult for a surgeon to restore almost normal hearing. Eardrums or the middle ear bones may be missing or broken; in young children the middle ear may become filled with fluid secretions which prevent the bones moving properly; sometimes bone tends to grow so that the middle ear bones become cemented into the oval window and cannot move. This is known as otosclerosis. Most of the defects of the outer and middle ears can now be cured fairly reliably by surgery which is a considerable achievement considering that the middle ear is only one cubic centimetre in volume and most operations are conducted through the meatus. Deafness resulting from defects of this kind is known as *conductive deafness*. The effect is usually a simple one in that sounds merely have to be louder to be heard. Even without treatment sounds as quiet as 50 to 60 dB can just be heard except for some cases of otosclerosis. There is not usually much distortion of pitch or timbre and a hearing aid which makes sounds louder can be very helpful.

Defects of the inner ear, or the nerve tract leading to the brain or even parts of the brain itself are different. Sometimes such a thing as a tumour pressing on the nerve can be removed surgically but the inner ear itself is too intricate and fragile for operations. Furthermore this deafness which is known as *nerve deafness* or *perceptive deafness* is not usually simply a case of sounds being fainter. Frequently the mechanisms concerned with recording pitch and timbre are upset and these cannot easily be compensated for by the amplifying effect of a hearing aid as we shall see. Commonly conductive and perceptive deafnesses occur together.

Audiometry, the assessment and measurement of hearing defects, uses a variety of techniques, the most easily applied being pure tone audiometry. The sounds used are pure tones each of one frequency only without other frequencies mixed with it. They are presented to the patient either through a loudspeaker or through headphones and the loudness is adjusted to find the level at which the patient can only just hear the sound being used. 'Thresholds' of this kind are measured for a number of different frequencies and the results are presented as an audiogram thus:

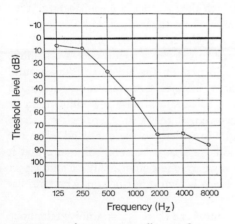

FIGURE 39. A pure tone audiogram for one ear showing a moderate/severe hearing loss

In this case the patient could, in his right ear, only just hear sounds of 100 c/s at 50 dB above the normal threshold (which is marked as 0), and this is described as a 'loss' of 50 dB at 100 c/s. The downward slope with the greatest loss in the high frequencies is a common shape for an audiogram, the part of the inner ear dealing with high frequencies being most sensitive to damage.

Pure tone audiometry is an important part of the picture of a patient's defective hearing but it is not everything. It records the level at which sounds can just be detected but this is not the level at which sounds can be used usefully. To make use of sounds so that different types of sound may be discriminated easily they must be above threshold. Usually the loudness of the sound as experienced by the person increases steadily as the intensity of the sound is increased above threshold level but this is not always the case. Sometimes when the intensity is increased slightly above threshold it can jump from being barely audible to being quite loud or even painful. This is called *recruitment*. Conversely the sound intensity may be increased above threshold but the subjective loudness does not increase much and the sound remains barely audible. These effects mean that two people with the same apparent hearing loss may be quite different in their ability to use sound.

An aspect of audiometry which has not received much attention yet is the nature of the 'threshold' itself. It is now fairly well established, largely as a result of the work of Swets, Tanner and Birdsall, (see Swets, 1964) that the concept of a sharp 'cut-off' point above which sounds are heard and below which they are not is unsatisfactory. Like information theory this is an area where theoretical work developed in connection with communication engineering has had fruitful results in psychology. Whether or not one can detect a sound over a telephone line or other channel depends in part on the amount of background noise and general distortion there is. When the sound to be detected is about the same intensity as the background noise it is difficult to be sure whether or not it has occurred. Rather than there being a sharp cut-off there is a threshold zone in which, on the one hand when the sound is relatively loud, one can be almost but not quite sure that it occurred ranging through cases where one cannot really be sure either way down to those cases where one is almost but not quite certain that it did not occur.

It is now appreciated that even where there is not a noisy telephone line to cope with there is always background 'noise' in varying degrees and from various sources including the nervous system itself. Noise is a technical term in this context used to cover all forms of distortion.

An interesting aspect of this phenomenon is that in this threshold zone our decision about whether or not a sound occurred depends partly on the loudness of the sound and the background noise but also partly on the effects of the decision. The shooting behaviour of a sentry guarding a military camp will vary with the penalties attaching to (*a*) shooting a friend accidentally (*b*) letting an enemy through accidentally.

If he is threatened with court martial for (*a*) but not for (*b*) he will make doubly sure of any faint movement or sound in the dark before shooting and vice versa.

It is usually accepted that most audiograms are only reliable within a zone of 5 or 10 dB on each side of the 'threshold' and part of the reason may be variation in an individual's desire to be completely certain about whether he heard a sound or not. While a narrow threshold zone probably applies in most cases and is not of great practical significance it is possible that in cases of nerve deafness where background 'noise' in the nervous system is a much bigger factor than usual, the threshold zone is much wider than usual and otherwise unexplained wide variations in threshold result.

Because of the recognised limitations of pure tone audiometry particularly in assessing a person's ability to distinguish speech sounds and other sounds of varying timbre other tests are commonly used. A pure tone audiogram enables one to make a rough assessment of someone's ability to discriminate speech sounds but for the reasons discussed above and through insufficient knowledge of the speech perception process it is not yet possible to make an accurate prediction of how well speech will be heard.

A much more direct approach is to use speech itself, the procedure being to use specially prepared lists of words or sentences which the tester speaks and the patient tries to repeat. Lips are concealed from the patient to avoid any clues from this source and the average intensity is recorded on a meter. The scoring may be in terms of whole items, right or wrong, or in terms of individual speech sounds. Three speech audiograms are shown here:

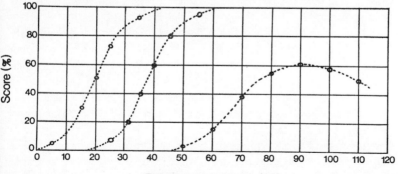

FIGURE 40

The first curve is typical of someone with normal hearing. When the speech is very faint, 10 dB or less, a very small percentage of the items is correct. As the intensity is increased the percentage correct rises to 50 per cent at 20 dB and levels off at 100 per cent around 35 to 40 dB.

The second curve is for someone with a simple conductive loss. The curve is a similar shape but a given score requires speech to be about 15 to 20 dB louder than for someone with normal hearing. An 100 per cent score is easily obtained by making the speech loud enough.

The third curve is typical of someone with perceptive or nerve deafness. In the beginning stages it is similar to the other curves, increasing intensity increases the score. However a point is reached where the score will rise no further and any extra amplification makes the hearing of speech actually worse. An 100 per cent score can never be obtained. This phenomenon reflects the effects of damage in the inner ear. Sounds are not merely fainter, they are also distorted; amplification not only increases the loudness of the speech but also increases the distortion produced by the faulty inner ear. The effect is similar to what may happen in a faulty radio where a turn of the volume control knob makes the programme louder but at the same time increases the background hum and crackle so that there is no benefit from the extra volume. The significance of this will be discussed later. A more technical account of these matters is available in Broadbent and Stephens (1970).

From the point of view of the assessment of individual patients speech audiometry also has its limitations. In particular it is obviously no use for someone without speech or language, which means the majority of young deaf children. Without some prior acquaintance with the words being used the patient has no means of deciding which word has been spoken.

In such cases then, if we wish to test a child's ability to discriminate speech patterns, yet another approach must be used. A common method is to say two 'words' (which may be nonsense syllables) which differ in only one phoneme (e.g. 'pat' and 'cat') and ask whether they are the same or different. There are various practical problems, including that of explaining the task to a child with no grasp of language, but most of these can be overcome in various ways. However there remains a theoretical limitation on the results of such tests because failure on such tasks does not demonstrate that the person is incapable of discriminating speech. As we saw in Chapter 6 the discrimination of speech sounds owes a great deal to learning. An important point is that audiometry of all kinds, except possibly some new techniques presently being developed, is particularly difficult with young children up to 3 or 4 or even older. The results of any tests have to be treated with great caution because if a young child fails to show any sign of hearing a sound this does not necessarily mean that he does not hear it.

The upshot of all this is that audiometric tests of various kinds are not yet capable of giving us more than a rough guide to a young child's potential to discriminate speech patterns and thus to comprehend and produce speech. Work on speech perception has made big strides but it is still early days to relate these results in detail to types and degrees of hearing loss. There are, however, some generalisations which seem to hold fairly reliably:

1. The most important frequencies for speech perception seem to be between 500 and 200 c/s (Hertz). Provided the losses are not too severe in this range there seems to be a good chance that speech and language can be acquired. Losses in this range can be compensated for somewhat if there is reasonable hearing in lower *and* higher frequencies.
2. Where the high frequencies are comparatively poorly heard, which is common, certain consonants which are distinguished by high frequencies tend to be either omitted or confused with other similar consonants. This is particularly true of [s], which is frequently omitted in deaf peoples' speech, and of other unvoiced fricative consonants [f, θ, ʃ].
3. As a general rule vowels have more energy and intensity than consonants so that errors are more likely in recognising the latter.
4. Where nerve deafness exists, which is the case in the vast majority of children whose hearing is bad enough to require special education, it is particularly difficult to correlate audiograms with capacity to discriminate speech sounds. The distorting effect of damage in the inner ear is likely to vary from individual to individual. This is a possible explanation of one result of a study of fifteen-year-old deaf children by Dr Esther Simpson (1963) who was able to find pairs of children in which all relevant factors (hearing, loss, age of onset, home background, I.Q., etc.) seemed to be the same but one of the pair had comparatively good speech and the other's was bad. In spite of these problems there is still a clear broad correlation between the degree of loss and the

ability to acquire speech (which is formally confirmed by such studies as that by Brannon & Murray (1966)) and language. Losses may be roughly classified thus:

$$\left.\begin{array}{l} 25\text{--}40 \text{ dB} - \text{slight/moderate} \\ 40\text{--}60 \text{ dB} - \text{moderate/severe} \\ 60\text{--}85 \text{ dB} - \text{severe} \\ 85/90 + - \text{profound.} \end{array}\right\} \begin{array}{l} \text{partially} \\ \text{hearing} \end{array}$$

These losses are usually taken to be the average loss for the frequencies 500, 1000 and 2000 Hz. Children with slight losses are likely to develop speech normally even without a hearing aid. Children with moderate or severe losses stand a fair to poor chance of developing speech and language if they have hearing aids and other amplification. Profoundly deaf children are those that would popularly be called 'stone' deaf and will be most unlikely to develop speech or language without special help. Even in this group, however, it has been shown that those with the greatest amount of residual hearing (smallest losses) stand a better chance of acquiring some speech than those with very little residual hearing. Conductive defects and perceptive defects may both contribute to losses of any degree but any loss greater than 60 dB is bound to have a perceptive component.

It will be clear from this discussion that deafness is rarely a case of nothing being heard and there is a sense in which every case is different. However the common thread linking all these cases is the harmful effect on language and speech caused by the hearing loss. In such a situation the best strategy is to consider the extreme or 'pure' case of complete deafness; if we can find a satisfactory solution to this problem this is bound to help us solve the less severe problems. In the remainder of the book we shall be concerned chiefly with profound deafness.

The problem of deafness

The problem of deafness is simply stated: if a child cannot hear the differences between phonemes, morphemes, words and larger syntactic patterns he cannot learn to recognise these patterns and to associate them with meanings. Even if he can understand language through some other medium, perhaps lip-reading, he cannot hear his own voice and cannot shape his own speech productions to match those of others.

A child born profoundly deaf and brought up without special help or tuition will certainly be unable to produce speech (although he can make noises with the speech organs) and will in all likelihood be unable to comprehend speech or language in any form. Hence the now unfashionable descriptions, 'deaf and dumb' or 'deaf mute'.

Where some useful hearing exists or where otherwise useless hearing is brought into use but not rendered completely normal with the help of an amplifying hearing aid or other amplification the picture is more complicated. In general the effect is that not all the elements of the language (phonemes, morphemes, words and syntactic patterns) can be distinguished one from another so that the recognition and production of these elements is patchy. That being so there will be problems in the learning of the meanings of the elements. To tease out the effects, in detail, of various degrees and kinds of hearing loss on language development is a task well beyond present knowledge and techniques. We have to be content with saying that the defects in language development are in rough proportion to the hearing loss. If an adult becomes deaf or if a child becomes deaf after he has acquired some language the effects of the deafness are different, the adult will retain his knowledge of language structure but the clarity with which he pronounces words tends to decrease over a period of months or years. The young child, even as old as three or four may lose much of the language he has acquired and behaves very much like a child who has been deaf from birth. It can be said with some confidence that a child becoming deaf up to one year and possibly up to two years will have very little advantage over a child born deaf. Such cases are said to be prelingually deaf.

The defect in a child's language has repercussions. At three or four or older, at the time a normal child is likely to be plying his parents and other adults with many questions about the world, the deaf child cannot. Not infrequently and understandably this inability to communicate effectively results in frustration and tantrums. Most deaf children come to accept their condition in time but it is obviously a bitter pill to swallow.

A child without language will not be able to learn to read unless reading is itself used as an instrument for teaching language. We shall be considering how this may be done. Normally, learning to read demands a prior knowledge of language. Thus the child without language is prevented from acquiring a general knowledge through normal social intercourse or through reading books and newspapers. The result is often an astonishing ignorance of elementary things not to mention normal school work.

The history of deaf education

There is no intention here of giving a complete history of the education of the deaf, this topic being admirably dealt with in other books e.g. that by Kenneth Hodgson (1953) which is freely acknowledged here. It is as well however to take a look at how the problem of deafness has been tackled over the years.

The inability to speak or to understand speech coupled with the unattractive vocal sounds which deaf people are apt to make has meant that they have frequently been regarded as mentally defective. The realisation that most deaf people are not defective in this way seems to have dawned very gradually and to have become universal only in the last two or three hundred years.

It is difficult to evaluate many of the early attempts at teaching deaf people either because the people concerned did not trouble to record what they did or in many cases, particularly when deaf education was becoming a profession in the eighteenth and nineteenth centuries, because the methods were regarded as trade secrets which had to be concealed to ensure the teacher's livelihood. More important perhaps is the problem of assessing the effectiveness of the methods in developing language. Even today there are many pitfalls in assessing a child's command of the complexities of vocabulary, syntax and semantics as well as speech intelligibility so that it is very difficult to be sure what was achieved in the past. In addition many of these early cases may well have been partially hearing in today's terms as audiometry was not available.

One of the first observations on the problem having a modern ring was made by Girolamo Cardamo, an Italian thinker of the sixteenth century, who is quoted by Hodgson as saying that '. . . writing is associated with speech and speech with thought; but written characters and ideas may be connected without the intervention of sounds.' This seemingly simple fact about language is not fully appreciated even today when people often find it difficult to think of language except as speech. The idea that one might by-pass the defective auditory channel by using another, e.g. vision, is obvious but has not yet been completely worked out.

Another idea for solving the problem also has quite a long history; from time to time attempts have been made to simplify and control the language presented to the deaf child so that what are considered to be the important patterns are emphasised and practised. One of the first people using this approach seems to have been Juan Pablo Bonet working in Spain in the seventeenth century. He was involved in a task which seems to have been responsible for much of the effort going into educating the deaf at that time and earlier: Spanish law had it that to inherit an estate a person had to be able to speak. So wealthy families with a deaf son employed tutors to try to achieve this; only the wealthy had the problem or could afford the remedy. In spite of this need to develop speech Bonet realised that language might be developed at first through the use of gesture, manual signs, writing and a manual alphabet.[1] Subsequently sounds were associated with letters and the effort for speech proceeded from there. In addition he appears to have used a carefully controlled scheme for introducing parts of speech progressively starting with nouns, excluding idiomatic and conversational language and also using special exercises for promoting mental development generally.

Lip-reading, which is an important part of many teaching methods today, did not seem to have been trusted as a possible medium of communication until relatively late. Jacob Rodrigues Pereira, a Portuguese teaching in France in the eighteenth century used it in conjunction with reading, writing, finger-spelling and signing. Bonet relied on his deaf pupils to learn to lip-read as a direct result of his lessons in articulation. He did not teach lip-reading explicitly. These days the term 'speech-reading' is preferred to cover information from the lips but also those movements and positions of other speech organs that can be seen, clues to meaning from facial expression and from residual hearing. The terms will be used interchangeably.

One of the most famous teachers of the deaf was the French Abbé, Charles Michel de l'Épée who developed an extensive and sophisticated sign language incorporating some mimes and other signs having an arbitrary relation to meaning. In addition there were ways of marking parts of speech so that the whole system probably approached ordinary language in its range and flexibility. He was not at all interested in trying to develop speech if only because with the numbers of children he was teaching, up to 60 at a time, it was impossible. He had as a priority that the deaf should have some efficient medium of communication

[1] For a description of sign systems and manual alphabets see Plate 3 and Appendix II.

and thought; in this it is clear that he was very successful. The advantages and disadvantages of such a system will be discussed later in the book.

The Abbé's work and general philosophy marks the beginning of a polarisation in approaches to deaf education since at the same period another famous teacher, Samuel Heinicke, was working in Germany but tackling the problem quite differently. His preoccupation was with speech; teaching approaches with this emphasis are known as 'oral' because speech is produced by the mouth. He used reading and writing as part of his method and pictures and miming also. However he was secretive about the details and in any case much of his method was apparently intuitive and not easily communicated. Hodgson writes that:

> 'Heinicke's work is the basis of modern oral teaching. He contended that the manual alphabet and signs have their dangers if speech is the aim. His predecessors had, many of them, seen these manual devices as a crutch to assist the deaf to walk mentally. It was left to Heinicke to argue that a crutch may itself be a handicap to those who have never walked, because it can make them disinclined to try. The only way to learn to speak is to speak.
>
> ' "The deaf mute can learn and should be taught to speak", Heinicke declared, "and language as spoken should be the instrument of instruction and . . . by such means will the unhappy one be restored to Society."
>
> 'This declaration has remained the manifesto of oral teaching. But in the hands of lesser teachers we have still the problem of how to avoid mental retardation when a child's speech is only embryonic and quite inadequate to the insatiable needs of growth. If a child fails to achieve a good oral standard, and is prevented from achieving a competence in manual language, then the child suffers the worst of both worlds.'

The polarisation then, and the accompanying controversy, one facet of which is illustrated in the above paragraph, was between those who advocated communication by some manual system using signs or letters of the alphabet signalled by various configurations of the hands and those who wished to try to develop actual spoken language with correct pronunciation of the sounds. The controversy continues to this day. One of the factors militating against a satisfactory solution to this issue is the fact that the terms 'manual' and 'oral' each apply not to one well-defined method but to a cluster of related methods and combinations of techniques. The protagonists in an argument are apt to find themselves using the terms in different ways and will thus be arguing at cross purposes. One of the aims of this part of the book will be to try to unravel some of the tangled strands.

The oral tradition was started in Britain by Thomas Braidwood working in Edinburgh towards the end of the eighteenth century. His ideas seem to have developed independently of Heinicke in the first place. His methods were kept a family secret and were passed on to a relative, Joseph Watson, who became the head of the first 'asylum' for the deaf. Watson in turn passed the method and the secure position on to his son.

In the early and middle parts of the nineteenth century deaf education reached a very low ebb for various reasons. There was at the same time a swing to manual methods through disenchantment with the inadequately applied oral approach towards the end of the Braidwood/Watson 'dynasty' (1760–1819). So when interest in the condition of deaf children revived at the end of the nineteenth century the asylums and the silent manual methods were both associated with the 'bad old days' and were thrown out together. In the flush of new concern for the deaf the feeling was that only speech was good enough for them and oralism was resuscitated. It remains the received doctrine in Britain today.

A significant strand of development in America began in fact in Edinburgh. Alexander Melville Bell invented a system of written symbols, 'visible speech', which represented the position of the speech organs for various speech sounds. This system was intended primarily for elocution lessons with hearing people but he and his son, Alexander Graham Bell, later applied it to teaching speech to the deaf. When father and son emigrated to America in 1870 they effectively started the oral tradition there. Visible Speech was the popular mainstay at the start but is not favoured today and, ironically, the Alexander Graham Bell Association for the Deaf is now one of the chief opponents of any form of supplement which might draw a child's attention away from lip-reading.

There are broadly three approaches now current in America. Some schools use oral methods with fairly strict control over signing or finger spelling. Most schools use what is there known as the 'combined system'; this is a broad term which does not mean oral methods and manual methods used at the same time, which is the meaning of the term here but means that in a given school some children are taught orally and some manually according to what is thought to suit them best. The third method is the Rochester method which is like the oral method but one-handed finger spelling accompanies and is synchronised with the spoken word. Only finger spelling is used, signs being rigidly excluded.

In Russia the most important development in the education of deaf children was a series of trials and experiments begun in 1950 in which a method similar to the Rochester method was introduced. These trials seem to have been so successful that the method was officially adopted for use throughout Russia and is now universal there.

Before we leave this subject of methods we should look more closely at oral education as it has developed in this country since the majority of schools and teachers subscribe to it. The method has been defined in a report of a government committee chaired by Professor M. M. Lewis (1968) as: '. . . the combined teaching of speech, lip-reading, reading and writing for the development of language and the acquisition of knowledge through these media of communication.' (para. 27)

The strongest influence in promoting this approach has been from Professor A. W. G. Ewing, now knighted, and his first wife, the late Irene Ewing, who for some years were in charge of the Manchester Department of Audiology and Education of the Deaf.

With the technical developments of war time, electronic hearing aids started to become freely available after the war and their use became an integral part of oral teaching. The most articulate advocates of the benefits of hearing aids have been the late Edith Whetnall and Professor D. B. Fry (1964).

The chief ingredients of the oral method seem now to be:

1. Great importance is attached to early diagnosis of deafness so that a start can be made on education as soon as possible.
2. It is also considered important for the parents to receive help and guidance so that they may be actively involved in their child's language development.
3. Amplification is provided as early as possible with a hearing aid which the child wears and also by the periodic use of a speech trainer, a larger amplifying apparatus.
4. Efforts are made to give the child experience of a wide range of different sounds and he is trained to discriminate progressively finer differences between them. This is auditory training.
5. Receptive language is developed not only through residual hearing but also by the use of speech-reading from the earliest ages. To this

end parents and teachers aim to speak always so that their faces can be clearly seen and the child's attention is brought to the face.

6. The development of expressive language is promoted partly through residual hearing, the child matching his own speech to what he hears like a normal child but also through direct instruction in the positioning and use of speech organs.

7. It is usually considered important for the language experience of deaf children to be as spontaneous and natural as possible. To this end children are exposed to as much language as possible related to naturally occurring situations and interests. However, in the early stages and particularly with profoundly deaf children simplification of sentences with emphasis and much repetition of key words related to the child's interests is recommended. Structural aids of various kinds are often used.

8. Reading and writing are used with older children to supplement the incomplete patterns from lips and residual hearing.

9. The majority opinion of the National College of Teachers of the Deaf, which speaks for the oral method, is that 'finger spelling is not suitable for use with pre-school, nursery or infant school deaf children' or for 'general use in infant/junior schools'. (Lewis Report, para. 178.) This declaration is apparently followed fairly closely in practice in that 91 per cent of nursery and infant schools taking profoundly deaf children claim never to use finger spelling. The figures for Junior and Secondary schools are 63 per cent and 49 per cent respectively. Similar figures apply to the use of signs with a similar swing towards them in secondary schools. These figures presented in the Lewis report relate to the use of normal media in the classroom by teachers. It should be said that there is a strong tendency for deaf children particularly the older ones to use them informally out of school hours and thus graduate towards what adult deaf regularly use amongst themselves. This is usually mainly signs, gestures and mimes with odd words fingerspelt when there is no suitable sign.

The usual reason given for excluding finger spelling and signing is that they are easier than lip-reading and will thus divert children from the discipline of learning to lip-read. In a few schools this conviction is so strongly held that children are punished for using any manual communication. In most schools manual methods are not punished but they are generally discouraged.

In addition to these principles it may be said that the treatment of individual children will vary and must be tailored to their individual needs according to the intuitive skill and judgment of their teachers. Professor and Lady Ewing write (1958) that: 'There are many ways in which deaf children differ from each other and there is no one set of methods that can meet fully the needs of them all.' In the last analysis it is not thus possible to define the oral method precisely.

9 Principles and practice

In the last chapter the simple effect was described – complete absence of language – which would result from profound deafness without treatment. It will now be evident that in countries with well-developed education systems children very rarely go without help of any kind and their ultimate proficiency in language will depend partly on their degree and type of deafness and partly on the education they receive. Other factors such as intelligence are no doubt relevant. Here we shall see that in spite of energetic attempts to overcome the problem, often at considerable expense to local education authorities, the language development and general educational attainments of most deaf children still fall very far short of those of most hearing children.

The plan of this chapter will be first to consider what our aims are and secondly to review the results of present practices. Finally we shall begin to analyse the problem in the light of psycholinguistic principles. This analysis will be continued in Chapters 10 and 11.

Aims

It is as well first to define what it is we are trying to do, to establish our aims in educating deaf children. Naturally we want to wipe the slate clean and give the deaf children the same opportunities and skills as a hearing child. The purpose of listing aims is to underline those features of the deaf child's condition which require special attention:

1. We can say as a general principle that we should provide the child with some efficient means of communication. Whether we try to justify this principle on the grounds that to communicate with other people is necessary for a person's intellectual and emotional well-being or whether we regard it as an intrinsically good thing few would dispute that it is important and that a child or adult unable to communicate with others is likely to suffer in many ways.

The options include speech, lip-reading and the use of residual hearing: gestures and mimes, sign systems, finger spelling and reading and writing.

In evaluating any of these options we should consider: (a) How quickly and easily it may be learned. Ideally a child should be equipped with some system at least as early as a hearing child, say by three or four. (b) How efficient the system is – whether it can match natural language in its flexibility, range, subtlety and precision. (c) The people with whom the deaf person will be equipped to communicate. The interest in giving deaf people speech derives mainly from the fact that this is a medium that everyone knows. Any other medium should either be already known to hearing people e.g. reading and writing, or should be easily learned by parents, family and friends. (d) A further consideration is the possibility that the learning of one system of communication may help in the subsequent learning of others. This point and the other criteria will be expanded at relevant points later.

2. Having set down the rather general principle of providing the child with some efficient means of communication it may seem odd to list as a second aim, of the same order of importance, the desirability of teaching him to read and write. We are here begging some fundamental questions concerning the value of education generally but we shall assume that we want our deaf child to be educated in much the same way as a hearing child. That being the case writing, and reading in particular, become essential. They are not only potential means of 'conversation' as suggested above but they are the key to the huge reservoir of books and other written material – the means to both instruction and enjoyment. The other practical uses need no enumeration.

   The reason for emphasising this seemingly obvious point is that a grasp of language structure in the sense described in Part I is essential for reading and writing but not for some of the options listed under the first aim. We cannot avoid the problem of developing language structure by simply choosing a suitable option.

3. The third aim is the child's general education, both intellectual and, for want of a better word, moral. An efficient means of communication and the ability to read and write are obvious prerequisites for education in the ordinary sense of the word. It should be emphasised again that unless the basic skill of language is acquired reasonably rapidly then general education is bound to

suffer. The most elementary facts about the world are not known or are misunderstood; ordinary instruction in school or college is very difficult.

It has also been suggested that the quality of a person's thinking is influenced. This is a difficult subject which was touched on in Chapter 2 where we saw that language certainly is not necessary for thinking but, where a person has language, it is intimately involved in his thinking. In Chapter 4 it was suggested that the more conventional and abstract concepts are probably shaped in a person's mind by hearing the verbal label used in appropriate situations.

In addition to the possible direct involvement of language processes in thinking there is a sense in which we learn techniques of thinking through the medium of language. An obvious example perhaps is the scientific approach to the solution of many problems which is now, for better or worse, widespread in Western culture. The effectiveness with which technical problems are solved today as compared with many earlier centuries is partly the result of better basic knowledge of the world and more brain power applied but also due to the method of approach which has been disseminated more or less explicitly through the medium of language. Problem solving, one aspect of thinking, is frequently helped by people getting together and discussing – the saying that two minds are better than one assumes that language is the indispensable medium for the exchange of ideas.

Any dispute over aims is likely to concern the choice of options under item 1. If speech were easy to teach there would be no question but that it was the best medium of communication. The manual-oral debate is, on the one hand, a dispute about the best way of achieving agreed aims and on the other it is a debate about the choice of priorities: whether we aim for speech at all costs or whether we aim for *some* efficient means of communication, not necessarily speech. In subsequent discussion I shall try to keep these two parts of the question distinct.

It has been taken for granted that we are trying to develop language structure in a full sense even though it may not be in the speech medium. The role of syntax in conveying meanings should be obvious now and this is the main reason for regarding it as important. Sometimes the attitude is taken that it does not matter too much if deaf children are confused about word order – a random jumble of words can still convey ideas. This is very much a council of despair which may be forced on one but is really an admission of defeat.

Successes and failures

There is in this country more concern for the education of deaf children and more money spent on this than at any time in the past. Partially hearing children have benefited from amplification and many have learned to speak much better than they would have in earlier times. However, many studies of deaf children's language and educational standards show that they generally fall far short of hearing children. There are from time to time startling successes with children apparently having very severe or profound hearing losses. These often serve to mask the failings of the majority. Where failures occur mis-application of the method may be invoked as explanation: considering the number of unqualified teachers still in schools for the deaf there is some force in this argument, but when the omission of any one of the nine essential ingredients of oral education may be used as an explanation of 'oral failure' it smacks of special pleading. Professor and Lady Ewing wrote in 1954:

> '. . . we believe that many so-called "oral failures" in schools for the deaf are pupils who have rarely or never been enabled to enjoy the satisfaction of talking spontaneously in conditions in which they were understood. After leaving school such pupils have been known to avoid and even resent speech and to seek social life solely amongst others handicapped like themselves who will communicate by a sign language, supplemented perhaps by finger spelling. Such a reaction to a sense of inability to succeed in talking is completely understandable, but the writers believe that, in a majority of cases, it is a danger that effective teacher-parent co-operation can forestall.'

While 'effective teacher-parent co-operation' may have been the magic ingredient then it is now more usual to blame inadequate parent guidance at the pre-school stage or to suspend judgment until hearing aids have been in use long enough to prove themselves.

In the following discussion of deaf children's attainments the four main categories, comprehension and production of speech, comprehension and production of written language may be borne in mind. There do not appear to be any studies of deaf children's attainments in which oral methods are acknowledged to have been applied fully. The nearest to this, perhaps, is a survey by K. P. Murphy of pupils aged twelve in all schools in England, Wales and Eire. This appeared in 'Educational Guidance and the Deaf Child' (1957) edited by Professor Ewing.

Originally the intention was to use the Schonell Silent Reading Test A, but this was abandoned because 'an appreciable proportion of children could not attempt it'. This is in itself revealing because the test is designed to cater for children down to a reading age of six years nine months. Many of these twelve-year-olds could not make a start. The test is composed of short descriptive paragraphs each followed by questions requiring a choice from four possible answers each of one word or a small group of words. It requires fairly full comprehension both of the paragraph and of the question.

A test was substituted, the 'Gates Reading Vocabulary Scale', which is composed of a list of words each accompanied by five other words one of which has a meaning fairly close to the test word. The task is to choose this synonym and underline it, there being thus no demand on syntax. The average score of those 170 children with hearing losses greater than 80 dB was 7.57 which for normal children would be interpreted as a reading age of eight years and eight months. There is no question but that this score, low as it is, is an inflated measure of reading ability in deaf children since it does not touch syntax. It is in fact very close to the minimum possible on this test: if words were chosen purely at random, by the throw of a dice or toss of a coin, the test would still register a reading age of seven years and ten months. Multiple choice tests have many advantages but do have to be interpreted with caution near the lower end when scores are little better than chance.

The Schonell Essential Mechanical Arithmetic Test, Form A, was also given and this registered an average score equivalent to a normal child's performance at age eight years and seven months. Perhaps arithmetic could be taught without language but, like most other school subjects, it is much easier if it can be explained verbally. Incidentally the average IQ for these 170 children was 101.6 which is marginally above average.

This study demonstrates indirectly the difficulties with the comprehension of writing. There are many other studies, less recent and from other parts of the world, showing similar results but I have not been able to find any using assessment methods refined in the way outlined at the end of Chapter 5. The best I can offer is my own personal experience of testing deaf children using the Reynell Scale: it is rare to find a deaf child who can correctly follow either through writing or speechreading such simple instructions as 'Turn the little table upside down' or 'Pick up the smallest pink pig and show me his eyes.' Normal five-year-olds can do these things easily. Where tests probe deeper than ordinary reading tests the comparative poverty of the deaf child's language shows up more clearly.

Commonly children seem to be rather poorer at speech-reading the Reynell items than at reading them. There is a dearth of formal studies of speechreading, the nearest being one of deaf school leavers (Montgomery, 1968) average age fifteen years ten months in which the children's teachers estimated that 25 per cent of them 'could follow a normal conversation reasonably well'. The remaining 75 per cent apparently fell short of this. More precise measures are needed.

This same study contains a figure of 7 per cent as the proportion of these deaf adolescents whose speech was 'intelligible to the man in the street'. This is comparable with the results of another study by Dr Esther Simpson of the Department of Health and Social Security who conducted a survey of 359 fifteen-year-olds in schools for the deaf in 1962–3 (1963). The hearing losses ranged from as low as 31 dB to total losses and the group included some children who were post-lingually deaf. Of this whole group 22·3 per cent were considered to have intelligible speech but Simpson comments: 'If all children with a hearing loss of 70 dB or less are excluded from the survey then of the remaining 276 children, thirty-eight achieved good speech. There is another factor to be considered and that is that six of these thirty-eight became deaf after the age of five. One is left therefore with thirty-two – 11·6 per cent who have been successful as regards speech'.

Of the children with partly intelligible speech she says: 'It is doubtful whether the speech of many of the children in this group could be readily understood at the first attempt by anyone unfamiliar with the speech of deaf children and there were a large number of children in this group who appeared unduly optimistic about their speech, who obviously thought they were speaking intelligibly and who were puzzled by the interviewer's inability to understand them. Great skill is developed by teachers of the deaf in understanding the speech of their pupils and this skill may not always work to the children's advantage'.

Twenty-three per cent of the children had no intelligible speech although these tended to be those with other handicaps as well.

Simpson suggests that the results might be better in five years when the effects of early diagnosis, pre-school training, parent guidance and better amplification may have worked through. The second survey was carried out in 1969–70, seven years after the first. The results do indeed show an improvement: 38·9 per cent of the children were assessed as having intelligible speech, 44·9 per cent being partly intelligible and 16·2 per cent being unintelligible. The Encouraging as this appears to be Dr Simpson writes that: 'The many possible variations in the cause of hearing impairment and of combinations of additional handicap as well as changes in educational provision mean that it is impossible to compare directly a group of handicapped pupils with those of similar age several years later. What the survey does show, however, is that, as in the previous one, a significant proportion of children leave schools for the deaf with speech unintelligible to a stranger and with all that this failure of two-way communication implies. . . .' The second sample was smaller than the first and contained a greater proportion of pupils at the two selective secondary schools. More of the second sample had losses less than 80 dB and fewer had losses greater than 90 dB. The integration of the deaf with hearing communities through good production and comprehension of speech is one of the main arguments for oral teaching. Results cut most of the ground from beneath this argument. The Lewis committee (1968) have expressed 'disquiet' over standards generally (para 19) and psychologist H. R. Myklebust (1960) writes that: '. . . the child with deafness from infancy has a marked retardation in all aspects of language. Furthermore, no educational methodology known has been highly successful in overcoming this limitation. . . . While the approach which emphasises speech in the language development of the deaf child is logical, it has not been highly successful'.

Approaches to a solution

Psycholinguistics is a new field and is full of unanswered problems. It may seem premature, therefore, to try to apply existing knowledge to a practical problem like developing language in deaf children. Against this it may be said that some useful ideas have already emerged and in any case there is bound to be some value in seeing what a fresh approach can do for an old problem. In this section some guiding principles are considered as a preliminary to the rest of the book where we discuss possible ways of overcoming the language handicap.

It has been said already that the main language aims for deaf education are an efficient means of communication (speech if possible, with comprehension through lip-reading and residual hearing), reading and writing. The two major underlying problems are those of developing children's knowledge of the tools of language, especially syntax, (discussed in Chapter 3) and the relationship of these with meanings (discussed in Chapter 4).

These twin problems of syntax and semantics may be tackled in two distinct ways. We may attempt to write a set of rules for syntax and semantics and teach these systematically, or we can try to reproduce the kind of situation in which a hearing child learns these things (making provision for the child's deafness) and hope that the unconscious processes which normally ensure language learning will do the same for the deaf child! The first approach we shall call 'structural' and discuss in Chapter 10, the second, 'unstructured' approach will be the subject of the last chapter. This classification cuts across the manual/oral division because, from time to time, both approaches have been used under both the manual and the oral flags.

Before proceeding to examine these two approaches there are some observations to be made which apply to the problem generally.

One idea which I think needs emphasis is the distinction, described in Chapter 3, between the form and substance of a language. Modern linguistics has underlined the fact that language is a form or pattern of contrasted units or elements regardless of the particular substance which is used to convey those contrasts. Spoken sound is so very much the main medium for language in normal hearing people that it is not always easy at first to think of language except as based on these sounds. To go with this idea is a second one which was discussed at the end of Chapter 5: most educated people master at least two language media, speech and written language, but the processes operating in the two cases are very different. The first or primary medium is learned from scratch but once this primary system of contrasts has been learned it is relatively easy to transfer to a secondary medium provided the systems of contrasts in the two media are reasonably isomorphic. The basic patterns remain the same; all that changes is the substance.

If a child has no hearing he cannot learn through the natural primary medium and he must therefore use a *substitute primary medium* (S.P.M.).

The fundamental question facing educators is which medium (or media) is most suitable as a substitute primary medium for language learning. A related second question is whether some media might not be better left and developed as secondary media following primary language learning.

It is often said that all deaf children have *some* hearing which can help them develop language. This is largely true and we shall accept that where hearing losses are not too bad children may learn language relatively normally. Where hearing losses are severe or profound it is not safe to assume that residual hearing is simply a reduced form of normal hearing. For our purpose we shall treat residual hearing as a possible substitute primary medium and examine it alongside others.

Looking at the second question first the reader will remember from Chapter 1 how it often happens that where a pattern is patchy or distorted, although not excessively so, we may be able to recognise it in spite of these defects because our perceptual system can effectively bridge the gaps and correct the distortions. This only happens however where the pattern is already familiar to us. If it is not we have no means of knowing what the 'correct' version should be and can take the distorted pattern on its face value only.

Where a medium only conveys a patchy version of the language or is otherwise unsuitable as a substitute primary medium then it is probably developed best as a secondary medium when the child's established knowledge of the language can help him with the patchiness and distortion. With normal children it is generally accepted that it is a waste of time trying to teach reading before a certain age. Although this notion of 'reading readiness' is controversial and reading could probably be taught earlier than it now is, the idea is basically sound. This is not so much because written English is an incomplete version of English (although it is certainly a distorted version) but it is unsuitable in other ways as a primary medium.

To introduce such media to deaf children at an early age alongside the chosen primary media is not so much likely to harm their language development as to be a waste of effort.

Turning to the main question one can now ask what qualities our substitute primary medium or media should possess. Our knowledge of normal language learning indicates one important quality at least. This is that the *substitute primary medium should reproduce the structure of the language faithfully with all the essential contrasts easily perceived.* There are two reasons for this:

1. If the medium is to be used as a base for developing other media it is important that it should be a complete and accurate version of the language, isomorphic at least at phoneme level if not in the details of the speech sounds.
2. In discussing language learning in Chapter 6 we saw that recognition generally precedes reproduction and it was suggested that this is because not all the available details or distinctive features

need be used for recognition. Generally speaking most elements such as words have a generous range of distinctive features and even if some are not used the word in question is still distinct from other words. In the terms of information theory language is very redundant. The corollary of this is that the words are correspondingly easier to discriminate when there are many distinctive features. Where only few small differences distinguish words they are more likely to be confused than where there are many obvious differences. In the early stages of learning a language we can safely assume that a medium which offers the child all the distinctive features clearly will be more easily mastered than one where these differences are muted. The capacity of the medium to reproduce language patterns is one important principle for language learning. Others will be introduced at appropriate points in the next two chapters. The substitute primary media used in oral teaching are lip-patterns and residual hearing with written language following later but introduced relatively early compared with hearing children. Let us now examine them to see how clearly they reproduce the patterns of language.

Lip-reading or speech-reading

Professor and Lady Ewing wrote in 1954:

'If words could be seen by a deaf child as completely as they can be heard by one whose hearing is normal, the deaf child could and would acquire, through lip-reading alone, the living language that he needs to express his thoughts in intelligible speech. But words are *not* as clearly visible to the eye as they are audible to the ear. Therefore a deaf child has to learn to recognise many of them from incomplete patterns. Very often he learns to do this with a wonderful degree of skill.'

The last sentence is a remarkable exaggeration in view of the evidence presented earlier in this chapter. It has been pointed out that most tests of lip-reading are made artificially easy by restricting the range of words to be selected and by presenting single words. If one presents a deaf child with about a dozen common objects and asks him to pick them out singly on the basis of lip-reading he is likely to do quite well. This can easily mislead people into thinking that the child's progress is better than it is. As soon as one graduates to simple sentences in which the sentence structure is the only clue to meaning (as in the Reynell test) the task becomes very much harder for most deaf children.

A set of photographs illustrating the lip-patterns of the phonemes (excluding diphthongs) is shown in Plate 2 (between pp. 146–147). They are arranged in groups to illustrate how similar are many lip-patterns for different phonemes. There are two points to bear in mind when examining these. Firstly, they are still photographs which may not illustrate certain distinctive features available when the mouth is moving. Secondly, a difference which is evident between two phonemes on these photographs may or may not be a consistent clue in practices; it is inevitable that each phoneme is pronounced slightly differently on each occasion and by different speakers and it is necessary to know how variable two lip-patterns can be before one can assess whether they are likely to be told apart easily or not in practice. Notice how, even with a good front light, it is impossible in most of the pictures to see the precise position of the tongue inside the mouth; an important element in articulation is invisible.

Of course one can learn to utilise subtle clues which might otherwise be ignored and oralists pin some faith on this. But there is a limit to what can be learned when essential clues are effectively absent. The fact that a hearing person may learn to lip-read in a relatively short time as well or better than a deaf person who has spent his whole childhood at it lends support to this point. The relative ease with which many hearing people who have gone deaf learn to lip-read is a prime example of how prior knowledge of language patterns helps the recognition of incomplete patterns. It seems to be the case even for these people that they can lose the thread of a conversation rather easily if the topic changes too suddenly.

Residual hearing

The main plea for making maximum use of residual hearing has come from the late Edith Whetnall and D. B. Fry (e.g. 1964) who saw the portable hearing aid which became widely available shortly after the war as a panacea of the deaf child's ills: 'It was the study of the group of deaf-born children with "spontaneous" speech which led to the conclusion that in spite of all that has been said to the contrary *neither the degree nor the type* of hearing loss need prevent the deaf-born child from learning to talk through his hearing.'

This is a very bold assertion and requires extremely good evidence to back it: this evidence is simply not forthcoming.

The supposition that any kind of residual hearing can enable a deaf child to speak rests on the assumption that although residual hearing may not be much use to the child at the beginning he can learn to make use of it through auditory training.

Now even before we look for evidence we find that there is no general agreement about what auditory training means: 'As sounds become familiar they become easy to detect and interpret and therefore can be recognised and understood at fainter intensities and at greater distances than when first heard.' This quote from Whetnall and Fry indicates that they see auditory training as improving the threshold for detecting sounds as well as the ability to discriminate sounds. It is clear from elsewhere in their book that this is what they mean. But Raymond Carhart (1966) writes: 'We must clearly understand at the outset that auditory discrimination is not the same as sensitivity of hearing. . . .' and he adds that auditory training is concerned with improving the discrimination of sounds above threshold not the detection of sounds at threshold. There is no suggestion by any of these authors that auditory training is concerned with anything but audition; Professor and Lady Ewing (1954) think differently: '. . . auditory training in this book means a multi-sensory approach in which listening through aids is combined with lip-reading at all times except when it is necessary to concentrate on testing children's capacity to hear or to lip-read.'

Ignoring these confusions let us see what evidence there may be that either hearing thresholds or discrimination may be improved through training. All that appears, in fact, either in Whetnall and Fry's book or in the other studies they quote is a handful of cases described anecdotally with 'before and after' audiograms shown. As scientific evidence it breaks all established principles.

To know whether there has been a genuine improvement in thresholds which is what the audiograms purport to show it is necessary to know:

1. Whether a similar improvement might not have occurred without treatment. It is essential to have a control group of cases without treatment as a comparison.
2. Whether the apparent improvement might not represent normal random variations on repeat testing. Given the notorious difficulty of getting accurate audiograms from young children it is very likely that many of the 'before' audiograms were spurious. The use

of control groups and appropriate statistical tests would have shown up any problems of this kind.

3. Whether the audiometrician doing the audiograms had a knowledge of which children were 'before' cases and which were 'after'. Unconscious bias can easily creep into audiometric testing and the tester should be insulated from this knowledge.

In the last chapter we touched on modern signal detection theory and saw that a testee's 'set' either to detect the faintest sounds at the cost of making mistakes or to be more cautious affects thresholds. I am not suggesting that auditory training cannot affect thresholds but to prove it one would need all the controls listed above and a measure of the testee's 'set'.

Whetnall and Fry did not test discrimination ability as such but present their cases in a general way as successes in school.

Before leaving their work it is worth noting a point made by Moores (1970) that none of the cases which they present as successes had hearing losses greater than 75 dB averaged over 500, 1000 and 2000 Hz. Montgomery's study (1968), already mentioned, showed that even the smallest amounts of residual hearing have some influence on speech but this is a very different conclusion from supposing, as Whetnall and Fry have done, that '. . . neither the degree nor the type of hearing loss need prevent the deaf-born child from learning to talk through his hearing'.

As was pointed out in Chapter 8 people with severe and profound hearing losses inevitably have damage to the inner ear which not only makes sounds harder to detect but also distorts more or less seriously. The apparent loudness may or may not increase as sound is amplified above threshold and in many cases amplification can make sounds actually harder to discriminate. This is true even when high quality amplification is provided but additionally when speech trainers and hearing aids especially are used in practice a large amount of distortion comes from these sources themselves. A common fault is that the 'loud-speaker' on the child's ear does not fit snugly so that sound leaks out and finds its way to the microphone in a continuous feedback loop. This results in a loud feedback whistle which renders the aid useless; the whistling of the hearing aids is so common that it is almost an accepted feature of a group of deaf children. Even without whistling or the crackling from loose connections the miniaturisation required to make hearing aids portable inevitably requires a sacrifice in sound quality. A rule for the use of electronic apparatus which is frequently ignored is that the quality of reproduction falls off markedly when an amplifier is used near its maximum output. These snags taken with the fact that little of the apparatus sold for use in schools for the deaf is made robustly enough to withstand young children and is frequently needing repair all militate against a child's chances of getting a tolerably clear version of speech through his ears. In illustration of this last point are the remarks of Mrs Beatrice Ingall (1971), Principal of the Woodford School for the Deaf, Essex, which has 100 pupils:

'Take the position we were faced with when the children returned to school after the six weeks summer holiday. We found 11 broken aids, 4 broken spare aids, 25 spare aids not returned, 1 no aid at all, 3 broken receivers, 6 broken earmoulds, 2 completely dead batteries, 6 wrong receivers, 2 lost receivers, 4 earmoulds completely blocked with wax, 25 new batteries needed, 20 new leads.

'All this despite a detailed and regular parent guidance programme, frequent staff meetings on the use and care of hearing aids and sending spare leads, batteries and receivers home.'

'Electronic pox' is the cynic's term for such diseases of the deaf child's prostheses.

There are likely to be a few cases with profound losses who are helped considerably by amplification and who may become oral successes. The existence of such cases should not disguise the high probability that residual hearing is for the majority of severely and profoundly deaf children a quite inadequate medium for language development; the damage to the perceptual mechanism means that many of the essential distinctive features for phonemes have been obliterated. No amount of auditory training can provide distinctive features which are not there – it can only focus attention on features which are being ignored. This point needs emphasis because people sometimes assume that although deaf children hear sounds differently from normal they can learn to interpret them and to treat the sounds as normal from their point of view. This is true only for distortions which do not destroy distinctive features. Once these latter have gone they cannot be replaced by training. As Bonet recognised in 1620: 'In the deaf mute . . . the physical auditive power is lacking, because the organ does not afford the power of extension as far as to the spot where it has to receive the air conveying the sound to the ears . . ; whence we shall conclude that neither the loud sounds some make or cause the deaf to utter, nor their closest attention, will have any effect towards remedying this defect of sense but will only weaken it more. And if by so violent a method anything is heard it will be a confused noise, which will arrive at the brain in so inarticulate a form that the mind cannot form any conception of it. And so it is needful to choose some other more certain medium . . .' A substitute primary medium in fact.

When the National Deaf Children's Society asks in its advertisements: 'Won't you ever listen?' the answer is 'no' for many deaf children and it is pointless to try to make them listen. R. J. Winning, a congenitally deaf man, writes about his schooling ('Hearing', August 1971): 'We went to the Hearing Aids Group room regularly for half-an-hour each day. Most of us hated it. What did I do with aids? Doing nothing, just watched my teacher and see if fellow pupils got right answers. Teacher used to put a record on. One side was Robin Hood and another side was Davy Crockett. I remember very well. He put it on and asked us which one. I was able to tell difference. What was my hearing like? It was just a tick in my ears. When I got ticks twice it was Robin Hood, three times it was Davy Crockett. That's all I could do.'

Written language

Writing has the great virtue of being clear to see and although ordinary spelling does not reproduce phonemes very well, all words are fully differentiated, in some cases (e.g. there and their) better than speech itself. On the face of things it should be a very good medium for presenting language.

One problem which is relatively easy to overcome is the convention of left to right reading. In the early stages the sequence has to be shown with a pointing finger, or some similar method, until the convention has been learned.

There are rather special problems in the use of writing as a S.P.M. which can best be explained in the next chapter.

It is possible, of course, that while lip-reading and residual hearing may be insufficient in themselves to convey language patterns, perhaps in combination and with writing they may do the trick. If this was the case one would expect present methods to be far more successful than they are. One of the chief reasons for oral failure seems to be the unsuitability of the media presently in use.

10 Structural approaches
including the possible uses
of programming

The fact that language is such a problem for deaf children has led people to see whether it is possible somehow either to simplify language for them or to present it in a controlled, systematic way or both. These we shall call structural approaches to the problem. Careful control and presentation of subject matter has developed elsewhere on the educational scene as the technique of 'programmed teaching' or programmed learning as it is sometimes called. This is one possible aid for our task.

There is not necessarily a sharp distinction between structural and 'natural' methods because a teacher may use elements of both from time to time. This is particularly true of oral teaching which is predominantly 'natural' but in which props and aids of various kinds are used quite frequently. It is simply for convenience that they are separated here.

In this chapter we shall first describe and comment on some examples of this kind of method which have been used and then consider the theoretical basis to see what the prospects are for improvements.

Basic English

Basic English is a simplified form of English which was designed by C. K. Ogden (1944) mainly as an international language, easy to learn by people whose native language is not English. (The letters of BASIC stand for British, Americal, Scientific, International, Commercial.) Although people have thought of using it for the deaf the idea has not really caught on. We should look at it briefly to see what it may have to offer.

The total vocabulary in the sense of the number of different word forms is only 850 words excluding variations like plurals and -ing forms, etc. The parts of speech include the traditional 'nouns', 'adjectives', 'prepositions', 'adverbs', etc., but 'verbs' are replaced by a limited range of what Ogden calls 'operators'. These words like 'put', 'give', 'do', 'go', etc. which may be combined with other words to replace verbs.

Thus 'move' would be 'give (a thing) a move', 'push' would be 'give a push to (a thing)', 'enter' would be 'go into', etc.

The normal changes in words for plurals, tenses, etc. are used and the effective vocabulary is increased by the use of derivatives. Thus 'birthday' is allowed because 'birth' and 'day' are part of the vocabulary and so is 'copyright', etc.; '-er' and '-ing' may be added to make new words.

The suggested answer to the problem of word order is the use of model sentences in which other words of the appropriate parts of speech may be substituted. Here is an example of a simple sentence with parts of speech marked:

I	(will)	give	(simple)	rules	(to
Noun/pronoun	auxiliary	operator	adjective	noun	preposition

the boy)	(slowly)
noun	adverb

I have bracketed the optional parts of the sentence. The rules for expanding simple sentences into compound sentences are fairly explicit: dependent clauses having the same form as simple sentences may be added between a noun and a following operator, or at the end of the sentence and in some other locations. Ogden gives this example of an expanded sentence:

The camera man (who made an attempt (to take a moving picture) (of the society woman), (before they got their hats off)), did not get off the ship (till he was questioned (by the police)).

I have bracketed the optional additions to the simple sentence.

A mechanical device, a 'panopticon' (see-at-a-glance) is described for constructing simple sentences. It consists of a series of concentric revolving discs each with a list of words of one part of speech round the perimeter. The discs can be rotated so that varying sequences of words come into line but the order of the parts of speech is preserved. It is very similar to a device sometimes used in schools for the deaf in which cards bearing lists of words pass through slots in another card. By moving the lists up and down various sentences can be constructed on a simple word substitution principle.

It is claimed, with some justification, that Basic English is capable of expressing any idea which can be expressed in ordinary English although perhaps not as elegantly. Special supplementary vocabularies of technical terms may be required for scientific or other specialisms but the claim is broadly true. It can read quite acceptably and is intended to do so. Any oddities which appear are mainly due to circumlocutions which the larger vocabulary of ordinary English would short-cut.

On the face of it Basic English is an ideal simplified language for the deaf. The fact that the range of word forms has been reduced with the most generally useful words retained is an obvious plus and the apparent simplification of grammar is attractive too.

But Basic English is not in fact as simple as it appears and may not help the deaf as much as expected.

Although the number of word forms is limited to 850 the actual number of words in the sense of forms with distinct meanings is much larger, even ignoring simple derivations formed by adding '-er' and '-ing'. The compound words have meanings other than the simple combination of the meanings of the two constituent words: the meanings of 'daybreak', 'football', 'firewood', 'income', 'today', 'cupboard', etc. are all rather more than or simply different from the meanings of the word forms from which they are composed. To get the basic set of 850 words to do the work which several thousand normally do they all have to be very versatile. In a sense Basic English makes as much demand on a person's knowledge of meanings as ordinary English because he needs to know many related and metaphorical meanings for each word to get the full use out of it. 'Letter' has to serve for a letter of the alphabet as well as mail; 'glass' is a drinking vessel, window pane, magnifier, spectacle, barometer, etc. 'Round' functions both as an adverb and as an adjective. Prepositions work particularly hard because metaphorical uses replace many other words: 'inspiration' would be expressed as 'thoughts came *into* mind'; 'research' would be 'get *at* the details'; 'to attack' would be 'to go *against*'; a train goes *through* a tunnel but we also do things *through* a representative – a student of Basic English not knowing ordinary English but who does know the first meaning of 'through' is not likely to deduce the second one from it; 'by' has at least two distinct meanings. Ogden's example of an expanded sentence has: 'before they *got* their hats *off*' and also '. . . did not *get off* the ship . . .' The difference in meaning when 'off' is placed immediately after the operator or after the noun is something of which few people are consciously aware but which is important. We cannot expect a deaf person to appreciate it without explicit instruction.

There are at least some savings which can be counted in favour of Basic. 'Put (a seed) in (the ground)', 'put (the baby) in (the bath)', 'put (the tea) in (the pot)' 'put (an account) in', etc., are perhaps simpler than learning 'plant', 'immerse', 'infuse', 'render', etc. Even here the meanings of many everyday operator-noun combinations are established by usage and are not particularly logical – they have to be learned as if they were separate words. There is no particular reason why we should say 'make an attempt' rather than 'take an attempt' or 'get an attempt'. People say 'give a party' but it would be just as logical to say 'make a party'. Actually, the nearest colloquial expression is 'make up a party' which is quite distinct from 'give a party'. Incidentally the use of 'up' in this phrase is not related in any obvious way to the normal sense of 'up'.

The grammar also makes implicit demands on a native English speaker's skills as Ogden's example of an expanded sentence illustrates (p. 179). In that example the group 'who made an attempt' (1) might be thought by a novice to be grammatically equivalent to, say, 'who gave a push' (2) or 'who took a chance' (3). It is true that all three could be followed more or less acceptably by 'to take a moving picture' but they differ in other ways. The second group, ('who gave a push') can be followed by such groups as 'to a door', 'to a car', etc., but these would not fit acceptably after the first or third groups. The third group, ('who took a chance') could be followed by such groups as 'of falling in' or 'of hitting it' but they would not follow the second group acceptably and the first one only doubtfully (it would be more in line with ordinary usage to say 'who made an attempt *at* hitting it').

There are pitfalls even in the simple sentence which are not made explicit by the grammar. Most of the operators can be followed by an object but a few like 'go' behave oddly. We can 'go a mile' or 'go a walk' but we cannot 'go an apple' or 'go a brick'. Perhaps such expressions are ruled out because they are nonsensical; others like 'go a car' or 'go a ship' are just as sensible as the first two but are simply not used in practice; they sound peculiar when one is familiar with English.

In chapter 3 we discussed variations on the expression 'I go home', 'I go to the shops', etc. The person learning Basic and finding 'I go home' as acceptable would no doubt assume that 'I go theatre', 'I go bed', etc., were also acceptable. These particular solecisms do convey the meaning quite adequately but we have already discussed our reason for regarding bad syntax as evidence of a bad method of developing language.

Other irregularities concern the first and second nouns in the sentence which in the case of 'pronouns' and 'proper names', certain other singular nouns and most plurals (e.g. 'sleet', 'cheese', 'people') can be a single word but for most words an 'article' (Class A words in

Fries's terminology) is obligatory: we say 'The policeman gives rules' not 'Policeman gives rules', etc. Again, the optional addition of an adjective before a noun looks straightforward but some words such as number terms which seem to behave like any other adjective (e.g. 'the six men', 'the ten green bottles') can occur in situations which other adjectives cannot (e.g. 'One dancer . . .' without an article but not 'Graceful dancer . . .').

When one starts expanding the simple sentences the irregularities of idiomatic English become even harder to handle on a simple substitution principle. The main strength of Basic is in the reduction of vocabulary not in it's handling of the syntax problem.

Other ideas

Basic English was not designed specifically for use with the deaf but the word substitution principle which it embodies for teaching grammar is common to almost all other structural methods. (Occasionally grammar rules have been presented verbally but such an approach will obviously fail in the early stages before the child has enough understanding to follow the rules.) Much the same comments as were made on Basic apply to these other approaches.

The best known is probably the Fitzgerald key designed by Edith Fitzgerald (1937) of Virginia School for the Deaf. The teacher's blackboard has a series of symbols and words along the top which is intended as a framework for constructing sentences below. The subject/verb/object and subject/'to be'/adjective patterns are the main frames but there are other 'slots' to cater for more complicated sentences. Thus 'whose' before the subject indicates that one may say 'Miss Holt's coat is green' as well as 'The coat is green'. 'Where' further on shows that one may say 'Miss Holt's coat is *in the closet*'.

Towards the end of the last century George Wing of Minnesota School for the Deaf used a series of numbers and letters to mark parts of speech in a similar way and Katherine Barry at Colorado School for the Deaf used a 'five-slate system' in which the five slates were used for subject, verb, object, preposition, object in that order.

One drawback of all these methods is that they are based on traditional grammar with all its inconsistencies. Modern grammar perhaps offers a better chance of success because it is at least based on the principle of word substitution and attempts to record the sub classes and special cases in these terms. We cannot be too sanguine about our chances of success even with modern grammars because of their incompleteness.

As far as one can tell, these methods were not altogether satisfactory and they have tended to fall out of favour. The common criticism made is that they lead to rigidity – it was difficult for children to graduate from the patterns they had been taught to the permutations and recombinations on them which gives normal language its richness and variety.

The swing against formal methods in the mainstream of education has been echoed in the deaf world so that 'free expression' and 'creativity' in language is now the fashion. This otherwise laudable trend is misplaced because it overlooks important problems: normal young children can create large numbers of new sentences and express themselves creatively but they will do so within the grammatical discipline which they learned at their mothers' knees. The deaf child without these skills can only produce a random jumble of words rather as a novice violinist would make a mess of trying to play Brahm's concerto creatively – he cannot even attempt the thing, let alone add artistry and expression.

Programmed teaching

By now the reader will be looking for a ray of sunshine to relieve the gloom. Could it be that programmed teaching, which has proved itself elsewhere, will provide an answer? The results of attempts to date are not in fact very encouraging, but this could be because the field has been insufficiently explored. Whether or not this is likely is considered at the end of the chapter.

Programmed teaching grew out of work by the psychologist B. F. Skinner using a device now known as a 'Skinner box'. This is really a cage for a rat, pigeon or other animal which has a lever, bar or button of some kind in a position that the creature can reach. It is usually arranged so that a pellet of food is released into the cage when the bar is pressed. A novice will only press the bar by chance but after this has happened and he has obtained some food a few times he usually learns the trick and presses the bar whenever he wants food.

Skinner and others have explored variations on this arrangement and have found that they can teach quite complicated routines by simply waiting until the animal does some particular action or approximation to the action and then rewarding or 'reinforcing' it with some food. A complicated series of actions cannot be taught all at once but must be built up in a series of small steps.

A teaching programme does the same thing but cues and clues are given in the early stages to help the pupil get the right answer; the reinforcement is usually some signal to say that the right answer has been given (or not as the case may be). If the correct answer is given then the pupil proceeds to the next 'frame' but if he gives the wrong answer he either tries again or a series of frames are presented to help him understand the difficulty.

It is often said that a good teacher teaches in the same way, presenting his subject in a graded series of small steps, giving his students problems and exercises and correcting them. The particular features of a programme which distinguish it from good classroom teaching are these:

1. The teacher relies on judgment and experience to grade the steps correctly, neither too big nor too small. A programme should have been tested and revised several times so that the steps are the right size (too many 'programmes' appear on the market which have not been). The programme preserves this grading in a permanent form which is available to teachers, good and bad, experienced and inexperienced alike.
2. A programme gives reinforcement immediately after each answer in a way that a teacher can achieve in classroom discussion but not in individual written work.
3. Each pupil works on a programme at precisely the pace which suits him best. Classroom teaching is always something of a compromise between the needs of the ablest and the slowest pupils.

Programmes cannot replace classroom teaching, they can merely complement it because they are laborious to prepare and test and they usually lack the flexibility which is possible in ordinary lessons where the teacher can pursue an interesting topic which is off his schedule if he feels the class is ready and interested. In many subjects discussion is a valuable teaching tool which cannot be included in a programme. The great advantage of a programme is the very close and detailed control of the material which it makes possible and the fact that errors by the student are nipped in the bud quickly and not allowed to become ingrained.

Typical of programmes for vocabulary is one by G. A. Falconer (1961). Twelve 4 ins × 8 ins cards were mounted on a rotating drum and the children registered their 'answer' to each card by inserting a stylus into one of five holes. If the answer was correct the drum moved on to the next card but if it was not the child had another try. The first card or frame for each word showed a picture with the appropriate word underneath. The same word was written next to one of the choice points and other wrong words next to the other four holes. Only a straight match was required in this case. In succeeding frames the clue word was 'faded' by removing letters, and the wrong answer words were made increasingly similar to the correct answer words.

The children undoubtedly learned to associate words with pictures by this means and apparently they enjoyed the task. The main criticism of the idea is that it is a laborious way of teaching something which normally intelligent deaf children will learn easily enough anyway. Falconer does comment that: 'The extent to which language can be developed by this technique is undoubtedly fairly limited'.

The very much more difficult problem of syntax has been tackled by Birch and Stuckless (1963) with a programme based on the Fitzgerald key. They used a simple teaching machine with the programme on a roll of paper mounted in a box so that the frames could be seen singly through a window in the side of the box. Another window was backed by a plain paper roll to receive written answers. Each teaching sequence started with a picture and a simple descriptive sentence with parts of speech marked with Fitzgerald symbols. The children's task was to write the sentence in the blank window with the cue sentence covered. They then uncovered the cue and corrected their answers. In successive frames syllables were removed progressively from the cue sentence until the descriptive sentence was written in response to the picture alone.

The overall result of trials with this programme was that the children learned the material no more or less accurately than when the same material was presented in the normal way but they did apparently learn it very much faster.

Little is said about the method of testing what the children had learned; it would be particularly interesting to know how well they could generalise the patterns they had learned to other combinations of words. One revealing feature of the study is the fact that the same picture was often used for several different sentences. It is obvious therefore that control over meanings was very loose. This is a good example of the difficulty of illustrating meanings from one picture or situation rather than the range of situations which is normally available to the hearing child.

Another study by Roy, Schein and Frisina (1964) exemplifies the general line of attack on the grammar problem. There was a preliminary programme to teach the mechanics of using an electric typewriter and then with the aid of a film projector and a variety of other mechanical and electronic gear the children were taught to respond to a short film sequence of, for example, a dog running with: 'The white dog is running' and after the film had stopped: 'The white dog ran.'

The results as measured by the tests used were not in fact very good, but even if they had been there would still be a query about whether the children had really learned some language in the full sense of the word. A full understanding of the linguistic uses of a form like 'The white dog is running' implies a knowledge of:

1. The range of situations where it is appropriate to use 'The' rather than 'A', 'One', 'His', 'Their', etc. (i.e. Class A words in Fries's grammar). The range of situations where one can say 'white' rather than 'grey', 'fawn', 'brown', etc. and the exact uses of 'dog' and 'run'.

2. The rather subtle difference in the way one uses 'The white dog is running' and 'The white dog runs.'

3. The fact that 'white' is an optional word in that context whereas all the others are obligatory. 'White' can be accompanied optionally by other modifiers some of which can precede or follow 'white' while others can only occur in one position relative to 'white'. One can say 'The fat white dog . . .' and, doubtfully, 'The white fat dog . . .', but one cannot say 'The guard white dog . . .', only 'The white guard dog . . .'. Other optional modifiers like 'with a collar on' must follow 'dog' and cannot precede it.

4. The range of words or groups of words which may be substituted acceptably at each position in the sentence.

5. Noun and verb inflections for singular and plural forms. One tense inflection has been taught but one can hardly call this a full knowledge of tense and mood forms.

The question 'What *is* language?' is always in the background when one is thinking about structural methods because the whole process of deliberately assembling a teaching scheme forces one to make conscious what is normally unconscious and automatic. Looked at in one way the task is very daunting because the complications proliferate so much, but it is also a useful exercise because it makes one realise what an intricate and finely woven fabric one is handling. Here is one final example.

My colleague, Miss Mair Lewis, and I have conducted some trials with the deaf mute Sam, mentioned earlier, to see what language he might learn in this kind of way and what difficulties we might encounter.

At the beginning we found that he already knew most but not all the letters of the alphabet (best in capitals because of his poor eyesight as we discovered later). Presumably he learned these during his short stay in a school for the deaf, but nothing else apparently.

At first we taught him the names of objects but he found this remarkably hard in the early stages. Later he accelerated considerably so that after a few months he could pick up new names almost as fast as we would. This may mirror the 'naming explosion' which normal children show after their first slow start.

In teaching sentence forms we did not use a programme in the strict sense but adopted most of the features of a programme: correcting all errors immediately, letting him know straight after each attempt whether it was right or wrong, simplifying and regrading a step when it proved too hard.

The first form was:

(1) A	boy	kicks	a	ball
	girl	throws		brick
	lady	touches		chair
	man	holds		table

Mair
Gerry
'Sam'

The substitution words are shown underneath. At first we used pictures, kindly drawn by Miss Christine Hart, with the people and objects labelled so that we could concentrate on the sentence pattern rather than divert attention to the naming part of the task. With a picture and the relevant sentence in view Sam copied the sentence a few times and then we covered up parts of it progressively until he could write it from memory. When he was thoroughly familiar with the first sentence we made one substitution and taught the relevant sentence. Eventually he was able to make appropriate substitutions in response to a picture at all three loci at once.

The one exception to this assertion is that he always found it very difficult to differentiate 'touches' and 'holds' even after we replaced pictures with dramatised demonstrations by Miss Lewis, myself and Sam himself. We interpreted this difficulty in terms of the distinction between natural and conventional conceptual groupings. Whereas 'ball', 'brick', 'chair', etc. are obviously different even without knowing that they have different names it may be that 'touches' and 'holds', which both involve static contact between a person and an object, are normally differentiated only after a child has learned that there are two words for the similar situations and he can then observe the different ways in which the two words are used.

Other patterns which Sam 'mastered' include:

(2) The	ball(s)	is/are	green
	brick(s)		red
	cup		yellow
	saucer		

(3) The	(red)	ball	is	on	the	(red)	brick
	(green)	brick		by		(green)	ball
	(yellow)	cup				(yellow)	cup
		saucer					saucer

(4) The same form but as an instruction: 'Put the . . .'

Only a selection of the objects used are shown here. He could also produce such forms as 'The red cup is on the cupboard' or 'The green chair is by the door.'

Forms (3) and (4) deserve comment because word order is crucially important to meaning. We always used objects in all possible relationships (e.g. saucer on cup as well as cup on saucer) so Sam was forced to get the meaning from the sentence form and not from the conceptual schema. Originally we tried to include 'under', 'behind', 'in' and 'in front of' but after prolonged failure to get Sam to distinguish these consistently we gave up. It may be that these are relationships which are not naturally conceptualised but are normally learned through language. 'On' and 'under' pose a special problem because two different sentences can describe the same situation – this was too difficult for Sam.

It came as a surprise to find him producing, with impeccable logic, sentences like 'The door is by the brick'. We had not bothered to teach him that the smaller object usually comes first in such sentences because we had not appreciated it consciously ourselves. This is typical of the stumbling blocks one is apt to find in structural methods.

An important question which we have only been able to explore to a limited extent is how he generalises these patterns once learned. Periodically we taught him a selection of new names for new objects which he had never used in any sentence pattern and then tested his ability to use them in sentences which he had learned using old names.

Appropriate statistical tests were used to make sure that his successes were not merely by chance but it was obvious that he generalised remarkably easily, at least as far as putting new object names in old sentences. This is an illuminating result because it does confirm that word classes can be formed through factors other than verbal context. As was said in Chapter 6 the correlation of Class 1 words with objects, Class 2 words with actions and Class 3 words with qualities probably helps word classification. Occasionally Sam would produce such a 'sentence' as 'The ball is on the green' showing that the conceptual distinction between an 'object' and a 'quality' could not be a completely reliable guide for him.

In teaching the singular/plural distinction in the second frame we tried to vary the number of objects used to show that the plural form applies to any number greater than one. Although we have not tested this formally it does look as though he has generalised this correctly to include numbers of objects which were never used in demonstration.

Having taught him two statement forms separately we wanted to know whether he could learn to give the right kind of statement in response to the appropriate question form when the two were presented in random order. The two questions were 'What colour is the ——?' and 'Where is the ——?'. He never mastered this task even after many lessons and the reason for this failure is not obvious. One possibility is that the answer forms were too similar, starting as they did with the same three words ('The —— is . . .'). By contrast he learned quite quickly to differentiate the question 'Where is the ——?' from the request 'Put the —— $\begin{Bmatrix} \text{on} \\ \text{by} \end{Bmatrix}$ the ——'. The reason why he failed in the one case and succeeded in the other is not clear.

There are many other questions one could ask about the way he generalised these patterns and without the answers one cannot be sure that he would generalise correctly without supplementary teaching. Although 'a' and 'the' have been used it is unlikely that Sam has grasped their ranges of use; 'is' is undoubtedly a meaningless element in the patterns at the present time because he has had no opportunity to see the alternatives (apart from 'are') which can fill that slot. He probably has some grasp of the fact that the colour terms are optional before object names but he does not fully appreciate the convention of word order in this case because he occasionally writes, e.g. 'The ball yellow. . . .' although, after we have corrected him on this a few times, he tends now to correct himself. A whole range of unanswered questions cover his use of individual object and colour names. By and large he seemed to apply most of them correctly but he was very uncertain of the right words to use when we produced odd shades of green and yellow (ties!) one day. One demonstration in this case was sufficient for him to identify these odd shades confidently in the same way as ourselves. Having learned the word 'bag' as applied to a handbag he overgeneralised it to describe a purse. Knowing the word 'box' as applied to a cardboard box with a lid he was unwilling to use it for children's plastic nesting cubes which we used one day and which could be described acceptably as boxes. Similar problems occurred in differentiating pens and pencils. In all cases he could handle the distinctions confidently once we had shown him where the words applied. These seem to be the expected problems arising in all cases where the boundaries of concepts are established by the conventions of language use rather than reflecting natural or salient regularities in the objects themselves.

These few sentence types could be of some limited use but obviously they are the bare rudiments. As the range of frames is increased problems are likely to arise in generalising word classes. With the few frames described the classes are interchangeable from one frame to another but this is by no means always true as we saw in Chapter 3. It is not possible to assess at this stage how far one could cope with this problem and develop genuine language facility using this kind of method.

If Sam's efforts are accepted as rudimentary language there is one interesting conclusion to be drawn. Many authors (e.g. Lenneberg (1967)) have asserted or assumed that there is a critical period for language learning in childhood after which it becomes difficult or impossible. If Sam has indeed learned some language then the second part of the proposition is disproved.

Structural methods have always looked like a promising avenue to be explored but none of the attempts to date enable one to decide whether one should continue exploring or give the search up as a bad job. A look at psycholinguistic theory suggests the latter.

The two major problems are those of syntax and semantics. It was emphasised in Chapters 3 and 4 that both these aspects of language involve patterns which, in their fine details, are extremely complex and which provide an almost inexhaustible source of material to be learned. In a sense our knowledge, especially of meanings, is being extended and refined throughout life. Most of this material is known implicitly and unconsciously by native speakers of English and only a relatively small part of it has been documented with any accuracy. Meanings of words have been fairly well covered in dictionaries but even these do not deal much with connotations and the variation of meanings in different contexts. Linguists are not yet agreed on how syntax should be described so that there is nothing like a complete record of syntactic patterns for any language much less of the meanings of these patterns. There are some records of idioms and their meanings but they are not in any sense complete. It follows from these facts that it is impossible to teach language entirely formally.

Of course no individual ever learns the whole body of language as known collectively by his speech community. We said in Chapter 3 that young children can produce a useful body of acceptable sentences even when they are familiar only with the main branches and a limited range of side branches and twigs of the language 'tree'.

The argument might run, then, that we could try to give deaf children at least the knowledge which, say, a normal five-year-old has of language. If we could get them to the stage where they could read simple text with reasonable understanding perhaps they could go on from there, learning syntax from the sequences of words in written text and inferring meanings of new words and structures, which they did not know, from the general 'cognitive domain' developed by the text, much as we learned the meaning of 'widge-driggler' in Chapter 5. (There is no doubt that normal people can enrich their language quite a lot in this way through reading. Occasionally one hears people mispronouncing words in a way that suggests that they have learned them only through reading. One such instance I know of is the word 'concerto' where the 'c' was given an 's' sound presumably by analogy with 'concert'.)

This is a worthy hope which may have some substance. Certainly it is the only possible way in which a structural method could be instrumental in giving deaf children useful language. The crucial questions are: 1. What levels of skill in understanding and using language is necessary before 'take off' of this kind can occur? 2. Are enough of the patterns up to this level well enough recorded to form the substance of a teaching scheme?

The first question is almost impossible to answer with any precision but a four or five-year-old child's skill with language seems to be a minimum. If this is the case the prospects do not appear very hopeful because even at this modest level the language patterns are more complicated than anyone has yet been able to describe adequately.

Ignoring this difficulty for the time being we can now look more closely at what features of normal language learning need to be preserved, or replaced by some alternative, in any artificial teaching scheme. This is also an opportunity to comment on the use of writing in oral teaching as a substitute primary medium.

1. The quantity of language exposure

Even up to the age of five children have normally been exposed to huge quantities of speech. This is true even of children who would, in the ordinary way, be considered to be relatively deprived of stimulation and attention.

What we know of the richness in detail of syntax and semantics indicates that a child probably needs this large amount of experience even to reach a five-year-old level. To develop an accurate knowledge of the contexts, both verbal and physical in which each word and group of words may or may not be used acceptably he must hear or see them used in a wide variety of contexts. The classes and sub-classes of words are progressively shaped and refined through this wide experience and meanings are refined in a similar way.

Any artificial teaching scheme has either got to provide this large quantity of material or has got to organise it so well that the same skills can be taught more efficiently than normal. The latter may look unlikely, stated like that, but in fact all teaching attempts to improve on what people would learn if left to their own devices.

In oral teaching writing seems to be the one medium which offers the deaf child a clear, precise version of language. Does it come in sufficient quantity or organised according to a proved structural scheme? The answer to the second part of the question is 'no' because no such scheme yet exists. Even the courageous and praiseworthy early attempts like the Fitzgerald key cannot be said to have succeeded. The quantity of written language to which deaf children are exposed is minute compared with normal speech experience because it is confined to only a part of school time, itself a small part of the child's waking experience.

The next two questions are how syntax and semantics might be organised so that they can be learned within the confines of formal lesson time.

2. Syntax

It is just possible that a transformational grammar such as Chomsky's could form the basis of a systematic scheme. Being incomplete, surrounded by controversy and very complicated it does not look like a starter at present.

The only obvious alternative is a grammar like Fries's based directly on the substitution principle. Our discussion of Basic English and of trials with Sam give a taste of the problems. The single large obstacle is that of sub-classes and irregularities.

3. Meanings

(a) *The use of pictures to illustrate meanings* The extreme form of any structural method will have every feature of language carefully controlled and, perhaps, recorded in a permanent form so that complete control is preserved. Whereas syntactic patterns can be written down, the same cannot be said of meanings. The usual way of including meanings in the 'package' is with 'pictures, but these have limitations.

They are reasonably adequate when all the distinctive features of a concept are visual. But few abstract concepts (e.g. 'liberty', 'pleasure', 'discipline', etc.) can be pictured properly and even everyday words like 'aunt', 'uncle', 'cousin' (and all other terms for relationships between people) or 'yesterday', 'today', 'last week' (and all terms for time relationships) require an understanding of the abstract frame in which they belong and which cannot be illustrated very easily with pictures.

Other words like 'hardness', 'taste', 'cold', 'plenty', 'crispness', 'pressure', etc. are non-visual or only partly visual. These meanings can be suggested only very indirectly with pictures. The same is true of all deictic words like 'he', 'it', 'here', 'there', 'these', etc., or of words like 'a', 'the', 'but', 'and', 'however', 'since', etc., where the function is mainly structural but there is some lexical meaning.

And then there are all the meanings of words and word groups which are not referential at all. It is difficult to see how the meanings of greetings, calls, exclamations or even questions, statements and requests can be satisfactorily conveyed except in the actual situations in which they are commonly used.

We seem to be forced to the conclusion that there is no satisfactory substitute for 'live' situations to illustrate a large proportion of meanings. These situations can still be organised on a structured scheme but the neat self-contained package or programme is ruled out. Incidentally this means we have lost one of the major advantages of most programmes, the fact that they enable pupils to work productively without individual supervision by the teacher.

(b) *The time delay in linking words and meanings* In Chapter 6 it was suggested that the mere regular association or correlation of words or word patterns with concepts and situations is sufficient to establish meanings. We saw that the time delay between words and the situations which illustrate their meanings should not be too great. The smaller the delay, the more easily will the correlation be recognised. This is true even when people are talking about things far removed in time or space provided that the child's knowledge of language is good enough for him to grasp the cognitive domain.

Now a programme using pictures to illustrate meanings can easily be arranged to ensure a close correlation between words and pictures but if, as seems to be the case, we are forced to use some kind of dramatisation then we have to rethink.

Lip-reading and residual hearing would be ideal media because they can be used just like normal speech but they are ruled out for other reasons. Writing is a clear medium but it is cumbersome to use like speech. Conceivably the teacher and others dealing with deaf children could carry a notepad and 'talk' to the children with it but by the time a remark had been written and the child's attention drawn to it, with a pointing finger to ensure that they read it in the right sequence, time would have been lost and perhaps the child's interest too. As we shall see in the next chapter there are easier ways of achieving the same effect.

Because of the difficulties of using writing spontaneously like speech, it is not often presented in the kinds of 'live' situations which seem to be necessary for meanings to be established. Even when it is used in dramatised situations it is very difficult to achieve the very close link between words and events which occurs in speech. When writing is related to things which happened at some other time or place it is even more difficult to correlate words and meanings accurately unless the deaf child already understands the writing well enough to grasp the schema fully and precisely. This rarely happens.

(c) *'Rotation' of meaningful situations* It is possible to illustrate simple referential meanings, particularly for objects, with single examples once the convention of pointing and naming or labelling pictures of objects is understood. Deaf children can learn large numbers of common 'nouns' (and to a lesser extent 'verbs' and 'adjectives') quite easily from a picture dictionary or from labels on objects around the classroom.

But it is often difficult or impossible to illustrate other meanings satisfactorily with single examples because the object, quality or action in question has to be shown in a situation with other describable things. One might try to show 'laughter' with a picture of a man laughing: 'the man is laughing', but the same picture would equally well illustrate 'the man has a jolly face', 'the man has a fine set of teeth' or 'the laughing man has fair curly hair'. Normally a child will hear 'laughter' or 'laughing', etc. in several different situations which will enable him to isolate the element, 'laughter', which is common to them all and to exclude the other variable features.

Even where the relevant feature of the picture or illustrative situation has been identified this is not the same as teaching a concept. The one example only locates the concept; it does not define its boundaries.

Fortunately this is not too serious with 'natural' concepts because children seem to understand fairly easily where a word applies and where it does not – they can usually group 'tables', 'chairs', etc. in the same way as people with language. With artificial or conventional groupings there are likely to be misunderstandings. A picture of a representative collection of tables, chairs, etc. may or may not be enough to define the concept of 'furniture' without the child perhaps thinking that anything found in a house counts as furniture or that things are not furniture unless they are made of wood. In the normal way such misunderstandings would be ironed out through everyday use of the word but this cannot be assumed with the structural method. A hazy picture of a bird might illustrate the concept of a 'bird' although ostriches and penguins might not be recognised as birds from this one example; a realistic picture of a robin or a blackbird would be even more likely to lead the child to apply the word too narrowly. To show a very general concept like 'animal' one would need a fairly comprehensive collection of animals in one's picture and even then the concept might be over-generalised, to include plants and all living things.

Any structural method really ought to be able to cope with all these possible misunderstandings and this means that a comprehensive range of illustrations has to be built into the scheme for every concept and for every other meaning. This would be a monumental task.

Trying to teach language artificially by controlling every facet is rather like trying to describe an abstract picture to someone verbally. There really is no substitute for seeing the thing at first hand. To quote

Bjorn Karlsen (1966) working in this field, it would need 'an almost unbelievable amount of programming'. Although programmes and other similar methods may have limited uses the answer to our problem is almost certainly in some method which reproduces the language experience of hearing children.

The limitations of writing as a primary substitute medium have been considered in passing. A few deaf children do seem to reach 'lift-off' so that they come to be able to read for pleasure and thus enrich their language. It is still true that written language has real limitations as a S.P.M.; it is difficult to arrange for it to come in large enough quantities, closely correlated with 'live' situations.

11 Unstructured methods

Normally speech is acquired without any conscious effort as it is heard in all the manifold situations of the daily routine. The situations to which it relates are real, the speech is closely geared to them and it comes in very large amounts. Could we recreate these conditions using a substitute primary medium and let the deaf child pick up language in the same way?

We can now consider more fully the questions from Chapter 9 of what medium is most suitable as a S.P.M. and which media are best learned as secondary media. We shall accept without further argument our conclusion from Chapter 9 that 'the substitute primary medium should reproduce the structure of the language faithfully with all the essential contrasts easily perceived'. It will also be taken as established now that lip-reading, residual hearing and written language are not suitable candidates. Speech, reading and writing will be best learned as secondary media.

On the question of aims and priorities it has been suggested that the deaf child should be offered an efficient medium of communication which (a) can be learned at a speed comparable with that of speech for a normal child; (b) matches the range and efficiency of ordinary languages; (c) is either already known by hearing people or can be learned relatively easily by them; and (d) can act, perhaps, as a base of learning other media.

It is rather obvious that the S.P.M. and the 'efficient means of communication' are likely to be one and the same thing. We shall accept this position and now consider the main candidates which seem to be 'visible speech', manual sign language, finger-spelling or possibly a combination of signs and finger spelling.

'Visible speech'

One medium which reproduces the pattern of speech in every minute detail is sound spectrography, two examples of which have been given already (Plates 1a and 1b). The same amount of detail, but in a different form, can be produced on the screen of an ordinary oscilloscope. In the latter case it seems to be quite impossible to distinguish phonemes by their visual patterns – the best that can be achieved with an oscilloscope display is some control over pitch and loudness.

Sound spectrograph machines are of two kinds: those that produce a pattern immediately after the speech and those in which there is a few minutes delay. For some reason the former, which are the only ones suitable for our purpose, seem to be rarely made today but where they have been used (e.g. Kopp & Kopp, 1963) there has apparently been some success in teaching deaf people to recognise speech patterns visually and to improve their own pronunciation of speech by comparing the sound spectrographs from their own speech with those from normal speech. The chief problem seems to be that of getting a picture of sufficient quality to show the distinctive features of the phonemes. The same kind of apparatus has been used to produce vibrations in a series of ten 'tabs' on which the deaf person's finger tips rest (Fant, 1958). The amount of vibration in each tab shows the amount of activity in each of ten frequency bands and it is apparently possible to learn to recognise speech phonemes from feeling which tabs are vibrating and which are not.

The major disadvantage of all these devices is their considerable cost and the fact that they are not portable. There seems little prospect of their being made portable. This means that they are quite unsuitable for the everyday, and all day use which we want. They do however offer a possible means of teaching and correcting speech pronunciation once the main fabric of language has been laid down.

Sign language and signing

Manual signs, some examples of which are shown in Plate 3, are commonly used in conjunction with mime with little of the control over the form and order that constitutes grammar. This is usually called signing. However amongst many deaf adults the use of signs is rather more than this, the order of signs becomes important and the whole medium can be said to have a grammar – it can thus be termed a sign *language*.

The range and expressiveness of sign language in this sense is comparable with that of other languages, so a school of thought has developed to suggest that the deaf community has as much right to learn and use its own language as any other cultural or national group – that deaf children should not be forced through the blood, sweat and tears of learning speech but should be reared on sign language which a deaf child can pick up as quickly and easily as a hearing child learns speech.

Now this point of view, advocated most forcefully by William C. Stokoe (1971), is a value judgment which is little more open to dispute than someone's assertion of their personal preference for tea over coffee. But Stokoe recognises that deaf people do need to be competent to understand and produce, at least in its written form, the language of the hearing community: they should, he argues, be bilingual.

So one is brought back again to the need for the S.P.M. to be iso-morphic with English (or other spoken language) and it is in this respect that *this* form of sign language is deficient:

'The signs of sign language can occur in the same order as the words in an English sentence, or they can occur in quite different order. The sign sentence may seem to omit signs for words that are essential in the English sentence. Again the sign sentence may have signs where the English sentence has no equivalent word. Sign language grammar or syntax has its rules as well as its lexicon or vocabulary of signs, and both rules and lexicon differ from the rules and lexicon of English.' (Stokoe, 1971.)

A word-for-sign translation from typical sign language might be 'Yesterday, I go party drink much eat much'. Many forms from English like the impersonal 'It is the case that . . .' or 'There is a saying that . . .', a whole host of idioms or colloquial expressions, or the syntactic dis-tinction between questions, statements and requests, markings of tense, mood or number are not reproduced in sign language. None of the phonemic structure or spelling of English words is reproduced in pure sign language.

This point is recognised by Stokoe when he stresses that sign language *can* be made to model English forms provided it is used in conjunction with finger-spelling to fill in the gaps which are not signed. The usefulness of a combined sign language and finger-spelling will be discussed after our section on finger-spelling.

The drawback of ordinary sign language, that it does not reproduce the structure of English, has been rectified in the Systematic Sign Language originated by Sir Richard Paget and developed by Pierre Gorman and Grace Paget (1969). This is derived from ordinary sign language but contains markers for tense, mood, questions, requests, etc., it does not, however, reproduce the internal structure of words.

There is no doubt that the Paget System is learned by deaf children as quickly as a normal child learns speech and that, once learned, it can be a valuable base for transfer to written English. It has the full communicative efficiency of English itself.

The really serious disadvantage of the Paget System is that there are as many signs to be learned as words so that its mastery by hearing people is a task comparable in magnitude to that of learning the Chinese 'alphabet'. A further disadvantage is that the internal structure of words is not conveyed. Both these objections apply equally to ordinary sign language.

Finger-spelling

The structure of English can, as we have just seen, be reproduced at the word level by using manual signs. The main alternative is to use a finer 'grain' and reproduce smaller elements in the structure. Ordinary finger-spelling (the American one-handed and the British two-handed systems which are shown in Appendix II) reproduces English spelling exactly. There are also a variety of systems which have manual symbols for phonemes rather than letters.

One general advantage of any finger-spelling system is that more detail is conveyed so that secondary learning of other media will be facilitated not only in the larger patterns but in the details also. The other main advantage is that the large number of different words in English is constructed from a comparatively very small variety of different building bricks – twenty-six letters for written English and about forty-four phonemes for spoken English. This means that finger-spelling is very much easier for the hearing person (e.g. the deaf child's parents) to learn than is sign language. One can learn to spell out words, albeit fairly slowly, in a few hours and to read it in a rather longer time depending on the speed required. It is a task comparable with that of learning shorthand or typing.

As an illustration of the possibilities in some form of finger-spelling here is a classic case of how a deaf child was reared on pure alphabetic finger-spelling. Howard Hofsteater, a profoundly deaf man, born in Alabama in 1909 described his own case (1959):

> 'It has always been my belief that the exasperating problem of non-verbalism among deaf infants was quite adequately solved years ago by my parents when they set about giving me approximately the same language background as a normal hearing child possesses upon entering school.

'To the best of my knowledge, the program for my education, as conceived and carried out by my parents, was so revolutionary – yet so simple – that it had never been attempted before then, nor since. Although it caused some controversial discussion at the time, no one else seems to have cared to duplicate the experiment on which my parents gambled my entire intellectual life.'

He describes how his parents became deaf at early ages through accidents and how he became deaf at 'eight or nine months old' apparently following some kind of infection. He then describes how his parents tackled the task of teaching him:

'Quite logically they argued that if a normal hearing child effortlessly acquires spoken language by hearing it and imitating it, a deaf child should be able to do exactly the same by seeing it used. They saw no psychological – nor physiological – difference between a baby's using its vocal cords, tongue, and lips to imitate spoken language and a baby's using his hands to imitate the movements of finger-spelled words. Furthermore, they maintained that since I had become totally deaf at so early an age that I might as well be considered congenitally deaf, sound would for me be forever only a hazy, mental concept instead of the vivid thing it is to hearing people and to those who lose their sense of hearing at around ten years of age and to those with considerable residual hearing. Therefore, speech and speech-reading would be an entirely foreign and artificial means of mental development for me. Carrying their line of reasoning still further, it occurred to them that, since they had committed themselves to some form of manual English, they might as well go the whole hog and use nothing but English through the medium of finger-spelling.

'My parents then decided upon this course of action. They would (1) begin at once to talk casually and constantly to me on their fingers, just as hearing people do vocally to their babies – whether or not I was paying any attention; (2) talk to me just as naturally as hearing people do when attending to my physical needs, pausing only to emphasize key words tied to my bodily wants and interests; (3) use only finger-spelling between themselves when I was consciously present; and (4) in general, raise me as if I were a normal hearing baby with the sole exception of using the manual alphabet instead of speech.

'So, instead of spelling only the word "milk" to me at feeding time, they said something like "here is your milk – m-i-l-k", or

"Howard, it's time for your milk – m-i-l-k", and so on. Apparently from all reliable accounts, the results were astoundingly quick.

'Miss Eugenia Thornton, in her letter discussing my early education, writes, "The first vivid recollection I have of you was when you were very young. I am sure I saw you, before that time and many times when you were still a baby, but no other incident stands out clearly. You were lying in your crib. Your mother brought a bottle of milk to you. You reached for the bottle and at the same time spelled 'm-k' several times, just as spontaneously and naturally as a hearing baby of the same age would have attempted to say 'milk', and perhaps have said 'mik'. . . . This is not a story that I have heard about you but an occurrence that is clearly remembered."

'Then followed w, w-t, w-t-r, water; p, p-d, puddy (custard pudding of which I was inordinately fond throughout my childhood) c-t, cat; pa; ma; s-g-r, sugar; b-n, banana; a-pl, apple; and so on. My parents are authorities for the foregoing information as regards the first few words I learned. While I was stumbling through the spelling of the words that appealed to me right off, the deluge of natural, everyday English continued unabated.

'Anyone who knows the manual alphabet appreciates the fact that consonant letters are much more distinctly formed than the vowels. So I believe it was only natural for me to omit vowels at first. Miss Thornton compared this tendency of mine to "lisping" among hearing babies.

'My parents assured me time and again they never had to resort to formal teaching procedures to get me started in free, idiomatic language. I used more and more everyday English because I saw it used all the time and because I wanted to participate. Dad and Mother repeatedly emphasized to me this point – never did they physically force me to look at their fingers when they were talking to me; nor did they insist on my "copying" consciously or memorizing words or phrases or expressions. They, of course, helped me along when I struck out on my own to imitate.'

At some stage before the age of four and a half they taught him the correspondence between the written letters, A, B, C, etc., and the same letters which he had learned informally on his fingers. Presumably this helped him when he made the transition to reading.

'My parents began to tell me stories shortly before we moved to Birmingham and I quickly slid into the phase in which a child insists on a bedtime story as well as stories at various times of the day.

'When I asked for a story, Dad or Mother would always drop everything else to gratify me, and my appetite for stories became a great drain on their time and energy. I was pretty badly spoiled in that connection. They would ask me what story I wanted and, unless Dad had brought home a new book, I would ask for one of my old favourites for a repeat just as all children do. Then they would get the book and, with me comfortably snuggled in their laps, "spell aloud" the story. They would hold their hands pretty close to the pages and spell.

'I was about four and a half years or so old when I received such a shock that I can remember every detail of the event. I asked Mother one day to read me the story of Silver Paw – which I knew by heart and which always caused me to cry. It was a very sad story about a puppy that got lost. I got impatient with the rate at which Mother was spelling it out and turned a page before she had finished it. She stopped spelling, but I kept right on and sobbed and bawled through to the end. The next day when I asked for another story, she flatly refused, telling me to go read it myself. I was very hurt, but I did retire into a nook and read the story. That evening when Dad came home, I rushed to him and asked him to read me a story, only to be rebuffed likewise. That was how I was abruptly weaned away from having stories read to me.'

He says that he probably did not mix very well with hearing babies and when he was older '. . . my frequent illnesses and growing fondness for books kept me from mixing a great deal with hearing boys of my age. However, I did have a few cronies, all of whom quickly learned to spell on their fingers - *and* to read finger-spelling. I learned many colloquialisms and Southern expressions from them!' He was kept out of school until he was nine because of poor health and he claims that the two deaf governesses who looked after him successively until he went to school, taught him nothing. His excellent language obviously owes little to schooling. At school and college he was able to concentrate on normal studies without the constant drag of inadequate communication.

It would be a mistake to assume from one case that all children could be as successful. The case does answer any doubts which might arise about feasibility. There are no grounds for the common assumption that the sense of vision lacks some necessary mechanism only found in the auditory system or that one could never get a child to attend to finger-spelling. The age at which he learned to read (four-and-a-half) shows that his competence at that age and thus his speed of learning was comparable with normal hearing children.

Hofsteater has never made any use of speech or lip-reading but he is obviously very capable of communicating with hearing people by means of writing even if he could not perhaps sit on a committee or listen to speeches. Hearing people need make comparatively little effort to learn his finger-spelling. He is quite able to educate himself from books and to acquire general and academic knowledge in this way. It may be that good language very nearly compensates for lack of speech. His account of learning to read illustrates how easy it is when the secondary medium is absolutely isomorphic with the primary medium.

If one's main interest is in providing a base for a secondary transfer to written language then alphabetic finger-spelling is the obvious choice. If, however, one's chief concern is with the learning of speech then a phoneme manual system will be better.

It should be made clear that the intention of most such systems is not to pattern speech in its finest details but merely to effect a one-for-one correspondence between speech phonemes and arbitrary manual symbols. There is no suggestion that these manual symbols will give any guide to how the phonemes are to be pronounced but only to their order within words. The process of teaching the deaf child how each of the forty-four phonemes of English is pronounced is a separate problem which will be discussed briefly later. There is actually one system designed by Zaliouk (1954) in which the position of the fingers for each phoneme gives a clue to the manner in which that phoneme is articulated but it is intended primarily for correcting the faulty articulation of aphasic patients and would almost certainly be too clumsy for our purpose.

The main problem with most finger-spelling systems is that of speed. This was touched on in Hofsteater's account of how he learned to read. It is a particular problem with phoneme manual systems because these are usually intended to be performed concurrently with speech so that the deaf person may gain extra clues from lip-patterns and residual hearing. This problem of speed may have been the reason why one early phoneme manual system designed by Edmund Lyon and used by him for two years at the Rochester School for the Deaf (U.S.A.) in the 1890s did not catch on.

The speed problem seems now to have been adequately solved in an ingenious system designed by Dr Orin Cornett of Gallaudet College,

Washington, which is called Cued Speech (see Appendix III). The point of interest is that the consonants are signalled by the positions of the fingers but the vowels are shown by the position of the hand relative to the face. This means that each consonant and the vowel which follows it in the same word can be signalled at the same time and this speeds up the system considerably as compared with systems which signal all phonemes successively.

Speaking now generally of finger-spelling systems as possible S.P.M.s they meet all of the criteria we have set. We have seen some evidence for the speed at which the deaf child may learn such a system and more evidence will appear later. Being modelled on English or other sound-based language it has all the expressive potential of such languages except prosody. A finger-spelling system is relatively easily learned by a hearing person and the system provides a very detailed model for secondary learning. The main conclusion of this chapter will be that the 'exasperating problem of non-verbalism' amongst deaf children is most likely to find its solution in the use of such a system from an early age. The last section of this chapter will discuss some questions of detail in the design of such a S.P.M. and present a scheme for the phasing of primary and secondary media.

Finger-spelling and signing combined

The main difficulty with pure finger-spelling has been until recently that of speed and it is here that signs could be helpful since most words can be signed more quickly than they can be spelt (at least with ordinary alphabetic finger-spelling). A combination of some kind should meet all our criteria quite acceptably *provided that all the essential patterns of English are preserved.*

This means that morphological changes to words (e.g. addition of [s] for plurals and various tense suffixes) would have to be finger-spelt as would all function words. To gain speed in this way one is sacrificing the internal structure of those words which are signed. This need not be serious provided that an opportunity is given periodically for the finger-spelled version of signs to be seen and learned. A combined system like this would in effect establish the 'bilingualism' which Stokoe advocates but would put more demands on the parents of deaf children mastering a S.P.M. for the first time. It could be introduced later when parents and child have become proficient in pure finger-spelling.

Evidence for the value of finger-spelling in developing deaf children's language

We have already seen the dramatic effect on Howard Hofsteater of his parents merely substituting finger-spelling for speech. Although this is only one case and oral successes are available to offset it one should remember that oral teaching is widespread whereas the very simple idea adopted by Hofsteater's parents has been tried only once.

Results are not yet available from formal trials with Cued Speech but there is anecdotal evidence from one little deaf girl, Leah Hennegar, who has been brought up on it (Miles, 1967). Her parents began using it with her in September 1966, shortly before she was two. Early in October she began recognising common words and phrases and the names of members of the family. After four months her receptive vocabulary was estimated as fifty-four words and she had started using some expressively. After a year her expressive vocabulary was 300 words and receptive more. After three years and ten months (July 1970) her receptive vocabulary is estimated at between 2500 and 3000 words, and she 'says' such things as 'Mommy has new white fingernail polish' and 'Where is my rainscarf?' Her teacher claims that she is capable of picking out meanings from context when she is reading and of 'learning new words, ideas and concepts areas through reading'.

There are a number of scientific studies (e.g. Birch and Stuckless, 1964) which throw some light on the possible value of manual supplements to oral patterns. Many of them are not sufficiently well designed for conclusions to be drawn with confidence but they all without exception point to the benefits of manual supplements. The very best, with few design faults, is that by Professor Stephen Quigley (1969), which will be described briefly.

It is in fact two separate studies. The first 'survey' study involved annual tests of pupils in two sets of schools without any interference in the teaching methods. One set of schools used the Rochester method in which teachers accompany their speech with the American one-handed finger-spelling based on the ordinary Roman alphabet. The other set used the 'combined' method which means that oral and manual methods were used variously throughout the school the latter generally in cases of 'oral failure'. It is a pity that 'pure' oral schools could not have been found for comparison but inasmuch as the Rochester children were markedly (and, as measured by statistical tests, very significantly) superior to the comparison children in finger-spelling throughout the five years of the study we can trace a causal link between this and their superiority in other spheres of their education. There is always a logical problem in any study of this kind that some other factor might be the cause of such differences but in this case obvious things like intelligence, age of onset of deafness and degree of deafness had been controlled for.

A number of tests of language and educational attainments were used which need not be described in detail here. A crude indication of the pattern of results is the fact that of the twenty-three pairs of test scores taken throughout the five years which showed a significant difference (in a statistical sense) one favoured the comparison children and the remaining twenty-two favoured the Rochester children.

The one pair of scores was on one of the speech-reading tests at the end of the second year. This reflects the fact that differences were generally least marked in tests of speech-reading and speech intelligibility and most marked in tests involving the larger language structures. This in turn may well be the result of the fact that ordinary spelling as opposed to a phoneme manual system was used – ordinary spelling is rather a poor guide to pronunciation or lip-patterns.

While the first study started with children who were mostly teen-agers the second 'experimental' study was of four-year-olds. In this case the comparison was between the Rochester method and Oral teaching both being carefully controlled so that parents, housemothers, etc., were encouraged to use finger-spelling with the Rochester children out of school hours, and the Oral children were strictly insulated from any form of finger-spelling or signing at all times. After four years a similar pattern of advantage to the Rochester group showed clearly.

A weakness in the study was that the Rochester group acquired their deafness at an average age of 12·64 as against 1·79 months for the Oral group. Normally a child going deaf at thirteen months or even two years does not appear to get any benefit from his period of hearing and seems no better or worse than a congenitally deaf child. None the less this difference might be thought to account for the Rochester children's superior performance.

What is surprising about Quigley's results is not that the Rochester children were generally superior to the comparison groups but that they were not as good as hearing children in their grasp of language structures. One point of course is that even the four-year-olds had nearly a four year handicap compared with normal children. To see why they were not as successful as, say, Harold Hofsteater or Leah

Hennegar one would need to have a more precise knowledge of exactly how the manual supplement was used. It is possible that it was not used as extensively as speech is normally. In fact this is more than likely since Quigley writes: 'In the past, the Rochester Method has rarely been used in its pure form other than in the Rochester School for the Deaf. In some schools where this method has been attempted, the use of signs along with finger-spelling often becomes so common that the method in use could more appropriately be termed the Simultaneous Method.'

Reports of dramatic results come from Russia where one handed finger-spelling (below the chin) is apparently used in conjunction with speech, spelling being phonemically regular in the Russian language. The Lewis Committee record the claim that children of five who have been taught by this method for three years comprehend 1000 to 2000 words and use 70 per cent of these in their speech. The validity of some of these claims is sometimes questioned but the officers of the Department of Education and Science who visited Russia in 1966 wrote:

'It appears to us, from what we were shown, that the Russians are more successful than we are in the development of language, vocabulary and speech in deaf children once they enter the educational system. This seemed to us to be a strong point in favour of their method (use of finger-spelling from the very start as an instrument for the development of language, communication and speech), the investigation of which was the main object of our visit.'

A brief comment here on the condition of those rare unfortunates who are both deaf and blind. The famous Helen Keller who overcame her handicap so well had the benefit of an individual tutor who could not be led into the trap of teaching through lip-reading. She used a form of the manual alphabet adapted so that Helen could distinguish the letters and words by touch. That tutor, Anne Mansfield Sullivan, guessed that an unstructured approach should work provided that Helen could distinguish the manual letters clearly. After a short description of how Helen's fifteen-month-old cousin was learning language she wrote (1887): 'These observations have given me the clue to the method to be followed in teaching Helen language, I shall talk into her hand as we talk into the baby's ears. I shall assume that she has the normal child's capacity of assimilation and imitation. I shall use complete sentences in talking to her, and fill out the meaning with gestures and her descriptive signs when necessity requires it . . .' Helen was two-and-a-half when she contracted the disastrous scarlet fever and she was probably helped by previously established visual concepts and early speech. One suspects that the congenitally deaf/blind will find more difficulty especially as concepts will be mainly tactile. Hofsteater's principle of constant exposure to manual language will still apply.

While there is good evidence that language presented in a suitable visual medium is learned more effectively by deaf children than when it is presented through lip-patterns and residual learning, few surveys or experiments have been conducted to test the second part of the thesis, that the primary learning in one medium facilitates secondary learning in other media. This may be because it seems too obvious – certainly it is taken for granted that learning to read would be extremely difficult for a child with no language as indeed our earlier quoted survey (Murphy) of deaf children's reading attainments proves. Bearing on this question is one common objection to the use of manual aids that children having the opportunity to see phonemes through a clear visual medium will not bother with the more difficult task of lip-reading. Our theoretical arguments have been that an incomplete medium like lip-patterns becomes easier to follow when one knows the language thoroughly than otherwise and indirect support is available for this position in Montgomery's (1968) observation that there is a positive correlation between the manual abilities of deaf school leavers and their lip-reading abilities.

Design problems

Our provisional conclusion is that some form of finger-spelling is the most suitable S.P.M., alphabetic if one is not concerned to develop speech later, but otherwise phonemic. The best of the phoneme manual systems seems to be Cued Speech. The questions discussed here are of relatively minor details in the design and use of the system.

1. The role of lip-patterns and residual hearing

Cued Speech is designed to be used in conjunction with speech; it is a supplement to oral patterns – so much so that it cannot be used except in conjunction with speech. This is because the manual symbols do not in themselves fully differentiate the phonemes, only the lip-patterns and manual symbol together do this. The rationale of this is that the child will be forced to attend to lip-patterns and may thus ultimately be weaned off the need for a manual supplement. The reason behind the reason is that this will be more acceptable to pure oralists.

Although it is not a complete medium in itself it undoubtedly adds considerably to the information available from unaided lip-patterns and is very much in tune with the case being presented. The one criticism, however, is that there is still too much reliance on lip-patterns so that certain pairs of phonemes (e.g. [l] and [ʃ], [k] and [z], [d] and [ʒ], [ŋ] and [j], etc.) are still not clearly distinguished. To overcome this problem I have designed an alternative ('Augmented Cued Speech'), shown in Appendix III, in which every element is recognisable from the fingers alone. As with Cued Speech it is intended to accompany speech. There is a slight risk that children will not observe lip-patterns as readily when all distinctive features are available on the finger but, to my mind, this is completely outweighed by the need to ensure that all phonemes are clearly differentiated.

2. Secondary transfer to reading and writing

Most normal children cope reasonably well with learning to read and write in spite of the vagaries of English spelling. A child reared on Cued Speech or Augmented Cued Speech is in a comparable position provided his linguistic competence is that of a normal five-year-old.

But in exactly the same way that normal children learn i.t.a. more effectively than T.O. because the two media are isomorphic, our deaf child with a good knowledge of a phoneme manual system should also. There is a rather stronger case for using i.t.a. with the deaf child because it will strengthen his knowledge of phoneme sequences.

Now this idea that i.t.a. might be a good medium for teaching reading to deaf children has been seriously misunderstood. A very extensive study was made to compare i.t.a. and T.O. (reported by Miss Jean Palmer (1970)) but the question being asked was whether or not the children read better in i.t.a. than in T.O. Of course a deaf child with little or no prior knowledge of phoneme sequences should not find i.t.a. any easier and this is exactly what the study showed. The crucial advantage of i.t.a. for deaf children is likely to be in teaching phoneme sequences and thus guiding their learning of speech pronunciation. This side of the coin was not investigated, but Miss Palmer remarks that: '. . . some teachers in the i.t.a. schools commented spontaneously to the researchers that i.t.a. was helping the children to make sound/symbol relationships'.

3. Secondary transfer to speaking and lip-reading

It has already been said that the use of a phoneme manual system or i.t.a. or both will only teach phoneme sequences not the articulation of the phonemes themselves. Fortunately there is a relatively small set of phonemes and, although it is very difficult to shape pronunciation without auditory feedback, the problem is now circumscribed.

The various techniques already in use will no doubt be brought to bear. Diagrams may be used to illustrate the positions of tongue, lips, etc. Amplification may help. By a process of repeatedly attempting a sound and being corrected by his teacher a deaf child can usually achieve a tolerable version of most speech sounds. 'Visible speech' machines may eventually help with this problem.

One minor question concerns the choice of phonemes in the phoneme manual system. In everyday speech we frequently say [ənd] rather than [and], [tə] rather than [tu], [ət] rather than [at] etc. Cued Speech has been designed on the assumption that the neutral [ə] sound will be used whereas in Augmented Cued Speech the 'strong' pronunciation has been assumed. The difference is probably not very important, the first option perhaps leading to a slightly more natural sounding, but not more intelligible, speech while the second option is thought to make the transition to reading and writing slightly easier. Cued Speech is intended for use with the strictly phonemic Speech i.t.a. (or World i.t.a.) whereas Augmented Cued Speech is better adapted for use with ordinary i.t.a. in which small concessions are made to English spelling. My own view is that the slight advantage in naturalness of using the 'weak' pronunciation will be completely masked by the distortions in and thoroughly unnatural quality of even the best deaf speech.

The intention is that a phoneme manual system will at all times be accompanied by speech (the exception being that the deaf child himself will not be expected to produce speech until relatively late). This means that right from the beginning lip-patterns and residual hearing will have been available. The efficiency with which these incomplete media can be followed is likely to increase in proportion to the child's general linguistic competence.

Summary

For a deaf child to develop normal linguistic competence the over-riding priority must be for him to have the opportunity to perceive language patterns in a medium which preserves all the essential contrasts and which, like speech, comes in large quantities closely related to everyday situations and events.

Some variation is possible in the choice of substitute primary medium but the balance of advantage seems to lie with a suitably designed phoneme manual system, say Cued Speech or Augmented Cued Speech.

The task of providing this linguistic environment should, ideally, be that of the deaf child's parents and family but where this is not possible residential facilities would be necessary. In either case those closest to the child should, to use Hofsteater's words: (1) begin at once to talk casually and constantly to him on their fingers, just as hearing people do vocally to their babies – *whether or not he is paying any attention*; (2) talk to him just as naturally as hearing people do when attending to his physical needs, pausing only to emphasise key words tied to his bodily wants and interests; (3) use only finger-spelling between themselves when he is consciously present; and (4) in general, raise him as if he were a normal hearing baby with the sole exception of using the manual system in addition to speech.

These remarks apply to any child whose hearing is suspected to be not good enough to support speech directly and this may cover losses as small as 50 or 60 dB. The provision of a hearing aid to all deaf children, which is present practice here, is a safety precaution which ensures that the opportunity to use any useful hearing is not lost. If hearing does prove adequate to support speech then the S.P.M. is merely a 'safety-net'.

Reading and writing may be begun at any time but it is probably a waste of time until the deaf child has roughly a four or five-year-old's facility with language. The process will be comparable with normal learning of these skills but the case for using i.t.a. is rather stronger because it minimises confusion in the early stages and will also reinforce the child's knowledge of phoneme sequences. The transfer to T.O. will be made as usual when the child is fairly fluent and confident in i.t.a. Again there is no need for haste as the experience of reading in i.t.a. will reinforce learning through the manual medium.

The comprehension of unaided speech will become progressively easier to learn the better the child's basic knowledge. Exercises may be devised to give practice in this skill but the normal everyday use of finger-spelling should continue unabated. Practice at speech-reading may begin at any time but, as with reading, it is best left till later.

The teaching of speech articulation should not be introduced too early. When the child begins to try to reproduce manual patterns he should not be burdened with the additional task of trying to pronounce the words. The whole process of articulating words will be facilitated by a firm knowledge of the phoneme structure of words and should thus be left till later. The important thing at all times is to ensure that the flood of 'visible speech' continues.

The umbilicus through which language can flow is the S.P.M. and no attempt should be made to cut the cord or reduce the flow until or unless there is no doubt that it has become superfluous. To do so is to risk linguistic starvation and thus the stunting of language growth.

Always intertwined in the many arguments about this problem are the value questions of what we are aiming at and the empirical questions of how best to get there. In this part of the book I have tried to demonstrate, drawing on ideas from Part One, that even if one's overall aim is proficiency in speech one should not approach this goal directly but should first make whatever detour is necessary to establish language.

The other main conclusion with grows from the general study of language processes in Part One is that the whole phenomenon is wrought with such intricacy, and is so finely woven that it is unwise to try to synthesise it using the crude analyses available; it is probably better to sail with the natural currents of language growth, adapting the craft in such a way as to ensure it stays afloat.

Appendix I
Speech sounds
and symbols

The phonemes commonly recognised in English with symbols from a simplified version of IPA, symbols from i.t.a. and details of pronunciation.

	Phonetic symbol	Sample word	i.t.a. (symbols)		Voiced or Unvoiced	Place of Articulation	Manner of Articulation
1	iː	*eat*	єє		V		
2	i	*it*	i		V		
3	e	*get*	e		V		
4	a	*act*	a		V		
5	aː	*art*	ɑ, ɑr	VOWELS	V		
6	o	*on*	o		V		
7	oː	*saw*	au, or		V		
8	u	*book*	ω		V		
9	uː	*soon*	ω		V		
10	ʌ	*up*	u		V		
11	əː	*word* ⎫	–r		V		
12	ə	*ever* ⎭			V		
13	ei	*aid*	æ	—	V		
14	ou	*own*	œ		V		
15	ai	*eye*	ie		V		
16	au	*out*	ou	DIPHTHONGS	V		
17	oi	*oil*	oi		V		
18	iu	*due*	ue		V		
19	uə	*poor*	ω r		V		
20	eə	*air*	æ r		V		
21	iə	*hear*	єє r	—	V		
22	p	*paid*	p		UV	Bi-labial	Plosive
23	b	*been*	b		V	,,	,,
24	t	*tea*	t		UV	Alveolar	,,
25	d	*day*	d		V	,,	,,
26	k	*car*	c, k		UV	Velar	,,
27	g	*give*	g		V	,,	,,
28	f	*farm*	f	CONSONANTS	UV	Labio-dental	Fricative
29	v	*very*	v		V	,,	,,
30	θ	*think*	ʈh		UV	Dental	,,
31	ð	*these*	ʈh		V	,,	,,
32	s	*say*	s		UV	Alveolar	,,
33	z	*size*	z, ꙅ		V	,,	,,
34	ʃ	*she*	ʃh		UV	,, back	,,
35	ʒ	*measure*	ʒ		V	,, back	,,
36	r	*red*	r		V	Alveolar	,,
37	h	*hope*	h		UV	Glottal	,,
38	tʃ	*chair*	tʃh, ʧ		UV	Alveolar	Affricate
39	dʒ	*just*	j, dʒ		V	,,	,,
40	m	*met*	m		V	Bi-labial	Nasal
41	n	*near*	n		V	Alveolar	,,
42	ŋ	*long*	ɳ		V	Velar	,,
43	l	*life*	l		V	Alveolar	Lateral
44	w	*win*	w, wh		V		Semi-vowel
45	j	*yet*	y		V		,,

Note: For an illustration of the lip-patterns of speech phonemes see *Plates* (between pp. 146–147).

Appendix II
Manual Alphabets

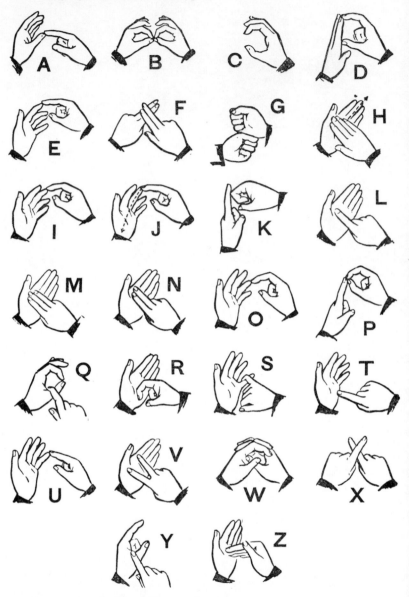

FIGURE 41. *The Standard Manual Alphabet*
This is the two-handed manual alphabet used for finger-spelling to the sighted deaf in Great Britain and many parts of the world. Note how each symbol forms, or at least suggests, the letter it represents.

From *Conversation with the Deaf* 9th ed., R.N.I.D., 1971

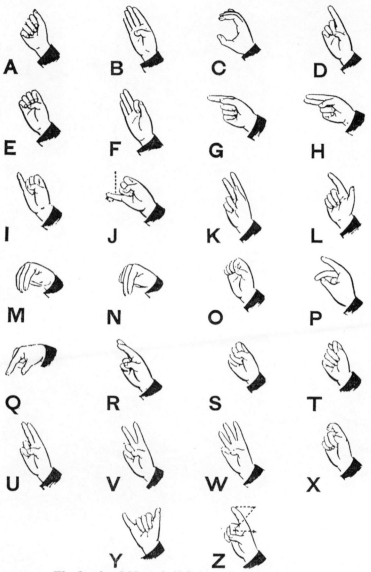

FIGURE 42. *The One-hand Manual Alphabet*
This is the one-handed manual alphabet used for finger-spelling to the sighted
deaf in some other parts of the world, including the United States of America.
Although there are occasional resemblances, the symbols are not so clearly
related to the written letter shapes, nor can they so easily be read at a distance.
From *Conversation with the Deaf*, 9th ed., R.N.I.D., 1971
Note. See *Plate* 3 for manual signs.

Appendix III
Cued and Augmented Cued Speech

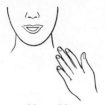

side position
α (father)
ɔ (nickel, the)
r (fur) (British)
œ (notation)

throat position
a (that)
i (it)
ω (book, put)

chin position
o (hot)
e (get)
ω (food, blue)

mouth position
u (butter)
ɛɛ (feet)
au (jaw, bought)

Diphthongs are cued as glides of the hand between the appropriate positions; e.g., ie from α to i, ou from α to ω, and œ from o to ω or e to ω.

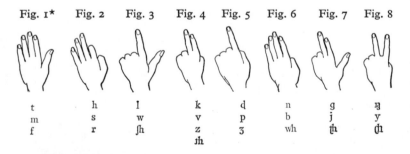

Fig. 1★	Fig. 2	Fig. 3	Fig. 4	Fig. 5	Fig. 6	Fig. 7	Fig. 8
t	h	l	k	d	n	g	ŋ
m	s	w	v	p	b	j	y
f	r	ʃh	z	ʒ	wh	th	dh
			ʃh				

★The hand shape shown in Figure 1 is also used with an isolated vowel – that is a vowel not preceded by a consonant.

FIGURE 43 *Cued Speech*
The system devised by Dr R. Orin Cornett to cover the variations of spoken English used in Britain, the United States of America and Australia. Symbols are from the Initial Teaching Alphabet.

AUGMENTED CUED SPEECH
CONSONANTS

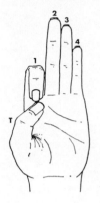

Fig. 44   1. *Unvoiced plosives*
[p]   [p] Thumb touches tip of finger 1
           [t] Thumb touches tip of finger 2
           [c] Thumb touches tip of finger 3

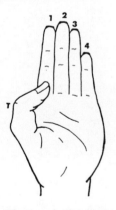

Fig. 45   2. *Voiced plosives*
[b]   [b] Thumb touches lowest section of finger 1
           [d] Thumb touches lowest section of finger 2
           [g] Thumb touches lowest section of finger 3

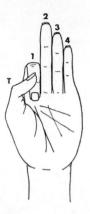

Fig. 46   3. *Unvoiced fricatives*
[f]   [f] Thumb over folded finger 1
            [θ] Thumb over folded finger 2
            [s] Thumb over folded finger 3
            [ʃ] Thumb over folded finger 4

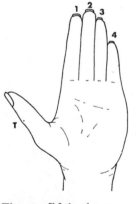

Fig. 47   [h] As shown
[h]

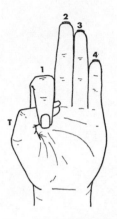

Fig. 48   4. *Voiced fricatives*
[v]   [v] Thumb under folded finger 1
           [ð] Thumb under folded finger 2
           [z] Thumb under folded finger 3
           [ʒ] Thumb under folded finger 4

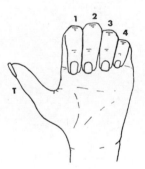

Fig. 49   [r] As shown
[r]

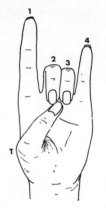

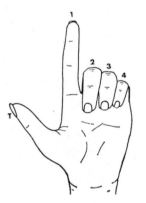

Fig. 50   5. *Nasal*
[n]   [n] Thumb touches tips of fingers 2 and 3
          [m] Thumb under folded fingers 2 and 3
          [ŋ] Thumb over folded fingers 2 and 3

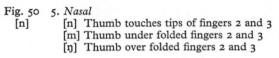

Fig. 51   6. *Affricates*
[tʃ]   [tʃ] As shown
          [dʒ] As for [tʃ] but with both fingers 4 and 1 extended

          7. *Others see* Fig. 44
              [l]   Thumb touches tip of finger 4
              [w] Thumb touches lowest section of finger 4
              [j]   Thumb touches tips of fingers 3 and 4

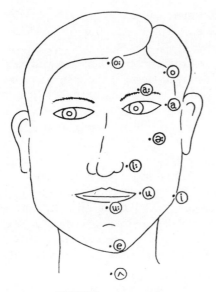

VOWELS

Fig. 52   *Diphthongs* – [ei], [ou], [ai], [au], [oi], [iu], [iə] [eə] [uə] – are formed by a glide from the first vowel to the second.

Notes on Augmented Cued Speech

As with Cued Speech a consonant and the vowel which follows it are signalled together provided they are both in the same word. It is assumed that right handed people will wish to 'speak' with their left hands so that the right hand is free for other things. Left handers will do the reverse. The consonant is signalled by the position of the fingers and thumb and the vowel position on the face is touched by the tip of the index finger for most consonants or with the tip of the second finger for [p], [f] and [v] or with the tip of the thumb for [r], [h], [tʃ] and [dʒ].

When a vowel occurs alone or at the beginning of a word then it is pointed by the index finger, the thumb being folded under the rest of the fingers. Where a consonant occurs without a vowel following then it is signalled an inch or two from the side of the face.

Diphthongs are modelled on a glide from the first vowel to the second. There is a slight possibility of confusion between such a glide and two syllables beginning with the same consonant. Thus [boi] might be confused with [bobi]. Context will almost always resolve such ambiguity but it is well to differentiate the two syllable case from the glide by lifting the hand from the face between syllables.

The 'spelling' employed is fairly strictly phonetic and thus will vary with regional variations in pronunciation. However the system follows i.t.a. in that the 'strong' pronunciation of such words as 'and', 'to', 'for', 'ever', etc., is used. Normally the vowel in such words is the neutral [ə] sound but in this Augmented Cued Speech the vowels [a], [u], [oː], [əː] would be used.

Most of the symbols are fairly easy to form. The critical element in most consonants is the relation of the thumb to one or more fingers. The other fingers may be held in whatever position is easiest provided they do not obscure the thumb. There is, with some consonants, a small amount of strain in keeping the palm of the hand facing forward. Again, all that is necessary is for the critical part of the symbol to be visible. Turning the body so that the right shoulder is forward will make this easier.

As with Cued Speech the system is intended to be used in conjunction with speech.

References

ATTNEAVE, F. (1954) Some informational aspects of visual perception, *Psychological Review*, **61**, 183–93.

BARTLETT, F. C. (1932) *Remembering: An Experimental and Social Study*, Cambridge University Press.

BERKO, JEAN (1967) Do children imitate? In *Oral Education of the Deaf*, II. International Conference convened by the Alexander Graham Bell Association for the Deaf.

BIRCH, J. W. AND STUCKLESS, E. R. (1963) Programmed instruction in written language for deaf children, *American Annals of the Deaf*, **108**, 317–36.

BIRCH, J. W. AND STUCKLESS, E. R. (1964) The relationship between early manual communication and later achievement of the deaf, Co-operative Research Project, 1969: University of Pittsburgh.

BONET, JUAN PABLO (1620) *Simplification of the letters of the alphabet and the method of teaching deaf-mutes to speak*, translation by H. N. Dixon (1890), published privately. Copies available from the Royal National Institute for the Deaf, 105 Gower Street, London W.C.1.

BRAINE, M. D. S. (1963a) The ontogeny of English phrase structure: the first phrase, *Language*, **39**, 1–13.

BRAINE, M. D. S. (1963b) On learning the grammatical order of words, *Psychological Review*, **70**, 323–48.

BRANNON, J. B. AND MURRAY, T. (1966) The spoken syntax of normal, hard of hearing and deaf children, *Journal of Speech and Hearing Disorders*, **9**, 604–10.

BROADBENT, D. E. (1970) In defence of empirical psychology, *Bulletin of the British Psychological Society*, **23**, 87–96.

BROADBENT, D. E. AND STEPHENS, S. D. G. (1970) Alternative to threshold measurements in the assessment of hearing, in G. E. W. Wolstenhome and Julie Knight (eds.) *Sensorineural Hearing Loss*, a CIBA Foundation Symposium, London: Churchill.

BROWN, C. (1954) *My Left Foot*, London: Secker & Warburg.

BROWN, R. W. AND BELLUGI-KLIMA, URSULA (1964) Three processes in the child's acquisition of syntax, *Harvard Educational Review*, **34**.

BROWN, R. W. AND BERKO, J. (1960) Word association and the acquisition of grammar, *Child Development*, **31**, 1–14.

BROWN, R. AND FRASER, C. (1963) The acquisition of syntax, in C. N. Cofer and B. Musgrave (eds.) *Verbal Behavior and Learning*, New York: McGraw-Hill.

BRUNER, J. S. (1957) Going beyond the information given, in *Contemporary Approaches to Cognition* (Symposium held at the University of Colorado), Cambridge, Mass: Harvard University Press.

BRUNER, J. S., GOODNOW, J. J. AND AUSTIN, G. A. (1956) *A Study of Thinking*, New York: John Wiley.

CARHART, R. (1966) Auditory training, in H. Davies and S. R. Silverman (eds.) *Hearing and Deafness*, New York: Holt, Rinehart and Winston.

CHOMSKY, CAROL (1969) *The Acquisition of Syntax in Children from Five to Ten*, Cambridge, Mass.: M.I.T. Press.

CHOMSKY, N. (1957) *Syntactic Structures*, The Hague: Mouton.

CORCORAN, D. W. J. (1971) *Pattern Recognition*, Harmondsworth: Penguin Books.

ERVIN, SUSAN M. (1964) Imitation and structural change in children's language, in E. Lenneberg (ed.) *New Directions in the Study of Language*, Cambridge, Mass.: M.I.T. Press.

EWING, A. W. G. (ed.) (1957) *Educational Guidance and the Deaf Child*, Washington D.C.: Volta Bureau.

EWING, I. R. AND EWING, A. W. G. (1954) *Speech and the Deaf Child*, Manchester: Manchester University Press.

EWING, I. R. AND EWING, A. W. G. (1958) *New Opportunities for Deaf Children*, London: University of London Press.

FALCONER, G. A. (1961) A mechanical device for teaching sight vocabulary to young deaf children, *American Annals of the Deaf*, **106**, 251–7.

FANT, G. C. M. (1958) The acoustics of speech, in A. W. G. Ewing (ed.) *The Modern Educational Treatment of Deafness*, Manchester: Manchester University Press.

FITZGERALD, EDITH (1937) *Straight Language for the Deaf*, Washington: Volta Bureau.

FLAVELL, J. H. (1963) *The Developmental Psychology of Jean Piaget*, Princeton, N.J.: Van Nostrand.

FRIES, C. C. (1952) *The Structure of English*, London: Longmans.

FURTH, H. G. (1966) *Thinking without Language*, New York: Free Press.

HAYES, J. R. AND CLARK, H. H. (1970) Experiments on the segmentation of an artificial speech analogue, in J. R. Hayes (ed.) *Cognition and Development of Language*, New York: Wiley.

HODGSON, K. W. (1953) *The Deaf and their Problems*, London: Watts.

HOFSTEATER, H. T. (1959) An experiment in pre-school education, *Gallaudet College Bulletin*, 8, 4–17.

HOSPERS, J. (1967) *An Introduction to Philosophical Analysis*, 2nd ed., London: Routledge and Kegan Paul.

INGALL, B. I. (1971) The audiology gap, *Hearing*, 26, 362–3.

i.t.a. FOUNDATION, 154 Southampton Row, London W.C.1.

JENKINS, J. J. (1965) Mediation theory and grammatical behaviour, in S. Rosenberg (ed.) *Directions in Psycholinguistics*, New York: Macmillan.

JOHNSON, N. F. (1965) The psychological reality of phrase structure rules, *Journal of Verbal Learning and Verbal Behavior*, 4, 469–75.

KARLSEN, B. (1966) *Teaching Beginning Reading to Hearing-impaired Children, using a Visual Method and Teaching Machines*, Minnesota: University of Minnesota.

KIRK, S. A., MCCARTHY, J. J. AND KIRK, W. D. (1968) *Illinois Test of Psycholinguistic Abilities*, revised edition. Board of Trustees of the University of Illinois.

KISS, G. R. (1972) *Grammatical Word Classes: A Learning Process and its Simulation*, Edinburgh: Medical Research Council Speech and Communication Unit.

KOHLER, W. (1924) *The Mentality of Apes*, London: Kegan Paul.

KOPP, C. A. AND KOPP, H. G. (1963) An investigation to evaluate the usefulness of the visible speech cathode ray tube translator as a supplement to the oral method of teaching speech to the deaf and severely deafened children. Final Report, V.R.A. Project No. RD-1526, Detroit: Wayne State University.

LASHLEY, K. S. (1951) The problem of serial order in behaviour, in L. A. Jeffress (ed.) *Cerebral Mechanisms in Behavior*, New York: John Wiley.

LENNEBERG, E. H. (1967) *The Biological Foundations of Language*, New York: John Wiley.

LEWIS, M. M. (Chairman) (1968) *The Education of Deaf Children. The Possible Place of Finger Spelling and Signing*, London: H.M.S.O.

LURIA, A. R. (1961) *The Role of Speech in the Regulation of Normal and Abnormal Behaviour*, Oxford: Pergamon.

LYONS, J. (1968) *Introduction to Theoretical Linguistics*, Cambridge University Press.

LYONS, J. (1970) Generative syntax, in J. Lyons (ed.) *New Horizons in Linguistics*, Harmondsworth: Penguin Books.

MARTIN, E. (1970) Toward an analysis of subjective phrase structure, *Psychological Bulletin*, **74**, 153–66.

MILES, A. C. (1967) Cued speech, *American Education*, November 1967.

MILLER, G. A. (1956) The magical number seven, plus or minus two: some limits on our capacity for processing information, *Psychological Review*, **63**, 81–97.

MILLER, G. A. (1962) Some psychological studies of grammar, *American Psychologist*, **17**, 748–62.

MILLER, G. A., GALANTER, E. AND PRIBRAM, K. A. (1960) *Plans and the Structure of Behavior*, New York: Holt, Rinehart and Winston.

MONTGOMERY, G. W. (1968) A factorial study of communication and ability in deaf school leavers, *British Journal of Educational Psychology*, **38**, 27–37.

MOORES, D. F. (1967) Application of 'Cloze' procedures to the assessment of psycholinguistic abilities of the deaf. Unpublished doctoral dissertation: University of Illinois.

MOORES, D. F. (1970) Oral versus manual . . . 'Old prejudices die hard but die they must', *American Annals of the Deaf*, **115**, 667–9.

MYKLEBUST, H. R. (1960) *The Psychology of Deafness*, New York: Grune and Stratton.

OGDEN, C. K. (1944) *Basic English: A General Introduction with Rules and Grammar*, London: Kegan Paul Trench, Trubner.

OLDFIELD, R. C. AND ZANGWILL, O. (1942) Head's concept of the schema and its application in contemporary British psychology, *British Journal of Psychology*, **32**, 267–86; **33**, 58–64 and 113–29.

PAGET, SIR RICHARD (1969) *A Systematic Sign Language* – general principles and list of first 2000 words. Published privately, and available from the Royal National Institute for the Deaf.

PALMER, JEAN (1970) A British experiment involving the use of i.t.a. with deaf children. Paper delivered at the seventh International i.t.a. Conference, London. London: i.t.a. Foundation.

PREMACK, D. (1970) A functional analysis of language, *Journal of the Experimental Analysis of Behaviour*, **14**, 107–25.

QUIGLEY, S. P. (1969) *The Influence of Fingerspelling on the Development of Language Communication and Educational Achievement in Deaf*

Children, Institute for Research on Exceptional Children: University of Illinois.

REYNELL, JOAN (1969) *Reynell Developmental Language Scales*, Windsor: N.F.E.R. Publishing Co.

ROMMETVEIT, RAGNAR (1968) *Words, Meanings and Messages*, New York: Academic Press.

ROY, H. L., SCHEIN, J. D. AND FRISINA, D. H. (1964) New methods of language development for deaf children. Co-operative Research Project 1383, Washington D.C.: Gallaudet College.

SCHULTE, K. (1967) Ausbau und Systematisierung Verwendbarer Lautzeichen zu einem Phonembestimmten Manualsystem, *Neue Blaetter fuer Taubstummenbildung*, **323**.

SIMPSON, ESTHER (1963) Survey of children born in 1947 who were in schools for the deaf in 1962–3. *Report of Chief Medical Officer*, Department of Education and Science.

STOKOE, W. C. (1971) *The Study of Sign Language*, Silver Spring: The National Association of the Deaf.

SULLIVAN, ANNE M. (1887) A diary entry reproduced in a supplement to *The Story of My Life*, edited by J. A. Macy (1903). Reprinted 1968, by Lancer Books Inc., New York.

SWETS, J. A. (ed.) (1964) *Signal Detection and Recognition by Human Observers*, New York: John Wiley.

WARBURTON, F. W. AND SOUTHGATE, VERA (1969) *i.t.a. An Independent Evaluation*, London: John Murray and W. R. Chambers.

WEIR, RUTH (1962) *Language in the Crib*, The Hague: Mouton.

WHETNALL, EDITH AND FRY, D. B. (1964) *The Deaf Child*, London: Heinemann.

WOODEN, H. Z. (1962) Dramatised language for the deaf, *Exceptional Children*, **29**, 155–63.

WOODWORTH, R. S. AND SCHLOSBERG, H. (1938) *Experimental Psychology*, 3rd edition 1954, London: Methuen.

YATES, A. J. (1963) Delayed auditory feedback, *Psychological Bulletin*, **60**, 213–51.

YNGVE, V. H. (1960) A model and an hypothesis for language structure, *Proceedings of the American Philosophical Society*, **104**, 444–66.

ZALIOUK, A. (1954) A visual-tactile system of phonetical symbolisation, *Journal of Speech and Hearing Disorders*, **19**, 190–207.

Index

DATE DUE